W0080944

Appointment of Judges to the Supreme Court of India

Appointment of Judges to the Supreme Court of India

Transparency, Accountability, and Independence

Edited by
Arghya Sengupta
Ritwika Sharma

OXFORD
UNIVERSITY PRESS

OXFORD
UNIVERSITY PRESS

Oxford University Press is a department of the University of Oxford.
It furthers the University's objective of excellence in research, scholarship,
and education by publishing worldwide. Oxford is a registered trademark of
Oxford University Press in the UK and in certain other countries.

Published in India by
Oxford University Press
2/11 Ground Floor, Ansari Road, Daryaganj, New Delhi 110 002, India

© Oxford University Press 2018

The moral rights of the authors have been asserted.

First Edition published in 2018
Third impression 2018

All rights reserved. No part of this publication may be reproduced, stored in
a retrieval system, or transmitted, in any form or by any means, without the
prior permission in writing of Oxford University Press, or as expressly permitted
by law, by licence, or under terms agreed with the appropriate reprographics
rights organization. Enquiries concerning reproduction outside the scope of the
above should be sent to the Rights Department, Oxford University Press, at the
address above.

You must not circulate this work in any other form
and you must impose this same condition on any acquirer.

ISBN-13: 978-0-19-948507-9
ISBN-10: 0-19-948507-0

Typeset in ITC Giovanni Std 9.5/12
by The Graphics Solution, New Delhi 110 092
Printed in India by Replika Press Pvt. Ltd

This volume is dedicated to
Anil Divan (1930–2017) and T.R. Andhyarujina (1933–2017),
stalwarts of the Indian Supreme Court Bar

Contents

II   The Analysis of the NJAC Judgment

III   Comparative Perspectives

Foreword

I am glad that Arghya Sengupta and Ritwika Sharma have decided to publish a book dealing with the appointment of judges to the Supreme Court of India.

From time immemorial, mankind desired to have wise and humane judges with the wisdom to discriminate between truth and falsehood. The legends of King Solomon and Dharmaraja and the like are proof of such desire. Mankind experimented with the process of identifying wise people to be made judges. No process is perfect. Experience demonstrates the shortcomings of every chosen selection process. So, the experiment goes on.

It is said that an independent judge is the hallmark of democracy. But there are also certain other attributes that go into the making of a good judge. They are efficiency and integrity.

Efficiency of a judge depends upon the judge's knowledge not only of law but also of various other branches of learning. The wider the range of knowledge, the greater the possibility of efficiency. However, the mere possession of information is not knowledge. The ability to analyse information systematically is an essential component to transform relevant information into knowledge.

The popular understanding is that an independent judge is one who is not afraid of deciding cases that come before him without troubling himself with the question whether his opinion would be palatable to the government. But there are other aspects of independence. Integrity is no doubt an aspect of independence. To decide cases without being influenced by considerations other than the law, such as personal and political beliefs, is a key manifestation of integrity and, consequently, of independence. Not seeking to secure monetary benefits for deciding a case in a particular way is perhaps its most critical manifestation.

Various societies in the modern world adopted different models of selection processes for appointment of judges. India chose a model when it became a republic. But the model is largely based on past colonial practice. With changing times and changing economic and political factors, the need to revisit the model was felt from time to time, both by successive governments and the civil society. The latest experiment was the Constitution (99th Amendment) Act, 2014, which was struck down by the Supreme Court in the case now known as the *National Judicial Appointments Commission (NJAC) Case*.

This book contains an examination of the legal history and background of the Constitution (99th Amendment) Act, 2014 and the views expressed by the Supreme Court in the *NJAC Case*. It also contains essays that examine models of appointment followed in some other democratic societies.

The experiment goes on. The critique goes on. The last word is not said. Perhaps it can never be said. The play must go on. The very fact that the play goes on proves that society is vibrant. Vibrancy is one of the vital elements for the sustenance of democracy.

This book is part of our vibrant democratic process. More are welcome.

Justice Jasti Chelameswar
Judge, Supreme Court of India
2018

Introduction

In the summer of 2015, for 32 days, the Supreme Court of India heard arguments in the *Supreme Court Advocates-on-Record Association and others v. Union of India and others*[1] (*NJAC Case*). The case concerned a challenge to the Constitution (Ninety-ninth Amendment) Act, 2014 (99th Amendment) to the Constitution of India which established the National Judicial Appointments Commission (NJAC). Also challenged was the National Judicial Appointments Commission Act, 2014 (NJAC Act), which contained the procedure to be followed by the NJAC in recommending appointments to the President of India. The NJAC was to be the defining judicial reform of the new National Democratic Alliance government that had swept into power in 2014. However, even before it could start functioning, petitions to strike it down had been filed in the Supreme Court.

From the initiation of proceedings itself, it was apparent that this was not going to be an ordinary case. First, the presiding judge of the Constitution bench, Justice Anil R. Dave, recused himself. In the reconstituted bench presided over by Justice Jagdish Singh Khehar, the government argued for several days as to why the matter must be referred to a larger bench. This argument was made so that the *Supreme Court Advocates-on-Record Association v. Union of India*[2] (*Second Judges' Case*)

---

[1] (2016) 5 SCC 1.

[2] (1993) 3 SCC 441. This is the second judgment in what are known as the three '*Judges' Cases*' in the Indian Supreme Court's jurisprudence. *SP Gupta v. Union of India*, 1981 Supp SCC 87 is known as the *First Judges' Case*, and *Special Reference No. 1 of 1998, Re*, (1998) 7 SCC 739 is known as the *Third Judges' Case*.

could be reconsidered and its ambiguities resolved. This request was, however, denied. The delays occasioned by the change of bench and the reference hearing meant that the Court continued hearing the matter through its summer vacation.

On 15 July 2015, the hearings concluded and the Court reserved judgment. As lawyers who were assisting the Union of India in preparing its written submissions for this case, the seemingly endless cycle of argument, counter-argument, rejoinder, sur-rejoinder by diverse petitioners, several governments, and public interest interveners demonstrated to us a massive gulf in legal scholarship—there was no single book that dealt with the politics, doctrine, and developments pertaining to judicial appointments in India. This edited volume uses the *NJAC Case* as the springboard to bridge this gulf—embarking on a larger political, doctrinal, and comparative enquiry into judicial appointments in the country and elsewhere.

Judicial appointments, the central issue in the *NJAC Case* and consequently the volume, have been the subject of empirical and sociological analysis in some prior, recent literature. Abhinav Chandrachud's *The Informal Constitution* (Oxford University Press, 2014) and George H. Gadbois, Jr's *Judges of the Supreme Court of India: 1950–1989* (Oxford University Press, 2011) are prominent examples. The volume of essays titled *Supreme but Not Infallible: Essays in Honour of the Supreme Court of India* edited by B.N. Kirpal, Ashok H. Desai, Gopal Subramanium, Rajeev Dhavan, and Raju Ramachandran (Oxford University Press, 2000) also discusses controversies around judicial appointments in some detail. This volume follows in their path, tackling this much-discussed yet little-researched subject with a distinctly doctrinal and comparative lens.

The centrality of judicial appointments in the narrative of the history of the Supreme Court derives much from the political intrigue surrounding several appointments and non-appointments. The sudden passing away of Chief Justice H.J. Kania appears to have led Jawaharlal Nehru to consider offering the Chief Justiceship to Justice B.K. Mukherjea, doing away with the seniority convention that would have meant Justice Patanjali Sastri taking the reins. Better sense prevailed and the seniority convention continued. The convention came under renewed stress following two supersessions—when the Janata government had to appoint a Chief Justice after Justice M.H. Beg's resignation, vociferous demands were made not to appoint Justices Y.V. Chandrachud or P.N. Bhagwati who had been party to the judgment of the Supreme Court in the infamous case of *Additional District Magistrate, Jabalpur v. Shivakant Shukla*.[3] Again, better sense prevailed and the convention continued. Today however the steadfast observation of this convention has meant that we have had Chief Justices with an average tenure of less than a year for Chief Justices in the last six years. Previously, tenures have been as short as 18 days (Chief Justice K.N. Singh) and 30 days (Chief Justice Rajendra Babu). Such anecdotes, personalities, and critical episodes have shaped the history and interpretation of law surrounding judicial appointments in India. These form the subject matter of Part I of the volume, which acts as a context-setter for the analysis to follow in Parts II and III.

Part I begins with Suchindran B.N.'s critical analysis of the dynamics of executive-judiciary relations in the matter of appointments from 1950 to 1973. Specifically, the essay traverses the historical journey of appointments to the Supreme Court from the tenure of the first Chief Justice of India, Justice H.J. Kania, to the appointment of Justice R.S. Sarkaria as Judge of the Court in 1973. This spans the tenure of 14 Chief Justices and 53 appointments made to the Supreme Court. It provides insights, and in some cases, hitherto unknown facts, about the factors that prompted the appointment of certain justices to the Court. The essay also documents the gradual incursion that the executive had begun to make in the latter half of the 1960s, particularly in light of certain judicial decisions which appeared to the executive to be confrontationist in nature. Appointments were not the focus of such confrontations, but it was only to be a matter of time before they did.

The tipping point was the judgment of the Supreme Court in *Kesavananda Bharati v. State of Kerala*[4] (*Kesavananda Bharati*). In the second essay that spans the tumultuous period between this judgment and the end of the Emergency when Indira Gandhi was Prime Minister, Late T.R. Andhyarujina brings appointments to the centre stage, demonstrating how judicial appointments became a proxy for a larger battle for control of the Constitution. Arguing that the independence of the judiciary was imperilled beyond redemption, Andhyarujina carefully

[3] (1976) 3 SCC 521.
[4] (1973) 4 SCC 225.

traces the pattern of executive interference up to and after the proclamation of Emergency. He argues that the severe blow dealt to judicial
independence in this period, in a way, determined the course of how
the process for judicial appointments was shaped in future decades.

So unprecedented was the assault on judicial independence perpetrated during the Emergency that its impact was felt long after it
was officially revoked. As a result, the 1980s have largely been seen
as a decade of executive consolidation over the judiciary, substituting
clandestine interference for overt attacks. A.K. Ganguli sets the record
straight by shedding light on the 1980s, particularly pertaining to the
First Judges' Case. This judgment, largely seen in academic scholarship as a genuflection of the judges before the executive, is defended
by Ganguli, arguing that it espoused the optimal balance that the
Constitution contemplated in the process of judicial appointments.
With the help of anecdotal examples, this essay tries to untangle the
case of the curious eighties, making the larger point that it is a decade
not amenable to easy typifying.

It is widely accepted in academic literature that the perceived diminishing of the role of the judiciary in the matter of appointments, and
consequently, the independence of the judiciary, led the Supreme
Court to wrest such power by means of a creative reinterpretation of
the Constitution in the *Second Judges' Case*. Arun Jaitley critically reflects
on the effects of the *Second Judges' Case* which created the judicial collegium of senior-most justices of the Supreme Court to primarily determine appointments to the higher judiciary, as concretised by *Special
Reference No. 1 of 1998, Re*[5] (*Third Judges' Case*). He explains how the
'collegium' came into being, without actually finding a mention in the
text of the Constitution. He makes a strong case for its reform through
practical examples of when the collegium failed in its constitutional
duties. Finally, he expresses an optimism that even though the NJAC
did not see light of the day, the intent to reform appointments processes would persist.

An important lesson that emerges from the four preceding essays is
that the process of judicial appointments is as much political as it is
legal. Unfortunately, petitioners in various cases as well as the Supreme
Court itself have constantly treated it as a matter of only constitutional

---

[5] (1998) 7 SCC 739.

law. While this is only natural considering existing separation of powers or lack thereof in India's constitutional framework, it is critical to be cognizant of the political drama involving successive governments and chief justices wresting the power to appoint judges. Pratap Bhanu Mehta provides a deep insight into this conflict, asking why and how the process of deciding upon a seemingly acceptable procedure for judicial appointments has become the source of an interminable confrontation between the executive and the judiciary, with neither of the two willing to concede. Taking a step back, he argues that while the government and the judiciary might individually be justified in their stance, as a result of this conflict, public credibility of both these institutions has been adversely affected. In any event, since reform of the judicial appointments process continues to remain a live issue, he offers some thoughts on what a possible NJAC-II, more amenable to all branches of state, might look like.

This segues neatly into Part II which contains a critical analysis of the various threads of judgment in the *NJAC Case*. Critical academic writing on judgments of the Supreme Court of India has been limited to essays and books by a few stalwarts, far less widespread than what a court whose judgments have pervasive consequences, requires. Specifically, sustained engagement with particular legal arguments in constitutional cases has been even rarer. In what will hopefully become a template for similarly significant constitutional judgments in the future, Part II of the volume offers a close critique of the opinions in the *NJAC Case*—where the judges got it right and where their reasoning is susceptible to criticism. Of course, the *NJAC Case* dealt with a multitude of issues—some such as laying down norms of judicial recusal—having little nexus with appointments. In dealing with the *NJAC Case*, this volume makes no claims to comprehensiveness, but instead, offers a close critique of the legal reasoning adopted by the Court in coming to its key conclusions that have a bearing on the future of judicial appointments.

It commences with an essay by Justice K.T. Thomas, who offers some preliminary thoughts on the judgment in the *NJAC Case*. Thomas rues the lack of any discernible attempt by the bench in the *NJAC Case* to read down the provisions of the 99th Amendment. He argues that neither the overwhelming majority with which the Amendment was passed in Parliament, nor the Court's own precedent, where it has tended to read down amendments, came to the aid of the 99th Amendment. He also argues how the mere apprehension of abuse of power by the eminent persons or the Union Minister in-charge of Law and Justice (Law Minister) ought not to have been deemed sufficient to invalidate a constitutional amendment. In parting, Thomas provides some lessons, to both legislators and courts, on how to ensure that future constitutional amendments do not meet the fate of the 99th Amendment and receive the respect they deserve.

So what exactly was wrong with the institutional design of the NJAC? Mukul Rohatgi examines the role that the executive, represented by the Law Minister, was expected to play on the NJAC. He succinctly charts a history of what the Constituent Assembly envisaged the role of the executive to be and how this role eventually panned out in the appointments process. This description culminates with an observation about how the collegium system, meant to counteract executive interference in appointments, has come to be mired in controversy itself. In its examination of the *NJAC Case*, Rohatgi notes how the Law Minister was viewed by the bench as capable of clouding the views of the other members of the NJAC in the process of appointment, or colluding with the eminent person(s) to act as a structured bloc against the judicial members. He contests this view on the ground that much of what led to the invalidation of the Law Minister's presence on the NJAC was based on conjectures and surmises, and not so much on principled constitutional grounds.

Equally contested, if not more, was the presence of two eminent persons envisaged by Parliament as civil society representatives on the NJAC. Madhavi Divan takes a deep dive into the role of the civil society in the judicial appointments process. She observes that the superior courts in India, especially during the last few decades, have assumed an activist role. Given such a role, at a time when several democracies around the world are making conscious attempts to include members of the civil society, or 'lay' members, in the appointments process, she argues that India should not stay far behind, especially given the visibly public role played by the Court. Eminent persons on the NJAC would have ensured a voice to the common people in appointments, who are the eventual consumers of the adjudication processes carried out by courts. More particularly, the inclusion of lay people in the appointments process would have positively impacted the cause of diversity in appointments.

The ninth essay in this volume deals with the ramifications of the judgment in the *NJAC Case* for the basic structure doctrine. The doctrine of basic structure places limits on the legislative power to amend the Constitution, and owes its origins to the judgment of the thirteen-judge bench of the Supreme Court in the *Kesavananda Bharati* case. While an exhaustive list of which aspects of the Constitution comprise the 'basic structure' eludes us, the judges in *Kesavananda Bharati* provided certain illustrations. According to Raju Ramachandran and Mythili Vijay Kumar Thallam, the judges in the *NJAC Case*, by striking down the 99th Amendment for violating the basic structure, appear to have conceptually expanded the remit of the basic structure doctrine significantly. They conclude that the contents of what was held to be part of basic structure in the *NJAC Case* are largely incapable of being defended normatively. Against this background, they chart the significance of the judgment on constitutional law and separation of powers questions in the future.

A different perspective on the judgment is provided by Arvind Datar who launches a scathing indictment of the NJAC Act, and presents what he calls the 'fatal flaws' in the legislation. If the legislative enactment is as flawed, Datar argues, the judgment can scarcely be anything but a resounding invalidation. It calls out the NJAC Act for its faulty drafting, and how it was open to challenge on eight specific grounds. He believes that the NJAC Act was not the fruit of a particularly thoughtful exercise in drafting of laws, a view which was also accepted by the Court. The presence of an even number of members, absence of qualifications for eminent persons, the susceptibility of the appointments process to be amended by Parliamentary law, and the possibility of misuse of the veto power were some of the grounds which indicated that the NJAC was doomed to fail.

The doctrinal device on which the *NJAC Case* was won and lost was the effect of the amendment on judicial primacy. Gautam Bhatia, through a close reading of the *NJAC Case*, assesses both whether as a descriptive fact the judgment held judicial primacy to be part of the basic structure, as well as whether such reading was normatively justified. Bhatia also expresses reservations about the extent of the Court's engagement with the concept of 'primacy'—its importance for the independence of the judiciary, and whether it is part of the basic structure of the Constitution.

While much discussion on the *NJAC Case* has centred on Justice Khehar's lead opinion, it was our firm belief that Justice Lokur's concurring opinion merits a standalone piece in the volume. Alok Prasanna Kumar comments on the robust defence of the collegium system as espoused in Justice Lokur's opinion. Justice Lokur's defence of the collegium makes for a compelling read at a time when the collegium system has been receiving all-round criticism for its manner of functioning. While Justice Lokur's defence is vehement, Kumar highlights certain principled (and pointed) deficiencies of the collegium which might have not been considered adequately. Equally, he argues that the notion that the collegium upholds judicial independence does not, by itself, mean that an alternative system of appointments would be likely to disturb it, or would not be able to satisfactorily uphold it.

In a judgment which invalidates a constitutional amendment by a majority of 4:1, the dissenting opinion is bound to stand out, more so if it is as incisive as the one delivered by Justice Chelameswar in the *NJAC Case*. Arghya Sengupta dissects the methodology adopted by Justice Chelameswar for assessing the validity of a Constitution amendment tested against the basic structure, and applies this methodology to test the validity of the 99th Amendment. He brings to light Justice Chelameswar's careful understanding of the constitutional relationship between the executive and the judiciary in light of the separation of powers principle, lost in his brethren's over-emphasis on select instances from constitutional history.

Part II of the volume ends with a few key thoughts by Gopal Subramanium on how the judgment in the *NJAC Case* is a befitting affirmation of judicial independence by the Supreme Court. This essay provides a conceptual understanding of judicial independence, against the backdrop of certain pivotal instances from India's judicial history. The highlight of this essay is Subramanium's discussion of *Union of India v. Sankalchand Himatlal Sheth*[6]—a judgment crucial for establishing the contours of judicial independence in the context of transfer of High Court judges. This essay gives this case the attention it merits by addressing the issue of judicial independence against its backdrop.

The Supreme Court of India has had an inconsistent record in its approach towards comparative law. While in a judgment dealing with the role of public prosecutors,[7] it quoted extensively from laws in

---

[6] (1977) 4 SCC 193.

[7] *National Human Rights Commission v. State of Gujarat*, (2009) 6 SCC 767.

Commonwealth countries, in *Suresh Kumar Koushal v. Naz Foundation*,[8] upholding the criminalization of intercourse against the order of nature, it refused. A similar reluctance to embracing comparative experiences was seen in the *NJAC Case*. Whether such reluctance was justified, and a reference to some experiences that might have justified a fuller embrace of comparative law, is the subject matter of Part III of this volume.

This part begins with Suhrith Parthasarathy's overview of the use of comparative law in the *NJAC Case*, calling out the judgment for its absence of a reasonable analysis of the comparative experience. He shows how the Supreme Court adopted an isolationist approach by shunning international experience from fifteen countries cited before it by the Union of India to drive home the point that executive presence in judicial appointments does not, by itself, impinge upon judicial independence. Parthasarathy contests the Supreme Court's cursory dismissal of relevant international experience on the ground that India, with its peculiar set of circumstances, cannot replicate the experiences of other nations in judicial appointments. He argues that this is self-serving and the judgment would have been better served by a surer grasp of comparative law and its rationales.

Part III then proceeds to examine the judicial appointments processes in select jurisdictions across the world. These essays are an exercise in analysing the relationship between appointment processes in various jurisdictions and independence of their judiciaries. The selection of jurisdictions is reflective of the currently active state of debates and developments around judicial appointments in each of them together with their relevance for India.

The country which has made rapid reforms despite a well-established and fairly well-functioning appointments system has been the United Kingdom (UK). Chintan Chandrachud discusses the transition to the commission model of judicial appointments in the UK with the advent of the Constitutional Reform Act of 2005 (UK CRA). Besides remodelling the office of the Lord Chancellor, the UK CRA also established a new Supreme Court for the UK. Chandrachud describes the historical reasons which were instrumental in the enactment of the UK CRA. Most significantly, the commission model in the UK provides for a sustained participation of 'lay' members, who are expected to be representatives

---

[8] (2014) 1 SCC 1.

of the civil society. This, Chandrachud argues, did not receive adequate consideration by the Indian Supreme Court in the *NJAC Case*. As a result, the judgment is either incorrect, or highly reductionist, when it says that the appointments process in the UK shows an increasing trend towards judicialization.

From the UK, the volume proceeds to another Commonwealth jurisdiction—South Africa—where the Judicial Service Commission (JSC) has been established in accordance with the South African Constitution and is regulated under the Judicial Service Commission Act, 1994. Chris McConnachie analyses the JSC's performance over the last two decades, about which opinion appears to be divided. McConnachie describes how the JSC has been successful in enhancing transparency in the selection process and improving the diversity of the judiciary. At the same time, the substantial number of politicians on the JSC has constantly irked its detractors, who apprehend undue political interference in appointments. Notwithstanding these concerns, McConnachie remains categorical about the South African judiciary being independent and credible. In this context, McConnachie makes an important point, one which holds immense significance for India—that the independence of the judiciary remains contingent on several variables, and the identity of those making the appointments is just one such.

From the commission model, the volume turns to look at a system where appointments are made primarily at the behest of the executive. Peter McCormick, traces the genesis of the Supreme Court of Canada under the Supreme Court Act of 1875 (Supreme Court Act), and the procedure for appointment of judges. The procedure as described in the Supreme Court Act is brief, and only envisages that judges are to be appointed by the Governor in Council. However, the way judicial appointments have actually worked in Canada constitutes an important lesson for India. A reformed procedure for appointments involves the Prime Minister and the Minister of Justice interacting with various Chief Justices, law school deans, and provincial justice ministers to solicit names of potential appointees. McCormick argues that the widening of the pool where consultation is made has resulted in the appointment of persons with diverse credentials. Thus, the Canadian experience demonstrates variations in appointment mechanisms for broad-based consultation even in the absence of a commission model. McCormick however rues that most innovations in the appointments process have been short-lived, and there has been a general reversion to a more secretive process.

The volume then turns to the sub-continent and an analysis of appointments processes in Pakistan, Sri Lanka, and Nepal, countries culturally closer, in many ways, to India. Sameer Khosa discusses the landmark developments pertaining to judicial appointments in the last decade in Pakistan. Pakistan began its experiment with the commission model of appointments with the Constitution (Eighteenth Amendment) Act, 2010 (18th Amendment) which established the Judicial Commission of Pakistan, comprising members from across the judiciary, political executive, and the bar. Much like the 99th Amendment to the Indian Constitution, the 18th Amendment in Pakistan was also challenged before the Supreme Court of Pakistan. However, unlike in India, the Supreme Court of Pakistan upheld the 18th Amendment in *District Bar Association, Rawalpindi v. Federation of Pakistan*[9] (*District Bar Association*). Khosa discusses the appointments process in Pakistan that existed prior to the 18th Amendment, followed by a close examination of the judgment in *District Bar Association*. He argues that even though the 18th Amendment, which ushered in the commission model in Pakistan, was upheld, by means of interpretation, what the Supreme Court has upheld is different from the process envisaged by this Amendment.

Rehan Abeyratne describes the trajectory followed by judicial appointments in Sri Lanka under its constitutions, each of which, he argues, has been successively less protective of judicial independence. Abeyratne analyses the switch to a transformed appointments process in 2001 when the power to appoint judges of the Court of Appeal and the Supreme Court was vested in the Constitutional Council, a ten-member body comprising largely of members of the Legislature. He also analyses the eventual reversion to President-led appointments in 2010. The controversial impeachment case of Chief Justice Shirani Bandaranayake reveals how processes for removal were as politicized as that of appointments. Abeyratne argues that politicization, in part, was also the consequence of the excesses perpetrated by the previous government, and hopes that the coming into power of a new government under President Maithripala Sirisena will assist in depoliticizing the judicial appointments process.

---

[9] PLD 2015 SC 401.

The volume culminates with a discussion around the live topic of judicial appointments in Nepal, in its recently enacted Constitution of 2015 (which is Nepal's seventh). Semanta Dahal's essay analyses how Nepal has consciously made attempts to depoliticize judicial appointments—while appointments to the Supreme Court were originally made at the behest of the executive (the monarch), the fifth Constitution onwards (in 1990), appointments became the prerogative of the 'Judicial Council', a body chaired by the Chief Justice of Nepal, comprising members from the executive as well as the bar. By the time Nepal enacted its Interim Constitution of 2006, judicial appointments involved all three branches of the government. The procedure required judges nominated by the Judicial Council to attend a compulsory hearing before the Parliamentary Hearing Special Committee. Dahal observes that the 2015 Constitution retains the Judicial Council and the Parliamentary Hearing Special Committee, and by necessary implication, the model of power-sharing between the three branches of government. Though still largely untested, Dahal believes that the appointment procedures under this Constitution may lead to appropriate selections being made, though its complicated power-sharing devices might quite easily descend into a gridlock.

The Supreme Court of India has rightly been described by a commentator as the most powerful Court in the world.[10] Within the powers vested in it by the Constitution, it awards the death penalty, overthrows elected governments, and lays down which parts of the Constitution are immune to amendment by Parliament. The *NJAC Case* reflects a particular constitutional vision—that sustaining the credibility of such a powerful court requires careful and impartial selection that a non-partisan commission without a clear majority of judges is institutionally ill-equipped to do. The history of judicial appointments, the reasoning employed by the judges in the case as well as a comparative understanding of appointments processes in other jurisdictions, suggest that the reality is perhaps a little more complex. It is some of this richer and more complex reality that this volume attempts to capture.

---

[10] S.P. Sathe, 'Judicial Activism: The Indian Experience' (2001) 6 *Washington University Journal of Law* 29, 43, 87.

I

The History of Judicial
Appointments in India

From Kania to Sarkaria

1 *Judicial Appointments from 1950 to 1973*

SUCHINDRAN B.N.*

On 26 January 1950, the founders of the Indian Republic created the Supreme Court of India. In an act of great faith and trust, they bequeathed to its judges the product of their great labours. The Court, in the words of one its members, was intended to be the 'sentinel on the qui vive'.[1] To say that this bequest was made without any reservations would be untrue. There were apprehensions expressed as to how the new Court would respond to the 'new deal' legislation attempting to create a new social order through radical changes to property rights and social equality laws.[2] But the Assembly was equally clear that they wanted an independent and not a subservient court. As Nehru put it,

* The author would like to thank Vikram Raghavan for his encouragement and discussions; and two law students, Gaurav Natarajan and Akshay Nagarajan, who provided research assistance for this essay. He would also like to add that most of the facts for this essay have been taken from interviews conducted by scholars such as George H. Gadbois, Jr and Granville Austin, autobiographies of the judges themselves, or persons involved in the appointment process. It can be safely presumed that with regard to their own appointments, the judges might have glossed over any canvassing that they might have done and, in many cases, did not know the actual deliberations that led to their appointment.

[1] *State of Madras v. V. G. Row*, 1952 SCR 597 [13].

[2] As Nehru put it: 'Within limits no judge and no Supreme Court can make itself a third chamber.' *Constituent Assembly of India Debates*, vol 9, no 4 (Lok Sabha Secretariat) 10 September 1949, 1195–6.

the 'judges should not only be first rate, but should be acknowledged to be first-rate in the country, and of the highest integrity, if necessary, people who can stand up against the executive government, and whoever may come in their way'.[3]

Such an independent court was not unknown to colonial India, but the founders knew that this could only be ensured by an untainted appointment process. After some debate, and considering various options and suggestions, the Assembly accepted the suggestion that the President (i.e., the executive government) shall appoint the Judges of the Supreme Court after consultation with such judges of the Supreme Court and High Court as she would deem necessary, provided that the Chief Justice of India shall be consulted in all appointments except his own.[4] On this basis, a practice developed by which the Chief Justice of India initiated appointments. Indignantly, Home Minister Govind Ballabh Pant wrote, after publication of the Law Commission's adverse findings of political interference, that every appointment had actually followed the final advice of the Chief Justice of India.[5]

The first phase (1950–73) saw the Court traverse all possible jurisprudential philosophies on the journey from the literalism of *A.K. Gopalan v. State of Madras*[6] in 1950 to becoming an unapologetic and *de facto* third chamber of the legislature restricting the parliamentary right to amend the Constitution itself in *Kesavananda Bharati v. State of Kerala*[7] in 1973. They did this by following a judicial method best illustrated by American Chief Justice Charles Evan Hughes, Sr., who once said that we are under a Constitution, but the Constitution is what the judges say it is. This period saw 14 Chief Justices and a total of 53 appointments to the Court.[8] The story of these appointments is the story of how providence, manipulation, and destiny can influence an institution.

[3] *Constituent Assembly of India Debates*, vol 8, no 3 (Lok Sabha Secretariat) 24 May 1949, 247–60.

[4] Constitution of India, art. 124(2), as originally enacted.

[5] Prasad Papers, Letter from Pant to Setalvad, 22 August 1957 (National Archives of India, File 47). He was talking about High Court appointments.

[6] AIR 1950 SC 27.

[7] (1973) 4 SCC 225.

[8] The full strength of the Court began with 7 and was increased to 14 in 1960, and this continued to be the position till 1977.

The Early Years (1950–64)

Justice Harilal Jekisondas Kania took over as the first Indian Chief Justice of the Federal Court at the dawn of Independence. Controversies relating to appointments had already begun in the Federal Court at that time.[9] Justice Kania himself was recommended to the Court because of a wrong that the incumbent Chief Justice of Bombay, Sir Leonard Stone, felt had been committed when he was passed over for his own post because of an altercation with the previous Chief Justice.[10]

Justice Kania initiated all further appointments to the Federal Court, but under the watchful eyes of Sardar Patel's Home Ministry. With the exception of Justice Saiyid Fazl Ali who had been appointed just prior to Independence, Justice Kania extended invitations to Justice Mundakathalur Patanjali Sastri, Justice Meher Chand Mahajan, Justice Bijan Kumar Mukherjea, and Justice Sudhi Ranjan Das to join the Court.[11] After the constitution of the Supreme Court, Justice Nagapudi Chandrashekhara Aiyar and Justice Vivian Bose were also extended invitations by Kania himself. Most of these appointments were based on exemplary judicial records and seniority in the High Courts, but also keeping in mind the necessity of regional and religious representation.[12] Most of these judges were from either privileged or legal,

[9] Chief Justice Maurice Gwyer had not been consulted in the decision to supersede Sir S. Varadachariar and appoint Sir Patrick Spens as his successor. When Gwyer protested, Viceroy Linlithgow replied, 'I think there is no doubt so far as the memorandum of procedure is concerned, that there has been a serious error in procedure for which, so far as responsibility rests here, I must apologise to you.' Kuldip Nayar (ed.), *Supersession of Judges* (Indian Book Company 1973) 18.

[10] Motilal Setalvad, *My Life: Law and Other Things* (NM Tripathi Pvt Ltd 1971) 56, 82 ('Setalvad'). *See also* interview with H.M. Seervai mentioned in George H. Gadbois, Jr, *Judges of the Supreme Court of India (1950–89)* (Oxford University Press 2011) 20 ('Gadbois').

[11] He also extended an invitation to Justice Mahommedali Currim Chagla who declined. This fact is documented in letters from Kania to Chagla, dated December 1, and 22, 1949. *See* Abhinav Chandrachud, 'My Dear Chagla', 31(2) *Frontline* (February 2014) <http://www.frontline.in/the-nation/my-dear-chagla/article5589838.ece> accessed 28 September 2016.

[12] Justice Das and Justice Mukherjea represented the East; Justice Kania and Justice Bose the West; the North was represented by Justice Fazal Ali and Justice

families.[13] While none of these appointments were shrouded in any controversy, Justice Kania's role in appointments to the High Court had caused some significant flutters. At one point, Nehru even questioned his suitability to be the first Chief Justice of India.[14] It was only Patel's pragmatism that had enabled him to 'manage' Justice Kania.[15] Both Patel and Justice Kania however passed away in quick succession.

Mahajan, and the South by Justice Sastri and Justice Chandrasekhara Aiyar. Three of the judges were Brahmins, Justice Fazl Ali was a Muslim, and Justice Bose was a Christian. The only significant representation absent was from the Scheduled Castes and Scheduled Tribes but that might have been because of unavailability of eligible candidates, clearly showcasing the urgency of social reform.

[13] All except Justice B.K. Mukherjea came from privileged backgrounds. Justice Patanjali Sastri was the only one not to have a close family legal connection but was a close friend of Justice Srinivasa Varadachariar of the Federal Court.

[14] Specifically, because of Justice Kania's interference in the appointments of Justice Bashir Ahmed and Justice Koman to the Madras High Court, and the appointment of Justice K.N. Wanchoo as Chief Justice of the Rajasthan High Court. See Vikram Raghavan, 'A Collegium of Nehru, Patel and Rajaji' (Livemint, 21 October 2015) <http://www.livemint.com/Opinion/vUddils2Sq2ote1ndPKBjN/A-collegium-of-Nehru-Patel-and-Rajaji.html> accessed 28 September 2016; Granville Austin, Working a Democratic Constitution: A History of the Indian Experience (Oxford University Press 1999) 126–7 ('Austin').

[15] Letter from Patel to Nehru dated 23 January 1950. Patel had interfered in the permanent appointment of Justice Bashir Ahmed by going ahead with it on his own and telling Justice Kania that any adverse action would be regarded as communal. Justice Kania's objection to Justice Koman of the ICS would have become a larger issue, but Patel refused to place the intemperate letter written by the Chief Minister on the file and himself redrafted a reply to be sent reiterating the support by the Chief Minister and the Chief Justice. Kumaraswami Raja's letter to Patel dated 12 November 1950 and Patel's to Kumaraswami Raja dated 20 November 1950; in the case of Justice Wanchoo's transfer and promotion; objections were raised by the acting Chief Justice, who, supported by Kania, was canvassing for himself; objections from the Chief Justice, Allahabad, who did not want to lose one of his star judges. The matter was settled by Patel sending his secretary to meet the Allahabad Chief Justice, whom he knew personally. See Austin (n. 14) 126–7.

Following Justice Kania's unexpected passing, it appears that the government did contemplate bypassing the rule of seniority in favour of Justice B.K. Mukherjea, Justice S.R. Das, or Justice M.C. Chagla. The idea of supersession does seem to have been entertained since there was a delay of more than 6 weeks in appointing Justice Sastri as the next permanent Chief Justice. The claims of all three candidates were equally strong: Justice B.K. Mukherjea was a true scholar and is still considered amongst the most brilliant judges who ever sat on the Court;[16] Justice Das was a favourite student of Rabindranath Tagore and hailed from a family that had strong judicial pedigree and political links to the Indian National Congress;[17] not only was Justice Chagla a nationalist Muslim, but he was also a close associate and colleague of Jinnah with whom he parted ways when Jinnah began propounding the two-nation theory. Equally strong might have been the disqualification of Justice Mahajan, who had some disagreements with Nehru during his tenure as Prime Minister of Kashmir over Sheikh Abdullah.[18] With Patel gone, this would have been a significant factor, but Justice Mahajan's threat to resign might have been the tilting factor to heed the principle of seniority.[19]

Significantly, during Justice Sastri's tenure, out of the four appointments, two had Madras connections—Justice Tirunelveli Lakshmanasuri Venkatarama Ayyar filled the vacancy created by Justice Sastri's own retirement, thereby protecting the 'Tamil Brahmin' seat on the Court. Justice Bachu Jagannadhadas was also from Madras but came via the newly constituted Orissa High Court. Both knew and had

[16] This was also the opinion of Justice Rohinton Nariman, expressed to Vikram Raghavan, and as told to the present author.

[17] His younger brother, Justice Prafulla Ranjan Das, was a Judge of the Patna High Court, and another brother was a barrister practicing in Calcutta. His extended family included the eminent lawyer politician 'Deshbandhu' Chittaranjan Das, J.R. Das, who was a judge of the High Court of Rangoon, and Satish Ranjan Das, who held the post of Advocate General of Bengal and was also a law member of the Viceroy's Executive Council. His daughter was a lawyer and his son-in-law was Ashoke Sen, a prominent lawyer and later law minister. *See* Gadbois (n. 10) 31.

[18] Mehr Chand Mahajan, *Looking Back: The Autobiography of Mehr Chand Mahajan, Former Chief Justice of India* (Asia Publishing House 1986) 277.

[19] Setalvad (n. 10) 189–90.

practiced with Justice Sastri at Madras and had very short tenures in the High Courts before being appointed to the Supreme Court. Justice Venkatarama Ayyar would distinguish himself as a brilliant judge and a master of constitutional law despite his short tenure on the Court. The regional and religious representation followed from the beginning of the Court would continue with the appointments of Justice Ghulam Hassan to the 'Muslim seat', and Justice Natwarlal Harilal Bhagwati to the 'Bombay seat'. Justice Sastri also offered a seat to Justice P.V. Rajamannar, who had been serving as Chief Justice of Madras since Independence, but he cited his duties towards his aged father to decline the invitation. If he had accepted, it would have been the most significant appointment of Justice Sastri's tenure since Justice Rajamannar would have served as Chief Justice of India for almost 7 years.[20] But his slightly younger brother-in-law, Koka Subba Rao, would make it to the Court and serve as Chief Justice of India.

Justice Jagannadhadas would have also known Justice Chandrashekara Aiyar, whose seat he filled, from his days at the Madras bar. He was also the first appointment to the Court who had actually fought elections, having served a term in the Madras Corporation. Apart from this, Justice Jagannadhadas also found support from the then President of India, Dr Rajendra Prasad, as well as from future President, V.V. Giri. President Prasad had interned with him in the Quit India Movement in 1942.[21] Giri, who was serving as India's High Commissioner in Colombo, in a letter to the then Orissa Chief Minister, H.K. Mahtab, wrote that 'My friend Jagannathdas' be recognized for his seniority and be appointed to the Court. Since Mahtab also canvassed unsuccessfully for Chief Justice B.K. Ray, it can be assumed that it was Justice Jagannadhadas's Congress connections that helped him supersede his former Chief Justice.[22] The *Cuttack Law Times* had noted that his long friendship with Congress Party Leaders had 'helped him in being elevated to the Bench in 1948'.[23] His political

---

[20] Gadbois (n. 10) 77.

[21] Gadbois (n. 10) 40.

[22] H.K. Mahtab, *While Serving My Nation: Recollections of a Congress Man* (Vidyapuri 1986), as cited in Austin (n. 14) 129.

[23] Gadbois (n. 10) 45.

links could be further evidenced by the fact that he resigned before his tenure to take up the politically significant post as Chairman of the Second Pay Commission.

During Justice Mahajan's tenure, it is reasonably certain that Justice Bhuvaneshwar Prasad Sinha was sworn in earlier to ensure that he becomes Chief Justice and to cut short the tenure of Justice Syed Jafar Imam in that post. Nehru's preference for Justice Imam to be sworn in first since the Muslim seat had been vacated was overruled by the full Court being convinced by Justice Mahajan.[24] Justice Imam would only be sworn in 3 months later after Justice Mukherjea took over as Chief Justice, but fate would conspire to deny him even this shortened tenure as Chief Justice. A debilitating stroke incapacitated him, and after obtaining Setalvad's opinion and a medical report from the All India Institute of Medical Sciences, Nehru reluctantly persuaded him to resign.[25]

It was Chief Justice S.R. Das who demonstrated the full extent of the Chief Justice of India's power to influence appointments to the Court. During his tenure at least three appointments were made from Calcutta. Two were close personal friends—Justice S.K. Das[26] (member of the Indian Civil Service (ICS)), with whom he shared a Brahmo Samaj connection, and Justice A.K. Sarkar, who was a junior in his own chamber. K.C. Das Gupta (also from the ICS), then serving as the Chief Justice of the Calcutta High Court, was also well known to S.R. Das. He had offered an appointment to the first Indian Chief Justice of the Calcutta High Court, P.B Chakravartti, and it had been approved, but the latter declined.[27] Complaints had been received about Justice A.K. Sarkar's appointment by Home Minister Pant since he superseded many judges senior to him in the Calcutta High Court, but by this time it was well settled that the Chief Justice has the unofficial determinative voice in appointments. That no other Supreme Court judge protested might also be a testament to the affable personality of Justice S.R.

[24] Gadbois (n. 10) 50.

[25] Gadbois (n. 10) 55; Setalvad (n. 10) 507–8; P.B. Gajendragadkar, *To the Best of My Memory* (Bharatiya Vidya Bhavan 1983) 158–9 ('Gajendragadkar').

[26] He was later also related to Chief Justice S.R. Das by marriage.

[27] P.B. Chakravartti, 'Appointment to the Supreme Court', *Calcutta Weekly Notes* LXXVIII (1 September 1969), as cited in Gadbois (n. 10) 59.

Das, who seems to have been a popular Chief Justice.[28] At the same time, he also extended invitations to some brilliant young judges who had been making a significant mark in High Courts—Justice Prahlad Balacharya Gajendragadkar, Justice K. Subba Rao, Justice Kailas Nath Wanchoo (ICS), Justice Mohammad Hidayatullah, and Justice Jayantilal Chhotalal Shah. These recommendations could have been an understanding with, and driven by, Home Minister Pant, since he had also urged making invitations to two relatively young and brilliant lawyers who were serving as Advocates General—H.M. Seervai and Lal Narain Sinha—who declined. Pant also extended an invitation to Nani Ardeshir Palkhivala at the incredibly young age of 41. If Palkhivala had accepted then he would have been Chief Justice for an incredible 14 years (from 1971 to 1985). These were tumultuous years for the Court and the nation, and it could be argued that Palkhivala might have made a greater difference as Chief Justice of the Court than as lead counsel for the petitioners in some of the most momentous cases of the period.

Justice B.P. Sinha inherited a young and stable Court when he took over as Chief Justice. He managed to overrule Home Minister Pant to appoint Justice Raghubar Dayal over another judge of the Allahabad High Court.[29] He also seems to have taken a stand for the 'Madras seat' by appointing Justice Narasimha Rajagopal Ayyangar.[30] He enjoyed a cordial relationship with President Rajendra Prasad and when the latter raised some doubts over the recommendation of Justice Janardhan Raghunath Mudholkar, he had only to point out that the candidate's father had been a former President of the Indian National Congress. For much of this time, and for some time after President Prasad demitted office, it was believed that the President had a voice independent from the government in the matter of appointments to the judiciary.[31]

---

[28] 'I do not think any other Chief Justice was so universally loved and respected.' See M. Hidayatullah, My Own Boswell (Universal Law Publishing Co. 2015 rep) 196; 'In the time of S.R. Das, the atmosphere of the Court was very friendly.' See Gajendragadkar (n. 25) 133.

[29] B.P. Sinha, Reminiscences and Reflections of a Chief Justice (B.R. Publishing Corporation 1985), as cited in Gadbois (n. 10) 96.

[30] Gadbois (n. 10) 96.

[31] See A.G. Noorani, 'The Prime Minister and the Judiciary' in James Manor (ed.), in Nehru to the Nineties: The Changing Office of the Prime Minister (C. Hurst & Co. Publishers Ltd 1994) 100.

Justice Gajendragadkar was a dynamic and relatively young Chief Justice. His tenure would encompass three Prime Ministers. It was Justice Gajendragadkar who seems to have begun a more formal practice of getting the concurrence from the senior-most associate justice[32] for appointments to the Court. Previously, the Court had been too small for the need to differentiate between senior and junior associate justices. Justice Gajendragadkar also seems to have taken some interest in meeting and interviewing candidates before forwarding a recommendation.[33]

The first appointment of Justice Gajendragadkar's tenure was Justice Sarv Mittra Sikri, a former Advocate General of Punjab and the first appointee taken directly from the bar. There had been attempts to appoint someone from the bar since the Chief Justiceship of S.R. Das, but none had fructified. The man behind this idea seems to have been Home Minister Pant. Chief Justice Sinha had been against the idea but had nominated Sikri after meeting him for tea with Justice Gajendragadkar.[34] In the case of Justice Ranadhir Singh Bachawat from Calcutta High Court, Justice Gajendragadkar had not taken his consent but had consulted K.C. Das Gupta, who was retiring.[35] Justice Jayendra Manilal Shelat was a long-standing colleague of Justice Gajendragadkar in the Bombay High Court and was a replacement for the latter's own seat. After retirement, Justice Gajendragadkar, still an influential figure, would also play a pivotal role in the elevation of Justice V.R. Krishna Iyer and Justice Yeshwant Vishnu Chandrachud.

The Indira Gandhi Era: Political Assertion (1967–73)

Justice A.K. Sarkar recommended the names of Justice Vashistha Bhargava (ICS) and Justice Gopendra Krishna Mitter. However, Justice

[32] Justice K.N. Wanchoo confirmed this in an interview to Gadbois. *See* Gadbois (n. 10) 104.

[33] He went to meet Vaidyanathier Ramaswami in Patna and also met Penmetsa Satyanarayana Raju before recommending their names.

[34] Gajendragadkar (n. 25) 152–4. Sikri in an interview to Gadbois admitted that it was Gajendragadkar's effort which resulted in his appointment. *See* Gadbois (n. 10) 106.

[35] Gajendragadkar (n. 25) 180–1.

Mitter's name ran into some controversy since the serving Chief Justice of West Bengal, D.N. Sinha, was interested in the appointment for himself and complained in writing to the Chief Minister of West Bengal and Home Minister Gulzarilal Nanda. However, the appointment was made since Justice Sarkar would not withdraw the name and he had also taken the trouble of getting concurrence from the incoming Chief Justice Subba Rao.[36]

Justice Subba Rao appointed his long-time partner and friend Justice Chittur Anantakrishna Vaidialingam. This caused some controversy, as V.A. Seyid Muhammad, a Member of Parliament, wrote in response to Palkhivala's *Our Constitution, Defaced and Defiled*[37] that if one were to adopt the objectionable method of Mr Palkhivala, one could easily say that Justice Vaidialingam was deliberately and intentionally brought over to the Supreme Court to get support for Justice Subba Rao's point of view.[38] Justice Subba Rao had also, with Chief Justice designate Wanchoo's concurrence, recommended the name of Justice Kawdoor Sadananda Hegde as his own replacement. The delay in making the appointment may have been due to Justice Subba Rao's resignation to become the joint opposition candidate for President. But he was ultimately sworn in after three months when Justice Wanchoo threatened to resign.[39] Justice Hegde was the first appointee to have prior parliamentary experience having served two terms in the Rajya Sabha and resigned during his second term to join the Mysore High Court on Pant's invitation. The latter seems to have been impressed then with his legal knowledge while preparing the draft of the States Reorganisation Act, 1956.[40]

Justice Hidayatullah invited Justice Ajit Nath Ray, Justice Jaganmohan Reddy, and Justice Inder Dev Dua. Justice Hidayatullah's nominees were a surprise to many of his colleagues but nobody inquired and no explanations were volunteered. Justice Dua was a neighbour in Delhi. Justice Ray was junior to Justice Jaganmohan Reddy but was sworn in first. At the time, it was only a question of status as both were not in

---

[36] Gadbois (n. 10) 118, 122.

[37] N.A. Palkhivala, *Our Constitution: Defaced and Defiled* (MacMillan 1974).

[38] Gadbois (n. 10) 123.

[39] Gadbois (n. 10) 128.

[40] Gadbois (n. 10) 129–30.

line to become Chief Justice, but when the supersession took place for Justice Ray to take over as Chief Justice of India, it would have been necessary for the government to supersede Justice Reddy also. Justice Hidayatullah's explanation for this departure from the seniority rule in swearing in was that Justice Ray was from the Calcutta High Court, which was higher in status.[41] This seems an unlikely explanation and far from satisfactory. Justice Reddy might have let it pass since neither was meant to be the Chief Justice. Just before retiring, Justice Hidayatullah had recommended the names of two of his close friends, S.P. Kotwal, then Chief Justice of Bombay, and M.S. Menon, who had just retired as Chief Justice of Kerala. The executive did not respond on either of these names. This was possibly the first time that the executive had completely ignored the names recommended by the Chief Justice of India.

The erosion of mutual respect and the suspicions building up between the government and the judiciary can be seen from the fact that there were rumours of supersession in the cases of Justice Hidayatullah, Justice Shah, and Justice Sikri but none of them fructified.[42] In retrospect, the government was obviously gauging the political climate and preparing to take on the Court after suffering a string of judicial setbacks in *Golak Nath v. State of Punjab*[43] in 1967, and *Rustom Cavasjee Cooper v. Union of India*[44] and *Madhav Rao Jiwaji Rao Scindia v. Union of India*[45] in 1970. Justice Hegde and many others believed that Mohan Kumaramangalam would be brought in as an outsider, but instead, he was made Minister for Steel and Mines and would ironically not supersede anyone but become the brainchild of supersession and court packing.[46]

---

[41] Gadbois (n. 10) 137. The reason that Hidayatullah does not mention any of the appointees to the Supreme Court in his autobiography might be because of the nepotism involved in many of his recommendations, as discussed later in this essay.

[42] Gadbois (n. 10) 136, 148, 151–2. *See* also K.S. Hegde, 'A dangerous doctrine' in Kuldip Nayar (ed.), *Supersession of Judges* (India Book Company 1973) 47 ('Hegde').

[43] AIR 1967 SC 1643 ('*Golak Nath Case*').

[44] (1970) 1 SCC 248 ('*Bank Nationalisation Case*')

[45] (1971) 1 SCC 85 ('*Privy Purses Cases*').

[46] Hegde (n. 42) 47; Gadbois (n. 10) 148.

Justice Shah had recommended Justice Prafullachandra Natwarlal Bhagwati, but this was also ignored. Justice Bhagwati would later be appointed in 1973, but had he been appointed earlier he would have had a stint of almost nine-and-a-half years as the Chief Justice. His appointment had also been delayed because of a warning from Justice Shelat, his former colleague from Gujarat, that he was given to pleasing the government on occasion and was too ambitious.[47] Although Justice Bhagwati would later receive much acclaim as a judge, he did receive criticism for an adulatory letter he wrote, as a sitting judge, to Indira Gandhi on her return to power stating that the 'reddish glow of the rising sun is holding out the promise of a bright sunshine'.[48] A few years earlier, Seervai had pointed out in his criticism that the same man had stated in a judgment that her electoral defeat was not just an ordinary defeat, but also a massive vote of no confidence in the ruling party. He had said in that case that '[w]hen there is such crushing defeat suffered by the ruling party and the people have expressed themselves categorically against its policies, it is symptomatic of complete alienation between the Government and the people'.[49]

Justice Sikri's Court would mark the end of the unofficial primacy enjoyed by the Chief Justice. Never before could any of the judges who were appointed be seen to have a primary political sponsor. It had been accepted that appointments will be initiated by the recommendation of the Chief Justice to the Law Minister. Law Minister H.R. Gokhale initiated the appointments of his erstwhile Bombay High Court colleagues, Devidas Ganpat Palekar and Yeshwant Vishnu Chandrachud; Siddhartha Shankar Ray recommended Subimal Chandra Roy and Arun Kumar Mukherjea; Mohan Kumaramangalam recommended Kuttyil Kurien Mathew; C. Subramaniam recommended his classmate Alwar Naicker Alagiriswami; and Indira Gandhi herself recommended Mirza Hameedullah Beg and Surendra Narayan Dwivedi[50] from her

---

[47] Gadbois (n. 10) 161.

[48] See Abhinav Chandrachud, 'Voice of a bygone era', 30(2) Frontline (January–February 2013) <http://www.frontline.in/static/html/fl3002/stories/20130208300208500.htm> accessed 30 August 2016.

[49] State of Rajasthan v. Union of India (1977) 3 SCC 592.

[50] Dwivedi was also related to H.N. Bahuguna, who was Minister of State for Communications at the Centre at the time.

family's hometown, Allahabad.[51] While Justice Reddy and most of the other judges at the time believed that Justice Hans Raj Khanna was the Chief Justice's nominee, Justice Sikri denied this in an interview to Gadbois and said that the initiation had come from Gokhale.[52] He might have done this in order to distance himself from the charge of cronyism as Justice Khanna was a close friend. Justice Khanna would go on to distinguish himself during the Emergency and would himself be superseded as the Chief Justice of India.

Justice Sikri exercised a veto against two other government nominees. Nagendra Singh, later elected to the International Court of Justice as India's nominee and who also served as Secretary to the President, was rejected by Justice Sikri although his candidature was vehemently pressed by Gokhale. Justice Sikri confirmed that he had threatened to resign if this appointment was pressed any further[53] and Justice Hegde told Kuldip Nayar that Indira Gandhi after being informed of his stand gave instructions that the name be withdrawn.[54] Justice Krishna Iyer was the other candidate rejected as Justice Shelat and Justice Hegde[55] had convinced Justice Sikri that he was a Communist and should not be appointed.

During Justice Sikri's period, the unofficial primacy of the appointment process had clearly shifted to the executive. Most of these judges, though deserving in their own right, had political patrons. Justice S.C. Roy's widow while confirming the fact that Siddhartha Shankar Ray had initiated her husband's appointment also added that Indira Gandhi had sent a message to her childhood friend, a nephew of former Bengal

---

[51] See P. Jaganmohan Reddy, *We Have a Republic Can We Keep It?: Lecture Delivered under the UGC Teachers Exchange Programme* (Sri Venkateswara University 1984) 34–5; A.N. Grover, 'Questions that must be answered' in Kuldip Nayar (ed.), *Supersession of Judges* (India Book Company 1973) 64; and Gadbois (n. 10) 154–5. Khanna himself believed that he was a Sikri nominee. *See* Gadbois (n. 10) 158.

[52] Gadbois (n. 10) 154–5.

[53] Gadbois (n. 10) 156.

[54] Kuldip Nayar, 'The Thirteenth Chief Justice' in Kuldip Nayar (ed.), *Supersession of Judges* (India Book Company 1973) 31.

[55] Gajendragadkar had also pressed Hegde on his morning walks to support Krishna Iyer, who was at the time working at the Law Commission. *See* Gadbois (n. 10) 195.

Chief Minister Dr B.C. Roy, that he 'must come to Delhi to help her'.[56] Justice Dwivedi had apparently declared at his farewell function that he was going to the Supreme Court to overrule *Golak Nath*.[57]

Justice Ray remains to this day the most controversial appointment to the office of the Chief Justice of India. The former Attorney General for India, C.K. Daphtary, with his mastery of the pithy phrase, put it bluntly in Parliament by stating that the 'boy who wrote the best essay got the first prize'. The 'best essay' was, of course, the sole dissenting judgment in the *Bank Nationalisation Case*. In the *Privy Purses Case* also he was the only judge who accepted the arguments of the government on merits. In the only interview he has given on the issue since his retirement he said that he accepted the Chief Justiceship because he was told that he would be superseded also. This could be true, since Justice Mathew was the first to have been offered the post and it was believed that Mrs Gandhi was willing to supersede all judges senior to him if it became necessary.[58] But in an act of great judicial propriety and courage, Justice Mathew declined the offer as improper.

The appointment of Justice Ray however was a grievous blow to the independence of the judiciary. Future aspirants to the Court were put on notice of the importance of governmental support for their appointment. Although supersession was only carried out once more in the case of Justice Khanna, judges clearly felt the hand of the executive on their shoulders. From that time on, a judge who ruled against the government became a 'brave judge'—a euphemism for a judge who was not looking for a post-retirement sinecure.

Justice Bhagwati and Justice Krishna Iyer were clearly 'court packing' appointments. Justice Krishna Iyer was the junior-most High Court judge ever appointed to the Supreme Court and had less than 3 years of experience. He was also the first appointee to have served all three branches of government—the legislative as the Member of the Legislative Assembly (MLA) for the Madras constituency, the executive as a minister in the E.M.S. Namboodiripad government, and the judiciary as a judge. He was also the first judge to have suffered imprisonment after Independence, giving him a lifelong interest in

[56] Gadbois (n. 10) 157–8.
[57] Jaganmohan Reddy, *The Judiciary I Served* (Orient Longman 1999) 228.
[58] Gadbois (n. 10) 175–6.

prison reforms. Together, they did mark a change in the trajectory of the Supreme Court's jurisprudence.

Keeping in mind the need for regional and religious appeasement (no longer merely representation), and to offset the radical appointments of Justice Bhagwati and Justice Krishna Iyer, the government and Justice Ray invited the first Assamese representative, Justice Parbati Kumar Goswami; and the first Sikh, Justice Ranjit Singh Sarkaria, to offset the radical nature of the previous two appointments. The latter would become more famous for the work he would do as head of the Commission on Centre–State Relations, in 1983.

Conclusion

The trust that had been placed in an elected political executive in the matter of judicial appointments had clearly been belied by the time Indira Gandhi had become Prime Minister. It was her government that began to question and assert against the unwritten predominance of the Chief Justice of India in making appointments. The more the Court flexed its judicial muscles, the greater the interest that was shown by the political executive in the appointment process. Towards the end of the period under study, several judges could be identified by their political sponsor and political views. Even earlier there were signs of nepotism and regionalism shown by the Chief Justices in recommending appointments, but overall there seems to have been a sense of duty and cordiality before making a recommendation. In retrospect, despite the creeping politicization of the judiciary, this was still a glorious phase of the Supreme Court with some of its best and most conscientious judges serving in this period.

'Republics are created,' said Sachidananda Sinha quoting Joseph Story, 'by the virtue, public spirit, and intelligence of the citizens. They fall, when the wise are banished from the public councils, because they dare to be honest, and the profligate are rewarded, because they flatter the people, in order to betray them.'[59] The first phase is an illustration of this statement. If we have not yet fallen, it is because we have not banished the wise completely from our public institutions and the Supreme Court. But we have been close to the precipice and back many times. One can only hope that we do not slip in the future.

[59] *Constituent Assembly Debates*, vol 1, no 1 (Lok Sabha Secretariat) 9 December 1946, 5.

A Committed Judiciary

2 *Indira Gandhi and Judicial Appointments*
T.R. ANDHYARUJINA[*]

The period of Emergency from 1975 to 1977 in India was characterized, generally, by excesses of the executive branch of the government in several facets of life. The Supreme Court of India also could not escape the oppressive atmosphere of the time, and its functioning in several respects became a matter of grave concern. The Emergency is remembered in the Court's history for having dealt a severe blow to the independence of the judiciary, as was evident from actions of the executive as well as from certain decisions rendered by the Supreme Court during this time. At the same time, the Emergency is also remembered for being a period where the Supreme Court itself, as an institution, failed the citizens as well as the Constitution. In fact, the Court also failed one of its own for having stood up to the excesses of the Emergency. Only two judges of the Supreme Court stood out as strongly independent during and immediately before this period—Justice V.R. Krishna Iyer and Justice H.R. Khanna—for their powerful judgments that were neither tainted by fear of the government nor the lure of ambition.

This essay commences with a discussion of the gradual increase in executive interference in the matter of judicial appointments in the

[*] Parts of this essay appeared in T.R. Andhyarujina, 'When the Bench Buckled', *The Indian Express* (New Delhi, 8 July 2015) <http://indianexpress.com/article/opinion/columns/when-the-bench-buckled/> accessed 22 September 2016.

years immediately preceding the Emergency. It then proceeds to discuss the judicial background and circumstances which were consequential to the proclamation of Emergency. This discussion will reveal that the proclamation of Emergency was, among other things, a response to certain judicial developments of the time. Thereafter, the essay will discuss the period of Emergency, and the way it impacted judicial appointments and transfers, and by necessary implication, judicial independence. The essay will conclude with a few thoughts on how the Emergency turned out to be a decisive event in the constitutional history of India, and possibly was the reason behind the currently prevalent system of appointment of judges.

Executive Interference Prior to Emergency

In the years preceding the Emergency, the occurrence of certain specific events indicated that the ground had been laid for a confrontation between the Parliament and the Supreme Court, even before the formal proclamation of Emergency. From the coming into force of the Constitution till 1970, appointments to the Supreme Court were made by the government on the recommendation of the Chief Justice. This practice came into jeopardy with the prospect of some friction between the Court and the Parliament after the judgments in *Golak Nath v. State of Punjab*,[1] *Rustom Cavasjee Cooper v. Union of India*,[2] and *Madhav Rao Jiwaji Rao Scindia v. Union of India*.[3] In the background of these judgments, which largely involved judicial invalidation of measures taken by the government of the day or curtailment of the power of the Parliament,[4]

---

[1] (1967) 2 SCR 762 (*Golak Nath*).

[2] (1970) 1 SCC 248 (*Bank Nationalisation Case*).

[3] (1971) 1 SCC 85 (*Privy Purses Case*).

[4] These three judgments had the potential to create a major conflict between the Parliament and the Supreme Court. In *Golak Nath*, the Supreme Court held that Parliament could not amend or alter any fundamental right. In the *Bank Nationalisation Case*, the Court struck down the nationalisation of fourteen private banks, while in the *Privy Purses Case*, the Court struck down the abolition of Privy Purses. *See* Arvind P. Datar, 'The Case that Saved the Indian Democracy', *The Hindu* (Delhi, 24 April 2013) <http://www.thehindu.com/opinion/op-ed/the-case-that-saved-indian-democracy/article4647800.ece> accessed 22 September 2016.

it was to be expected that judicial appointments would be made keeping an eye on the judicial attitudes of the appointees.[5] The process of consultation with the Chief Justice became secondary to the primary process of government nomination.[6] The government of the day was making earnest attempts to appoint only such judges who were unlikely to be obstructive to its policies.[7]

The starkest instance of the government attempting to pack the Court with possibly favourable persons was the appointment of Justice A.N. Ray as the Chief Justice of India in 1973, superseding three judges of the Supreme Court who were senior to him. His appointment, which broke the long-standing convention of appointing the senior-most puisne judge of the Supreme Court as the Chief Justice of India, was the fallout of the judgment in *Kesavananda Bharati v. State of Kerala*,[8] which was delivered on 24 April 1973. The majority in this case, comprising seven judges, held that Parliament has no power to alter the basic structure of the Constitution. Six other judges, including Justice A.N. Ray, held that there were no restrictions on Parliament's power to amend the Constitution. The then Chief Justice S.M. Sikri who headed the majority on the bench, was to retire the next day on 25 April, after the judgments were delivered on 24 April. The government of the day, after having come to know of the contents of the judgments in advance, disregarded the seniority of the three senior-most judges who had been part of the majority for the appointment of the next Chief Justice, namely, Justice J.M. Shelat, Justice K.S. Hegde, and Justice A.N. Grover, and appointed Justice A.N. Ray as Chief Justice on the next day. Interestingly, Justice Ray had ruled in favour of Parliament in other cases as well, such as the *Bank Nationalisation Case* and the *Privy Purses*

[5] T.R. Andhyarujina, *The Kesavananda Bharati Case: The Untold Story of Struggle for Supremacy by Supreme Court and Parliament* (Universal Law Publishing Co. Pvt. Ltd 2014) 14.

[6] Andhyarujina (n. 5) 15.

[7] For instance, in 1972, Chief Justice Sikri had reservations about the appointment of Justice S.N. Dwivedi, who was related to a minister in Indira Gandhi's government. Ultimately, the government prevailed and Justice Dwivedi, who was considered 'pro-government', was appointed to the Supreme Court. *See* Andhyarujina (n. 5) 16–17.

[8] (1973) 4 SCC 225 (*Kesavananda Bharati*).

Case, apart from having held in *Kesavananda Bharati* that there was no restriction on Parliament to amend the Constitution. Unsurprisingly, Chief Justice-ship was conferred as a reward on Justice A.N. Ray. Thus, the first step in undermining the independence of the judiciary at the behest of executive overreach was successfully taken.

At a dinner party given by the Supreme Court gazetted staff on 25 April in his honour, the retiring Chief Justice Sikri incisively told the incoming Chief Justice, Justice Ray, who had been appointed Chief Justice after him, 'You will rue the day you accepted the Chief Justiceship.'[9] This sentiment was evoked by the fact that the supersession of the three senior-most judges and appointment of Justice Ray as Chief Justice caused tremendous dissatisfaction and agitation in the legal community, as he was considered to be a judge who was inclined to decide in favour of the government. In any case, the events immediately following *Kesavananda Bharati* were merely a precursor to what lay ahead for the future of appointments to the higher judiciary in India in the backdrop of the Emergency.

Proclamation of Emergency—A Brief Judicial History

In the tense climate prevailing in the Supreme Court after the supersession of Justices Shelat, Hegde, and Grover, an unexpected development took place on 12 June 1975 when, pursuant to an election petition filed by Raj Narain in the Allahabad High Court, Justice Jagmohan Lal Sinha held Prime Minister Indira Gandhi guilty of two corrupt electoral practices under the Representation of People Act, 1951, and disqualified her for 6 years. Incidentally, the Allahabad High Court's decision was made when the Supreme Court was on vacation. An urgent application for stay of the judgment of the Allahabad High Court was made before a vacation bench of the Supreme Court, which was presided by Justice V.R. Krishna Iyer. Within a short time of the delivery of the Allahabad High Court judgment, the then Union Law Minister, H.R. Gokhale, sought to meet Justice Krishna Iyer at his residence. Upon being queried by Justice Krishna Iyer on the purpose of the meeting, Gokhale said that the government would file an appeal to seek stay of the Allahabad High Court judgment. Much to Gokhale's consternation,

[9] Andhyarujina (n. 5) 83.

Justice Krishna Iyer declined to meet the Law Minister keeping every possibility of perceived executive interference in the manner of deciding Mrs Gandhi's election petition at bay.

On 23 June 1975, when the matter came up for hearing before Justice Krishna Iyer, senior advocate Nani Palkhivala appeared for Mrs Gandhi and pleaded passionately for an immediate unconditional stay of her disqualification in national interest. However, in his order of 24 June 1975, Justice Krishna Iyer declined to grant a total stay of the Allahabad High Court judgment. Mrs Gandhi was allowed, as the Prime Minister, to participate in parliamentary proceedings, without any vote, pending the final decision in the election appeal.[10] Eminent jurist H.M. Seervai considers this decision by Justice Krishna Iyer as the finest hour of the Supreme Court.[11]

However, the immediate effect of Justice Krishna Iyer's order was the proclamation of Emergency, which was signed by the President of India, Fakhruddin Ali Ahmed early on 25 June 1975, a day after the judgment. However, it must be mentioned that the proclamation did not stop the government from making desperate efforts to validate Mrs Gandhi's election. Whilst the appeal was pending in the Supreme Court, Parliament enacted the Constitution (Thirty-ninth Amendment) Act, 1975 (39th Amendment) inserting Article 329A into the Constitution by which a dispute on a Prime Minister's election was retrospectively taken out of the jurisdiction of courts and freed from the rigour of ordinary election laws (such as the Representation of the People Act, 1951). The 39th Amendment was challenged before the Supreme Court. The decision in the appeal against the Allahabad High Court's judgment as well as on the challenge to the 39th Amendment was rendered by the Supreme Court on 7 November 1975 in the landmark judgment of *Indira Nehru Gandhi v. Raj Narain*.[12] While the 39th Amendment was struck down by the Court for abolishing the forum for adjudicating upon a dispute relating to the validity of the elections of the Prime Minister and Speaker, Mrs Gandhi's appeal, on facts, was allowed.

---

[10] *Indira Nehru Gandhi v. Shri Raj Narain* (1975) 2 SCC 159 [31].

[11] H.M. Seervai, *The Emergency, Future Safeguards, and the Habeas Corpus Case: A Criticism* (N.M. Tripathi Pvt. Ltd 1978) 260.

[12] 1975 Supp SCC 1.

However, a rather distressing development occurred during the course of the hearing of Mrs Gandhi's appeal. On 9 October 1975, suddenly, a bench of thirteen judges was ordered to be constituted by Chief Justice Ray, on his own accord, to review the judgment in *Kesavananda Bharati* without any reference by a bench of the Court, as is the usual practice. This move by the Chief Justice was a matter of surprise to his own colleagues as well. It was clear that the real purpose of the review exercise was to overrule the majority decision in *Kesavananda Bharati*, and possibly curtail the contours of the basic structure doctrine.[13] However, such was the prevailing atmosphere in the Court that it was believed that it would not be difficult for the government to have a favourable decision on the review it sought. This was because, apart from Justice H.R. Khanna, most senior judges in the Supreme Court were the ones who had dissented from the majority judgment in *Kesavananda Bharati*.[14] In the hearing of this review petition, Palkhivala reappeared to defend the majority decision in *Kesavananda Bharati* on the inviolability of the basic structure of the Constitution by an amendment. In what is considered to be the most eloquent arguments and impassioned address ever heard,[15] Palkhivala convinced the Supreme Court that no case had been made for reconsideration of the matter, more particularly at that time when Emergency was in full force.

Much to the good fortune of the Constitution, as well as of the Supreme Court, Palkhivala prevailed upon the judges not to reconsider the majority view in *Kesavananda Bharati*. Consequently, on 12 November 1975, Chief Justice Ray dissolved the *Kesavananda Bharati* review bench in front of a packed court and observed that for two days the arguments 'were in the air'. In this manner, Chief Justice Ray's attempt to review *Kesavananda Bharati* during the Emergency failed and the basic structure doctrine survived.

[13] Upendra Baxi, *The Indian Supreme Court and Politics* (Eastern Book Company 1980) 70 (Baxi).

[14] Baxi (n. 13) 70.

[15] Justice Khanna believed that 'the height of eloquence to which Palkhivala rose on that day had seldom been equalled and never surpassed in the history of the Supreme Court'. *See* H.R. Khanna, *Neither Roses Nor Thorns* (Eastern Book Company 2015) 78.

However, what could not escape anyone's attention was the manner in which the judiciary was beginning to succumb to the pressures of the government of the day. The executive's intention to secure a pliant judiciary was being realized in small, albeit significant ways.

ADM Jabalpur and What Ensued

The prevailing sentiment about the years of the Emergency has been that it marked a collective failure of all constitutional functionaries including the members of Parliament, the President, as well as Supreme Court justices.[16] The judiciary could not remain untouched from the excesses of the Emergency, and the government's attempts to secure a pliant judiciary were becoming evident. The government made no qualms about being considerate to judges who were favourable to them in their rulings. In fact, it is believed that it was during the Emergency that for the first time in its history, a credible threat was posed to the Court's survival as a major institution of State.[17] The Court was feeling pressures from the outside in the form of executive inroads into their decision-making, as well as the inside when judges of the Court readily gave in to executive pressure.

In the history of the Supreme Court, there have been two egregious instances of bypassing the seniority convention in the appointment of the Chief Justice of India. Both these stark instances of supersession of the senior-most judges of the Supreme Court for appointment as Chief Justice have been premised on landmark decisions rendered by the Court. As mentioned earlier, the first such instance followed the judgment in *Kesavananda Bharati*. The second instance of supersession occurred after what is considered to be the most deplorable decision of the Supreme Court during the Emergency—*Additional District Magistrate, Jabalpur v. Shivakant Shukla*.[18] On 28 April 1976, after a marathon hearing, a five-judge bench of the Supreme Court, with the majority comprising Chief Justice Ray, Justice M.H. Beg, Justice Y.V. Chandrachud, and Justice P.N. Bhagwati, held that by reason of the proclamation of

---

[16] This view was voiced by Fali S. Nariman in his autobiography. *See* Fali S. Nariman, *Before Memory Fades: An Autobiography* (Hay House 2010) 171.

[17] Baxi (n. 13) 38.

[18] (1976) 2 SCC 521 (*ADM, Jabalpur*).

Emergency of 25 June 1975, any petition to question the legality of detention orders (made under the Maintenance of Internal Security Act, 1971 [MISA]) even if they were made *mala fide* and without authority of law, could not be judicially reviewed.[19] Chief Justice Ray was categorical that liberty is confined and controlled by law, and is not an unregulated freedom.[20] He also held that Article 21 is the sole repository of the right to life and personal liberty, and any claim to a writ of *habeas corpus* for enforcement of Article 21 during Emergency is barred.[21] In rendering this decision, the Supreme Court set aside the contrary view taken by nine High Courts. Upon consideration of the legality of the detention orders, these High Courts had upheld the right of a detenue to move the court for a writ of *habeas corpus* even when the proclamation of Emergency was in force.

In the context of judicial independence, two important consequences flowed from the judgment in *ADM Jabalpur*—first, sixteen High Court judges, who had previously held opinions contrary to the Supreme Court paid the price for their judgments by forced transfers to other High Courts; second, Justice Khanna of the Supreme Court, who gave a powerful dissenting opinion in this case, was superseded for appointment as Chief Justice despite being the next in line in terms of seniority.

The mass transfer that took place in 1976 concerned sixteen judges of the nine High Courts who had upheld the rights of the persons detained during the Emergency. These judges were transferred around the country from their original High Courts, without their consent, and overriding their objections.[22] In other cases, judges initially appointed for two years prior to their confirmation were not continued if they were critical of the government.[23] The sixteen judges who were transferred were not guilty of any misbehaviour or wrong-doing.[24] On the

[19] *ADM Jabalpur* (n. 18) [452].

[20] *ADM Jabalpur* (n. 18) [33].

[21] *ADM Jabalpur* (n. 18) [137].

[22] Granville Austin, *Working a Democratic Constitution: A History of the Indian Constitution* (Oxford University Press 2003) 344 (Austin).

[23] Austin (n. 22) 344.

[24] H.M. Seervai, *Constitutional Law of India*, vol. 3 (4th edn, Universal Law Publishing 2008 rep) 2802 (Seervai [2008]).

contrary, they had performed their constitutional duties with utmost sincerity, and had only 'erred' in delivering judgments which were not to the liking of the government.[25] As Seervai put it incisively, 'The sixteen judges were transferred not for doing anything wrong but for doing right to all manner of people according to the Constitution and the laws.'[26]

The government's intent was also reflected in its decision to prohibit all newspapers from publishing the names of the sixteen judges who were transferred as well as any discussions around the issue.[27] Further, a threat of transfer to forty other judges was expressed by a deliberate leaking of their names[28]—a warning of their prospective shared fate with the other sixteen judges in the event they failed to conform to the government's diktats. This was a blatant governmental attempt to control the judiciary, by the threat of transfer of High Court judges who were considered by the government to be confrontational.

The judgment in *ADM Jabalpur* is as much remembered for the tainted judgment delivered by the majority as it is for the powerful dissent delivered by Justice Khanna. In his dissent, Justice Khanna held that there was no sufficient ground to interfere with the view taken by the nine High Courts. Most significantly, he held that Article 21 cannot be the sole repository of the right to life and personal liberty, which is the most precious right of human beings in civilized societies governed by the rule of law.[29] In an atmosphere that was characterized by widespread curtailment of civil liberties, Justice Khanna's dissenting opinion was the beacon of hope for protection of the constitutional rights of the citizens.

On several occasions, his dissent has been likened to the famous dissenting judgment of Lord Atkin in *Liversidge v. Anderson*[30] for its

[25] Seervai (2008) (n. 24).

[26] Seervai (2008) (n. 24).

[27] Seervai (2008) (n. 24).

[28] Seervai (2008) (n. 24) 2803.

[29] *ADM, Jabalpur* (n. 18) [525], [593].

[30] 1942 AC 206. Lord Atkin delivered a celebrated dissent in this case where he invalidated an order of detention which was passed without trial during the days of the Second World War.

[31] V.R. Krishna Iyer, 'A Courageous Voice of Dissent', *The Hindu* (New Delhi 19 March 2008) <http://www.thehindu.com/todays-paper/

courage and for managing to keep the lure of ambition at bay.[31] For his bold judgment, Justice Khanna came to be held in great esteem by the judiciary and the bar, and later, as a mark of respect, his portrait was put up in the Supreme Court. However, while veneration may have followed, Justice Khanna was also made to pay a price for his powerful dissent. In January 1977, Justice Khanna was superseded by Justice Beg for being appointed as the Chief Justice. Justice Khanna's supersession was the government's way of sending out a strong message to anyone who refused to toe its line.

Evidently, the Emergency had a crippling effect on the decisional independence of the judges of higher judiciary. The transfer of sixteen judges across High Courts was the direct consequence of these judges having ruled independently and courageously in the MISA cases during Emergency.[32] Justice Khanna was also the victim of his independent and untainted decision in *ADM Jabalpur*. The government did not shy away from making career decisions for judges based on their allegiance to them, thereby ushering in a distressing time for judicial independence. Appointment of judges became a plaything of the government and consequently the site for future struggles around the independence of the judiciary.

The Long-Term Consequences of *ADM Jabalpur* and the Emergency

The aftermath of the Emergency, in general, and the judgment of the Court in *ADM Jabalpur*, in particular, concretized the government's policy of intolerance towards judges who dared to challenge the executive's

---

tp-opinion/a-courageous-voice-of-dissent/article1222615.ece> accessed 25 August 2016; Anil Divan, 'A Profile in Judicial Courage', *The Hindu* (New Delhi 7 March 2008) <http://www.thehindu.com/todays-paper/tp-opinion/a-profile-in-judicial-courage/article1215366.ece> accessed 25 August 2016.

[32] *Union of India v. Sankalchand Himatlal Sheth* (1977) 4 SCC 193, where Justice Untwalia noted that 'orders of transfers were made by and large in cases of Judges who had shown exemplary courage and independence even during the period of emergency in delivering judgments which were not to the liking of the men in authority, including the judgments in many MISA cases' [128].

unbridled exercise of powers. It also brought into focus the hitherto uncontroversial subject of appointment of judges.

The causes and impact of the supersession that occurred during as well as before the proclamation of Emergency have been documented and analyzed by the Law Commission in its 121st Report. The Report pertinently notes that,

> Supersession in the matter of selection of the Chief Justice of India, transfer of Judges, and non-confirmation of additional Judges of the High Courts in exercise of the power conferred by article 222 of the Constitution are some other developments which have given rise to an apprehension that the independence of judiciary, said to be the cardinal feature of the Constitution, is likely to suffer erosion at the hands of the Executive.[33]

The disregard for constitutional governance during the Emergency escaped no one, including the judiciary. Even the supersession of the three judges that occurred prior to the Emergency witnessed the emergence of two polarized positions. Those who condemned the supersession viewed it is a threat to the independence of the judiciary, as it amounted to an erosion of the judiciary's insulation against executive overreach.[34] On the other hand, those in support of the supersession relied on the Law Commission of India's seminal 14th Report, which while noting the entrenchment of the tradition of appointing the senior-most puisne judge, observed that not merely experience but competence must also play a role in the appointment process.[35]

Irrespective of these opinions, the judiciary was especially affected by debilitating executive interference. This impact was long-lasting and was apparent in the politics that informed the three *Judges' Cases*. While the *First Judges' Case* witnessed consensus of the majority on the issue that in the matter of appointment of judges to the Supreme Court, the

---

[33] Law Commission of India, *A New Forum for Judicial Appointments* (121st Report, Ministry of Law and Justice, Government of India 1987) para 3.4 (121st Report).

[34] 121st Report (n. 33) para 1.5.

[35] Law Commission of India, *Reform of Judicial Administration* (14th Report, Ministry of Law and Justice, Government of India 1958) (14th Report).

[36] The judicial trajectory that followed the decisions of the Supreme Court in the three *Judges' Cases* finds enunciation in Lord Cooke of Thorndon, 'Where

constitutional duty to consult did not imply a duty to obtain concurrence of persons consulted,[36] this position experienced a shift in the subsequent cases. The *Second Judges' Case* took a detour by holding that it was the Chief Justice of India who had primacy in the matter of appointment of judges, with such opinion being formed in consultation with a collegium consisting of two of the senior-most puisne judges of the Supreme Court, and that consultation was to be read as concurrence.[37] This position was further embedded in the scheme of judicial appointments by the *Third Judges' Case*, which unlike the first two cases was a unanimous opinion. The *Third Judges' Case* reiterated that it was the opinion of the Chief Justice that has primacy in the matter of appointment of judges to the Supreme Court, and clarified the *Second Judges' Case* to the extent that the collegium must constitute of four of the senior-most puisne judges of the Court.[38]

The need to read in primacy in Articles 124(2) and 217(1) was in response to the specific circumstances that prevailed during the Emergency. Evidently, the excesses perpetrated by the executive during the Emergency had the consequence of ushering in a major transformation in the manner of interpretation of the terms of the Constitution, as well as the manner of judicial appointments. As is evident from the majority judgment of the Court in the *NJAC Case*, the effect of these excesses continues till this day.

Conclusion

Needless to say, the Emergency had a palpable effect on the Indian judiciary, and appointments to the Supreme Court could not remain untouched. As Benjamin Cardozo, a judge of the Supreme Court of the United States of America, said, 'The great tides and currents which engulf the rest of men do not turn aside their course and pass the judges by.'[39]

Angels Fear to Tread', in B.N. Kirpal, Ashok H Desai, Gopal Subramanium, Rajeev Dhavan, and Raju Ramachandran (eds), *Supreme but not Infallible: Essays in Honour of the Supreme Court of India* (Oxford University Press 2000) 97–106 (Lord Cooke).

[37] Lord Cooke (n. 36) 101.

[38] Lord Cooke (n. 36) 101.

[39] Benjamin Nathan Cardozo, *The Nature of the Judicial Process* (Yale University Press 1946 rep) 168.

It would not be incorrect to say that the transition from the appointments process, as envisaged by the framers of the Constitution to the process that presently exists can, in good measure, be attributed to the Emergency. Unlike what was anticipated by the Constituent Assembly, the power equation between the executive and the judiciary in the appointments process over the last two decades has unnaturally titled towards the latter. This was a reaction to the domination of the executive during the period of the Emergency in key matters pertaining to the judiciary. The excesses of the Emergency are largely used to justify the vesting of primacy in the judiciary in the matter of appointments. However, as much as the executive was responsible for exerting undue pressure, the judiciary was responsible for succumbing to that pressure with least resistance. The decision in *ADM Jabalpur* is evidence of that.

The time has now come to correct the executive–judiciary imbalance in the appointments process, something that the National Judicial Appointments Commission made an attempt to do. Though struck down, the search for a mechanism for appointments that acts as a check against pressures from the government and from within the judiciary must continue if the Indian higher judiciary is to become truly independent.

Recovering Lost Ground

3

The Case of the Curious Eighties

A.K. GANGULI

The pronouncement of the Supreme Court in the *NJAC Case* raises serious questions concerning the interrelationship between the legislature, the executive, and the judiciary in the scheme of the Constitution of India. The majority ruled, taking a cue from the majority judgment in the *Second Judges' Case*, that the independence of the judiciary is part of the basic structure of the Constitution, and that the Constitution secures this independence by preserving 'the primacy of the judiciary in the matter of selection and appointment of judges, to the Higher Judiciary'.[1] Much moral justification for this judgment, as well as the majority view in the *Second Judges' Case* lay in the invidious interference with the functioning of the judiciary including in appointment of judges that began in the 1970s, reached alarming proportions during the Emergency, and purportedly continued through the 1980s. Particularly, the 1980s in popular perception and in the majority judgment in the *NJAC Case* was singled out for harsh treatment. The *First Judges' Case* was considered 'the solitary departure'[2] to a line of judgments that had vested the Chief Justice of India with primacy in the appointment of judges. The implication was clear—independence of the judiciary in the appointments process was not secure in the decade.

---

[1] *NJAC Case* [416].
[2] *NJAC Case* [89.3].

This essay contests this understanding of the 1980s. First, it provides context to the decade by looking at the events that preceded it. Second, it analyses the judgment in the *First Judges' Case* in detail to point out how it espoused rather than derogated from the fine balance that the Constitution envisaged in the process of appointment. Third, it looks at specific anecdotal examples to demonstrate the strength of the independence of the judiciary in this period. A combination of these three arguments leads to the inference that the 1980s were a curious decade—while the judiciary in its processes of appointment continued to remain largely independent as before, with well-established conventions being followed, the perception, based on seeming infirmities in the *First Judges' Case*, was otherwise. If this essay goes some distance in correcting this misperception, it would have served its purpose.

Independence of the Judiciary: Constitutional Roots and the Shaky Seventies

In view of the reasoning of the Supreme Court that the 99th Amendment and the NJAC Act were violative of the independence of the judiciary, it is worth recounting how and when judicial independence came to be recognized as part of the basic structure of the Constitution. Even though judicial independence was not explicitly mentioned as a facet of the basic structure in *Kesavananda Bharati v. State of Kerala*,[3] it came to be considered part of the basic structure through a process of progressive interpretation in several decisions. While the rule of law was recognized as part of the basic structure in *Indira Nehru Gandhi v. Raj Narain*,[4] in *Samsher Singh v. State of Punjab*[5] the Court held that by mandating consultation with the Chief Justice of India before appointing judges, the Constitution guarantees the independence of the judiciary.

---

[3] (1973) 4 SCC 225 (*Kesavananda Bharati*). The judges in the *Kesavananda Bharati* case conceptualized several elements as part of the basic structure, but independence of the judiciary was not one of these. A brief discussion of the elements recognized to be part of the basic structure takes place in Raju Ramachandran and Mythili Vijay Kumar Thallam, 'The Obvious Foundation Test: Re-inventing the Basic Structure Doctrine', 109–121 in this volume.

[4] 1975 Supp SCC 1 [664].

[5] (1974) 2 SCC 831 [149] (*Samsher Singh*).

By the time of the judgment in *Union of India v. Sankalchand Himatlal Sheth*,[6] the Court took the formulation of independence of judiciary being part of the basic structure to be *a priori*. In the *First Judges' Case*, the Court recorded that there was no dispute between the parties that the independence of the judiciary was part of the basic structure of the Constitution.[7]

In practice, the idea of independence of judiciary being integral to the Constitution is older. Even before the adoption of the Constitution, the Federal Court, established under the Government of India Act, 1935, was developing a practice that would come to entrench itself post-Independence. Though the Government of India Act, 1935 did not contemplate consultation with the Chief Justice in the matter of appointments to the Federal Court,[8] it was only based on the opinion of the then Chief Justice H.J. Kania that the appointments were made.[9] During the tenure of Justice Kania as Chief Justice of the Federal Court, Justice Patanjali Sastri, Justice M.C. Mahajan, Justice B.K. Mukherjea, and Justice S.R. Das were appointed to the Court. With the coming into effect of the Constitution, the system of consultation with the Chief Justice became concretized as a matter of convention. However, the precise meaning of the term 'consultation' would become the subject matter of debate over the subsequent decades owing to a break in a related though distinct convention pertaining to appointment of the Chief Justice of India.

The decade of the 1970s saw two instances of supersession, wherein a judge other than the senior-most judge was appointed as the Chief

[6] (1977) 4 SCC 193 [87] (*Sankalchand Sheth*).

[7] *First Judges' Case* [320].

[8] Government of India Act, 1935, s 200 merely provided that the judges of the Federal Court of India 'shall be appointed by His Majesty by warrant under the Royal Sign Manual...'

[9] The matter of appointment of Chief Justice does not seem to have enjoyed this amount of transparency. Upon the resignation of Chief Justice Maurice Gwyer, rather than appoint Justice Varadachariar, who was the senior-most judge, the Governor General appointed Patrick Spens as the next Chief Justice. This was met with great disappointment even among the Englishmen, including the outgoing Chief Justice Gwyer himself. However by the time of the next transition, the seniority principle was respected by the Governor General who appointed H.J. Kania.

Justice of India.[10] The first was when upon the retirement of Chief Justice S.M. Sikri, Justice A.N. Ray was appointed as the Chief Justice of India, superseding three judges—Justices J.M. Shelat, K.S. Hegde, and A.N. Grover—whose opinions in the *Kesavananda Bharati* case were perceived as unfavourable to the Government.[11] This move was criticized in the legal and political circles and was seen as a serious affront to the independence of the judiciary.

During the tenure of Chief Justice Ray, a seven-judge bench of the Court in *Samsher Singh* had the opportunity to examine the correct interpretation of the word 'consultation' in the context of termination of the services of subordinate judges. The majority opinion rendered by Chief Justice Ray dwelt upon the power of the Governor vis-à-vis the Council of Ministers. Justice V.R. Krishna Iyer, in a separate but concurring judgment on behalf of himself and Justice P.N. Bhagwati, struck a note of support for the theory of primacy of the Chief Justice, holding that the executive may not differ from the opinion of the Chief Justice of India.[12]

In 1975, through a set of circumstances in which the judiciary played a crucial role, Emergency came to be imposed and was in force for the next two years. Several persons had sought relief from various High Courts seeking the writ of *habeas corpus* to protect themselves from the coercive might of the state acting under the infamous Maintenance of Internal Security Act, 1971. The judgments of the various High Courts came to be challenged before the Supreme Court in *Additional District*

---

[10] The impact that the Emergency had on the judicial appointments process finds enunciation in T.R. Andhyarujina, 'A Committed Judiciary: Indira Gandhi and Judicial Appointments', p. 18 in this volume.

[11] Granville Austin, *Working a Democratic Constitution: A History of the Indian Constitution* (Oxford University Press 2003) 344.

[12] *Samsher Singh* (n. 5) [149]. Justice Krishna Iyer held:

In all conceivable cases consultation with that highest dignitary of Indian justice will and should be accepted by the Government of India and the Court will have an opportunity to examine if any other extraneous circumstances have entered into the verdict of the Minister, if he departs from the counsel given by the Chief Justice of India. In practice the last word in such a sensitive subject must belong to the Chief Justice of India, the rejection of his advice being ordinarily regarded as prompted by oblique considerations vitiating the order.

Magistrate (ADM), Jabalpur v. Shivakant Shukla,[13] where the Court, by a majority of 4–1, held that in view of the declaration of Emergency, no person could move the High Court challenging the legality of an order of detention. In his dissenting opinion, Justice H.R. Khanna held that even during the period of Emergency, High Courts would have the power to issue writs in the nature of *habeas corpus*.[14] The majority judgment in *ADM Jabalpur* was contemporaneously criticized by the media across the world, with an editorial in *The New York Times* having noted, 'The submission of an independent judiciary to absolutist government is virtually the last step in the destruction of a democratic society....'[15]

Even though Justice Khanna's dissenting opinion came in for all-round praise, immediately after this, he was superseded for the position of Chief Justice of India by Justice M.H. Beg. Combined with the first supersession, this created a serious dent in the belief in the seniority principle and, consequently, the independence of the judiciary. In the elections that ensued after the Emergency was lifted, there was a change of government at the centre. The new Janata Government was composed of persons who had suffered because of the judgment in *ADM Jabalpur* and were opposed to it. However, the convention of the senior-most judge being appointed as the Chief Justice was restored after supersession on the two occasions discussed here. This proved that though there had been deviations, there was no systemic deficiency in India's constitutional machinery when it came to appointing the Chief Justice of India.

To ensure that no systemic deficiency is given a chance to occur in the future, the 80th Report of the Law Commission of India[16] had

---

[13] (1976) 2 SCC 521 (*ADM Jabalpur*).

[14] *ADM Jabalpur* (n. 13) [593].

[15] *See* Editorial, 'Fading Hope in India', *The New York Times* (New York 30 April 1976) <http://www.nytimes.com/1976/04/30/archives/fading-hope-in-india.html?_r=0> last accessed 15 August 2016.

[16] Law Commission of India, *The Method of Appointment of Judges* (80th Report, Ministry of Law and Justice, Government of India 1979) (80th Report). This Report was submitted on 10 August 1979. The Chairman of the Law Commission of India at the time of preparation of the Report was Justice H.R. Khanna, who had resigned from the Supreme Court after having been superseded. However, the covering letter reveals that by the time the Report was prepared and signed, he had moved on from the Law Commission, though the

recommended that in the matter of the appointment of judges to the Supreme Court of India, the Chief Justice of India should consult his three senior-most colleagues and in the communication incorporating his recommendation, specify the result of such consultation and reproduce the views of his colleagues. Between 1977 and 1979 the Chief Justice of India started consulting two of his senior-most colleagues, and then expanded it to four of his senior-most colleagues.[17] Similarly, in the matter of appointment of judges to the High Courts, there was an informal acceptance of a Law Commission recommendation that the Chief Justice should consult two of his colleagues. But thereafter this practice was discontinued. It is in this context that the decade of the eighties began.

The *First Judges' Case*

The major development in the 1980s with regard to the appointment of judges was the *First Judges' Case*. This case is regarded as a landmark in India's constitutional history because, as Jill Cottrell notes, the real interest in this case is that it is *about* judges, and not only *by* the judges.[18] The Congress Government, subsequent to re-election in 1980, formulated a policy which contemplated that one-third of the judges of a High Court should be from outside the concerned state. Accordingly, while consent and preferences of judges for transfer was sought, it was made clear that there was no commitment on the part of the government to accommodate the preferences of the judges. Several writ petitions were filed in High Courts across the country challenging

---

Report had his full concurrence. Though Justice Khanna himself was a victim of executive interference in judicial appointments, he reposed faith in the existing system. At the commencement of the consultations for this Report, Justice Khanna had written to the Law Ministry proposing a Judges Appointments Commission consisting of the Chief Justice, Union Law Minister, and three retired judges or Chief Justices of the Supreme Court.

[17] Law Commission of India, *A New Forum for Judicial Appointments* (121st Report, Ministry of Law and Justice, Government of India 1987) para 3.4 (121st Report).

[18] Jill Cottrell, 'The Indian Judges' Transfer Case' (1984) 33 ICLQ 1032, 1035.

the letter laying down this policy, the ad-hoc extensions given to additional judges, and also the transfers of some judges, particularly Chief Justices of High Courts across the country. The question, as distilled by the Court, was whether 'consultation' with the Chief Justice of India would be binding or not on the President.

Justice Bhagwati, one of the majority judges, stated that the question of interpretation of 'consultation' was no longer *res integra* having been decided in *Sankalchand Sheth*.[19] However, he sketched out the concept of consultation in more detail, laying down that consultation with the constitutional functionaries[20] was to be interpreted as consultation with the Chief Justice of India, the Chief Justice of the High Court, and such other Judges of the High Court and of the Supreme Court, as President may deem necessary to consult. He further held that this consultation was to be full and effective. To this end, it was necessary that:

[T]he President must communicate to the Chief Justice all the material he has and the course he proposes. The Chief Justice, in turn, must collect necessary information through responsible channels or directly, acquaint himself with the requisite data, deliberate on the information he possesses and proceed in the interests of the administration of justice to give the President such counsel of action as he thinks will further the public interest.[21]

Though the contention that the opinion of the Chief Justice of India, as the *pater familias* of the judicial fraternity, would have primacy was rejected, it was held that the opinion of the Chief Justice of India was to enjoy great weight.

Justice Bhagwati, however, expressed some dissatisfaction with consultation with only the Chief Justice of India and said that it would

[19] *First Judges' Case* [30]. In *Sankalchand Sheth*, Justice Chandrachud opined on the true meaning and content of consultation as envisaged by Article 222(1) of the Constitution. He said, 'After an effective consultation with the Chief Justice of India, it is open to the President to arrive at a proper decision of the question whether a Judge should be transferred to another High Court because, what the Constitution requires is consultation with the Chief Justice, not his concurrence with the proposed transfer.' *Sankalchand Sheth* (n. 6) [41].

[20] Article 217 of the Constitution of India contemplates consultation with the Chief Justice of India, the Governor of the concerned state, and the Chief Justice of the High Court.

[21] *First Judges' Case* [30].

be appropriate if a collegium would make recommendations regarding appointments to the higher judiciary to the President and that the recommending authority be more broad-based. A similar recommendation was later made by the Law Commission in its 121st Report, where a participatory body for judicial appointments was contemplated in the hope that it would have greater acceptability and reduce the probability of arbitrary action.[22]

Though this suggestion was not given effect to in the *First Judges' Case*, it laid the foundation for future developments. Justice R.S. Pathak, as he then was, held that three distinct constitutional functionaries[23] were involved in the consultative process for the appointment of a judge of the High Court and each had a distinct role to play. This also meant that while the Chief Justice of India did not have primacy in the consultative process over the Chief Justice of the concerned High Court, the Chief Justice of India must be deemed to have taken into consideration the advice tendered by the Chief Justice of the concerned High Court.

Justice D.A. Desai, Justice S. Murtaza Fazal Ali, Justice Pathak, and Justice E.S. Venkataramaiah, for differing reasons, supported the proposition that while the opinion of the Chief Justice of India enjoyed great weight, it would not have primacy. While Justice Venkataramaiah unequivocally held that the President is not bound by the view of the Chief Justice of India,[24] Justice Pathak stopped short of recognizing the primacy of the Chief Justice of India though stating that the view of the Chief Justice of India would carry greater weight than the view of the Chief Justice of the High Court.[25] Thus, while the Court in the *First Judges' Case* declined to recognize the primacy of the Chief Justice of India in the consultative process for appointment of judges to the High Court and Supreme Court, the judgment substantially broadened the scope and interpretation of 'consultation'.

A salient aspect of this judgment that amply demonstrates the strong culture of independence in the judiciary at the time is the handling of the issue of Justice K.B.N. Singh, who was a Chief Justice of a High Court who had been transferred, he claimed, without due consultation.

---

[22] 121st Report (n. 17) [7.4].

[23] *First Judges' Case* [887].

[24] *First Judges' Case* [1030].

[25] *First Judges' Case* [891].

The Court identified that the case, heard along with others, was substantially a dispute between the Chief Justice of a High Court and the Chief Justice of India and, therefore, the Chief Justice of India filed a counter affidavit explaining his position.[26] The Court reminded itself:

> [W]e are sitting as Judges, who have taken an oath to perform the duties of our office without fear or favour, affection or ill-will and it is our solemn and sacred duty to do justice, irrespective of who is the litigant before us. We have the highest regard for the Chief Justice of India as we have for Chief Justice K.B.N. Singh, but they are both litigants before us and while deciding the contest between them, we must be blind to their status or position and we must adjudicate the controversy between them as we might do in the case of any other litigants before us.[27]

After examining the facts of the case, Justice Bhagwati held that there was no 'full and effective consultation' in the case of transfer of Justice K.B.N. Singh in light of the fact that the reasons that weighed with the Central Government in recommending the transfer were different from the reasons stated by the Chief Justice of India. Hence it was clarified that the purpose of the Government of India was to be made clear to the Chief Justice and consultation was to be carried forward on that transparent basis.[28]

Another important aspect of the judgment in the *First Judges' Case* is that it recognized the need for democratic legitimacy of the judiciary. While the nature of the appointment process is not democratically accountable as in the United States of America, it was recognized that the voice of the people in appointment of judges is indirectly recognized in India.[29] Justice Fazal Ali significantly noted that the vesting of the power to appoint in the President creates and subserves democratic

[26] Justice Bhagwati has come in for significant criticism from Seervai in this regard, a fact which has been recorded in the *NJAC Case. See NJAC Case* [390].

[27] *First Judges' Case* [111].

[28] *First Judges' Case* [112].

[29] *First Judges' Case* [332]. Justice Fazal Ali also notes that the power to appoint being vested in the President introduces a popular element in the matter of administration of justice, and links with judicial system the dynamic goals of a progressive society by subjecting the principles of governance to be guided by the Directive Principles of State Policy.

processes since the President (being the head of the executive) functions through the Council of Ministers, which is a purely elected body and is accountable to the people. Justice Bhagwati justified the vesting of the power of appointment in the executive on the ground that the executive is responsible to the legislature, and through the legislature it is accountable to the people who are the ultimate consumers of justice.[30] He went on to say that the power of appointment of judges is not entrusted to the Chief Justice because he does not have accountability to the people; consequently, the Chief Justice cannot be held accountable for a wrong appointment. Justice Venkataramaiah also pertinently noted that appointments made on the basis of recommendations of only judges might give rise to the sentiment that 'they will be Judges' Judges' and that 'such appointments may not fit into the scheme of popular democracy'.[31]

There was a severe indictment of the *First Judges' Case* by several legal commentators. It was felt that this judgment gave primacy to the executive in the matter of judicial appointments, and was an affront to judicial independence. While Upendra Baxi believed that the judgment was marked by 'incoherence, futility, and lack of perspective,'[32] Seervai regarded the judgment as having 'destroyed judicial independence'.[33] Baxi remained critical of both the supreme executive as well as the organized bar for aspiring for a judiciary which is not independent, and potentially unable to discipline their power and influence in any vital manner.[34] At the same time, he was scathing in his criticism when he said that this judgment signalled that independence of the judiciary means 'selective and opportunistic independence'.[35] An independent judiciary, as indicated in this case, was one which will have the choice

[30] *First Judges' Case* [30].

[31] *First Judges' Case* [1042].

[32] Upendra Baxi, 'Judiciary at the Crossroads' (1982) 9 *Journal of the Bar Council of India* 231, 231 (Baxi 1982).

[33] H.M. Seervai, *Constitutional Law of India*, vol. 3 (4th edn, Universal Law Publishing 2008 rep) 2854 (Seervai).

[34] Upendra Baxi, 'The Myth and Reality of Judicial Independence: The Judges Case and All That' in Upendra Baxi, *Courage, Craft and Contention: The Indian Supreme Court in the Eighties* (NM Tripathi Pvt Ltd 1985) 23, 55 (Baxi 1985).

[35] Baxi 1985 (n. 34) 42.

to make 'on whom to depend, how much and to what extent'.[36] Seervai, who had argued the case, was equally critical of the judgment in the *First Judges' Case*. He said that by exhorting Additional Judges not to seek redress in courts, Justice Bhagwati and Justice Fazal Ali failed in their duty to uphold judicial independence from illegal attempts to subvert it.[37] Seervai opined that the judgment required reconsideration on certain specific aspects (for instance, the interpretation of Article 217 as to 'suitability' and on 'reputation for lack of integrity' as a ground for dropping an Additional Judge), and unless such reconsideration, the judgment had inflicted an irreversible injury to judicial independence.[38]

However, much of this criticism is based on the perceived notion of executive overreach in judicial appointments, and on the specific circumstances prevailing in the preceding decade. If anything, the *First Judges' Case* stands as an illustration of the Court having accorded regard to the unambiguous language of the Constitution, specifically the term 'consultation'. Scholarly criticism, as well as the *NJAC Case*'s proclamation that the *First Judges' Case* was the 'solitary departure' from a line of cases which confer primacy to the opinion tendered by the Chief Justice does not give the judgment the credit it deserves.

The Chandrachud Era

Following this judgment, the decade of the 1980s saw four Chief Justices—Justice Y.V. Chandrachud, who was Chief Justice at the time of the judgment, followed by Justices Bhagwati, Pathak, and Venkataramaiah. Space precludes a detailed discussion of the tenures of each of these Chief Justices and is thus limited to Justice Chandrachud's tenure alone.

Justice Chandrachud's long tenure as Chief Justice, the longest in independent India, brought stability within the judiciary for the first half of the decade. The fourteen judges appointed to the Supreme Court during the tenure of Justice Chandrachud are noteworthy. This era saw for the first time the appointment of a member of the Scheduled Castes

---

[36] Baxi 1985 (n. 34) 42.

[37] Seervai (n. 33) 2781.

[38] Seervai (n. 33) 2762.

as a judge of the Supreme Court.[39] This era also saw, for the first time the appointment of a judge who was a member of the Parsi community.[40] In the course of this era, the Congress party under Indira Gandhi came back to power. While there was no other supersession, it appears that there was some muscle-flexing by the government in the matter of appointments, for which reason, appointments were stalled for some time in this period.[41] However, that appointments were made by the government without any meaningful consultation with the Chief Justice of India was never seriously alleged. On the contrary, several episodes brought out the trust and influence enjoyed by the Chief Justice of India in appointments casting aside any extraneous influences.

In this context, the unique set of circumstances surrounding the case of *A.K.M. Hassan Uzzaman v. Union of India*[42] is worth considering. In this case, an election candidate had approached the High Court seeking intervention of the Court to remedy large scale irregularities in the electoral rolls. The High Court having issued certain interim orders, the aggrieved party approached the Supreme Court. The Supreme Court passed an order requesting that the writ petition be placed on the board of the learned High Court judge (Justice Sabyasachi Mukharji) on a particular date, and that hearing be completed and order be pronounced on the very next day, and that the order be communicated by telex to

---

[39] Justice A. Varadarajan was appointed even though he was not the senior-most judge of the Madras High Court. The Scheduled Castes had not had any representation on the Supreme Court.

[40] Justice D.P. Madon was the first judge of the Parsi community.

[41] After having demitted office as Chief Justice of India, Justice Y.V. Chandrachud was quoted by Ramakrishna Hegde in *The Judiciary Today: A Plea for a Collegium* (Government of Karnataka 1988) as having said,

> The Government has a great power of filibustering. I will tell you what happens. I say this man must be appointed Chief Justice. The Government has got the power of appointing an acting Chief Justice. The Government says, 'We are not doing anything against you. But you see he deserves to be appointed. Let us consider it.' ... As I told Ms. Gandhi never overruled me ... The Government has got every power in its hands. It may not differ with you, but it may not agree with you. So vacancies are kept unfilled.'

[42] (1982) 2 SCC 218.

the Supreme Court. Justice Sabyasachi Mukharji took note of this order and expressed strong views opining:

> In my limited experience, as a Judge of this High Court for about 14 years, I have not known, read or heard of such type of request or direction or expression of hope by the Supreme Court. I do not know how far this, again, be it a request, direction or expression of hope, is consistent either with the dignity of the judicial process or comity amongst Court and judicial functionaries. I hope, that wiser heads in the future will decide.
>
> The contents and mode of communication to this Court were unprecedented. In my opinion, the aforesaid communication was unwarranted by the Constitution, law and precedence. As the dignity of this Court was concerned, I was hesitant to act on the said communication. But, keen as I am to maintain the dignity of the judiciary and subject as I feel myself to the judicial discipline and as I am anxious not to do anything to erode further judicial process, I have proceeded to hear and pronounce in the interest of justice, as indicated in the latest communication of the Supreme Court.[43]

Though this strong indictment of an order of the Supreme Court, passed by a bench consisting of Justice Desai, Justice A.P. Sen, and Justice Baharul Islam, was made by Justice Sabyasachi Mukharji, who was at the time a judge of the High Court, and later came to be considered for final disposal by a bench headed by Chief Justice Chandrachud, it does not seem to have been held against him by the Chief Justice. Despite reservations owing to this strident opinion being expressed, Justice Mukharji was elevated to the Supreme Court the very next year. This incident comes across as a shining example of the ability of the judiciary to remain truly independent, including of pressures from within the institution.[44] At the same time, it demonstrates the prominent role continued to be played by the Chief Justice of India as a matter of convention, notwithstanding his constitutionally delineated role in the *First Judges' Case.*

Conclusion

The 1980s were a curious decade when constitutional order in appointment of judges was restored. This was not achieved through any

---

[43] *A.K.M. Hassan Uzzaman v. Union of India,* 1982 (1) CLJ 291.

[44] The case was finally decided in *Lakshmi Charan Sen v. A.K.M. Hassan Uzzaman* (1985) 4 SCC 689.

particular act but rather a combination of a mature judgment by the Supreme Court coupled with a new-found respect amongst the political class for a judiciary that is independent at its core. However, with the *First Judges' Case* not laying down a fundamental proposition of law that would obviate any possibility of an executive takeover of the appointments process, together with stray incidents of interference in judicial functioning, the perception of the decade has been otherwise.

This essay contests that view. By demonstrating that the 1980s were in the shadow of the dramatic instances of judicial independence being affected in the Emergency and the 1970s on the whole, that the *First Judges' Case* was sound in law and that anecdotal instances of the independence of the judges in action coexisted with any incidents of executive interference in the judiciary, it makes the fundamental point that the 1980s could not, when considered holistically, provide grist to the mill for the holding in the *Second Judges' Case*, affirmed in the *NJAC Case*, that judicial primacy is necessary in the appointment of judges. Its reputation as a decade characterized by sustained attacks by the executive on judicial independence should thus be given a decent burial.

The Judicial Collegium

4

Issues, Controversies, and the Road Ahead

ARUN JAITLEY

The peculiar aspect of the manner in which judges of the Supreme Court and High Courts are appointed in India is that the primary appointing body is an invention of the Supreme Court itself. The judicial collegium, which, over the last two-and-a-half decades has had the last word on the appointment of judges, was born out of the decision of the Supreme Court in the *Second Judges' Case* and does not find mention in the text of the Constitution. The origin of the collegium was preceded by several episodes of severe confrontation between the government and the judiciary. While the genesis of the collegium was seen as an assertion of judicial independence, it has invited several controversies owing to its opaque functioning, questionable choices, and genuine lack of participatory involvement of interested stakeholders.

In this essay, I will commence with a discussion of the *Second* and *Third Judges' Cases* and how it led to the genesis of the collegium. Thereafter, I will provide some insights into the concerns that have affected the functioning of the collegium. Thereafter, in the backdrop of the judgment of the Supreme Court in the *NJAC Case*, I will provide a normative vision of what the road ahead for reform of judicial appointments in India should look like. I will address the twin questions of *how* appointments should be made, and *who* should make appointments. Through this analysis, my argument will be that the process of judicial appointments requires a fundamental transformation in order to inspire continued confidence of the citizens in the delivery of justice in India.

The *Second* and *Third Judges' Cases*—Genesis of the Collegium

With the best of intentions, the Supreme Court in the *Second Judges' Case* held that the power of appointment of judges of the Supreme Court and High Courts would hereinafter wrest with a collegium of senior-most judges of the Court. A judicial collegium to appoint judges of the Supreme Court and High Courts was a response to feared executive overreach in appointments. A seven-judge majority (with five judges speaking through Justice J.S. Verma) fundamentally altered the nature of the appointments process in Article 124(2) and Article 217(1) of the Constitution. They held that in the event of disagreement between constitutional functionaries involved in appointment of judges, the opinion of the Chief Justice of India would have primacy.[1] This opinion would be a collective opinion of the judiciary, speaking through the Chief Justice of India.[2] In reaching this opinion, representative of the judiciary as a whole, the Chief Justice of India would have to consult two of his senior-most colleagues, known as the judicial collegium and any other judge who may have knowledge in this regard.[3] Further, no appointment could be confirmed by the President if the Chief Justice of India had not positively opined in favour of such an appointment.[4]

This judgment had been hailed as a triumph of judicial independence. Academics praised it, newspapers editorialized it positively, and foreign judges were startled by its boldness. It was a leap of faith with the Supreme Court reposing faith in itself to ensure that the independence of the judiciary is systemically protected.

The reality however turned out to be quite different. Soon after the genesis of the idea of the collegium to appoint judges, there was a stand-off between the executive and the judiciary. Chief Justice M.M. Punchhi strongly reiterated the primacy of the Chief Justice of India in appointment; the government of the day however understood the judgment differently—it considered the role of the Chief Justice of India, acting in his personal capacity as having been whittled down in favour of a more broad-based judicial collegium.

---

[1] *Second Judges' Case* [411(1)].

[2] *Second Judges' Case* [466].

[3] *Second Judges' Case* [211].

[4] *Second Judges' Case* [478(12)].

The interpretive confusion led to a Presidential Reference where nine questions were asked of the Supreme Court by the President. By a unanimous opinion in the *Third Judges' Case*, the Court firmly underlined the significance of the collegium and gave a concrete shape to it. Contrary to the *Second Judges' Case*, which had specified that the Chief Justice of India would have to consult his two senior-most colleagues before reaching his opinion, the judgment expanded the collegium to the Chief Justice and his four senior-most colleagues for Supreme Court appointments and his two senior-most colleagues for High Court appointments. Additionally, the senior-most judge of the Supreme Court acquainted with the High Court from which the potential candidate hailed (for Supreme Court appointments) and to which High Court the candidate was proposed (for High Court appointments) would have to be consulted. Both these judgments traced their interpretation of Article 124 and Article 217 to the concept of judicial independence, which was a fundamental constitutional purpose and would be severely affected if the executive had primacy.

Evidently, the *Third Judges' Case* laid down differential sizes of the collegium depending on whether it was an appointment to the Supreme Court, High Courts, or a transfer of a judge from one High Court to another. However, in all cases, it firmly established that the last word on all appointments and transfers would be that of the collegium; the government could disagree, but if the recommendation was unanimously reiterated, then the person must be appointed. The collegium has thus played the focal role in appointing judges ever since—a process described by a retired Supreme Court judge and a former member of the collegium as 'one of the best kept secrets in the country.'[5]

Second and *Third Judges' Cases* in Practice—the Working of the Collegium

The operation of the collegium system in the last two decades has created much disaffection. The collegium was perceived to be a medium of insulating judicial appointments from executive interference and to

---

[5] Justice Ruma Pal, 'An Independent Judiciary' (5th VM Tarkunde Memorial Lecture, New Delhi, 10 November 2011) <http://www.commoncause.in/publication_details.php?id=59> accessed 29 August 2016 (Ruma Pal).

protect the independence of the judiciary. However, the functioning of the collegium has given rise to the fundamental doubt—though the judges might largely be independent of the executive, have they, particularly High Court judges, functioned in a wholly independent manner, including from pressures internal to the judiciary itself? Further, several selections of the collegium have been mired in issues pertaining to quality of appointments and lack of transparency in its functioning.

The key argument here is not that the collegium system inherently produces less worthy candidates, which is a matter of subjective opinion, but rather that it allows less worthy candidates to slip through, a matter of fact. While the reasons for substantive appointments and non-appointments are not known because of the completely opaque nature of the process and hence cannot be critiqued, certain egregious appointments have brought to light grave deficiencies in the process, or lack thereof, followed by the collegium in making appointments.[6]

In my experience, two particular features of the operation of the collegium system are pernicious. First, bargains are struck between members of the collegium. Often, members have their favoured candidates and are willing to accept other members' candidates if it means one's own can be appointed or elevated. As a result, merit often ceases to be the single most important criterion. It is replaced by community representation, caste, ideology, or plain familiarity.

At the same time, the relevance of seniority in elevations to the Supreme Court appear to be strategic. While often, the lack of seniority

---

[6] The appointment of Justice P.D. Dinakaran to the Supreme Court demonstrates the deficiencies of the process. At the time the proposal to appoint him was leaked, several senior members of the bar provided details of the judge's disproportionate assets (acquired when he was a judge in the High Court of Madras), obtained in purported violation of the law as well as several questionable judicial orders in matters where he had an interest in the outcome of the case. The statutory committee set up during the process of impeachment found 12 charges to be *prima facie* tenable. However, before their report could be tabled, Justice Dinakaran resigned lending further truth to these charges. Irrespective of their veracity, it demonstrated the complete lack of fitness for the task of the collegium, since it neither had the infrastructure nor the processes to check antecedents of candidates. *See* Chandrani Banerjee, 'What in the name of justice!' *Outlook* (13 June 2011) <http://www.outlookindia.com/magazine/story/what-in-the-name-of-justice/272096> accessed 29 August 2016.

is seen as a reason why appointment of competent judges is kept on hold, in other cases, seniority is seen as a criterion that can be overridden. The non-consideration of the names of Justice A.P. Shah, Chief Justice of the Delhi High Court, and Justice A.K. Patnaik, Chief Justice of the Madhya Pradesh High Court, by the collegium despite their seniority in comparison with the judges recommended raises considerable doubt as to whether seniority is a criterion or a self-serving tool to be used at will.

It was this collusiveness and lack of transparency within the collegium that was sought to be undone by a bipartisan parliamentary consensus establishing the NJAC. The 99th Amendment and the NJAC Act together sought to establish the NJAC, which was the culmination of nearly three decades of reform proposals. It sought to broad-base the appointments process by including members other than judicial members in decision-making while maintaining judicial preponderance. However, pursuant to the decision of the Supreme Court in the *NJAC Case*, the 99th Amendment as well as the NJAC Act have been struck down, taking us back to the collegium system of appointments. Since the principled and practical deficiencies in the operation of the collegium still persist and cannot be undone merely by tinkering with procedure, a wholesale reform of the hitherto ill-functioning appointments system is imperative.

The Road Ahead for Judicial Appointments: How to Appoint

The invalidation of the 99th Amendment and the NJAC Act does not take away from the fact that the judicial appointments process requires urgent reform. The frailties that exist in the collegium system, particularly the issues of lack of transparency and accountability, have also been acknowledged by the judges in the *NJAC Case*.[7] Taking a cue from Justice Lokur, who agreed that 'better institutionalising and fine tuning of the scheme laid down in these decisions (*the Second and Third Judges' Cases*) is required',[8] the time is ripe for some systemic changes to be made to the appointments' process. These changes merit attention,

---

[7] *NJAC Case* [1221] (Justice Chelameswar); [990] (Justice Joseph),
[8] *NJAC Case* [699].

irrespective of whether appointments in the future will be by the collegium, or another non-partisan commission within the framework of the Constitution.

For the process of judicial appointments to be more systematic and efficient, it is imperative that certain process-related details are clearly outlined. The discussion on reforming the appointments process should not concentrate only on *who* appoints, while overlooking the need to address *how* appointments are made. Merely changing the authority which appoints judges without specifying certain process-related details would not address issues relating to quality and competence of judges appointed. Such a constricted outlook towards the appointments process would possibly lead to a throwback to the genesis of the collegium.

To this end, the most imminent process-related details that must be etched out are—first, streamlining the process of shortlisting candidates, and second, laying down certain objective criteria for selection of candidates. To begin with, the process for shortlisting/nomination of potential appointees should be appropriately specified so as to give clarity on the number of people who have been considered by the collegium. Names cannot simply be picked out of a hat, as is often the impression that is rightly or wrongly held regarding the functioning of the collegium. This view is bolstered by the statement of Justice (Retd) Ruma Pal, who has candidly admitted,

> The 'mystique' of the process, the small base from which the selections were made and the 'secrecy and confidentiality' ensured that the 'process may, on occasions, make wrong appointments and, worse still, lend itself to nepotism.[9]

No process should allow such an institutional hijack. The appointing body should create a shortlist of names of candidates who could potentially fill the vacancy six months before a vacancy arises for a seat in the Supreme Court or the High Court. This should follow a clearly laid-out consultative process with members of the relevant bar and existing members of the bench. Additionally, there should be a specified zone of consideration of High Court judges it can consider eligible for judgeship for the Supreme Court. For High Court appointments, a

---

[9] Ruma Pal (n. 5).

similar zone of consideration of District Judges should be established. This would give clarity on the actual number of people who have been considered by the collegium, and ensure, to some extent, that its decisions are not alleged to be arbitrary, or appointments made by it considered out of turn. Creation of this shortlist would also ensure that the oft-cited criticism of opacity in the functioning of the collegium is addressed, and what transpires within the portals of the appointing body is also made known optimally to the public, and not just the ultimate result of the process.

Once the procedure for shortlisting assumes concrete shape, attention should be paid to devise certain objective criteria for assessing merit and suitability of a candidate. Currently, there are no written criteria for determining the suitability of a candidate, though certain unwritten rules are followed as a matter of convention. The need for devising objective criteria for selection of judges persists, irrespective of the nature and composition of the body tasked with appointing judges to the higher judiciary. The imminent concern for objective criteria was flagged by judges in the *NJAC Case* as well, which categorically stated that the revised Memorandum of Procedure to be prepared by the Government 'may indicate the eligibility criteria, such as the minimum age, for the guidance of the collegium (both at the level of the High Courts and the Supreme Court) for appointment of judges....'[10]

Clearly, the need for some objective criteria for appointment is worthy of consideration. While it may not be practicable to provide in intricate detail the process to be followed and every criterion to be appointed by the collegium, some objective factors can be contemplated that the collegium can resort to. Inspiration can be drawn from the United Kingdom (UK) Constitutional Reform Act, 2005, which mandates that 'selection must be on merit'.[11] Almost complimentarily, the Twenty-Fifth Report of the Select Committee on Judicial Appointments in the UK spells out the criteria to be followed in assessing the merit of a candidate.[12] The

---

[10] *NJAC Case*, order dated 16 December 2015 in W.P. (C) No. 13/2015.

[11] United Kingdom Constitutional Reform Act 2005, s 27(5).

[12] Select Committee on the Constitution, *Judicial Appointments* (House of Lords 2012, 272) [83]–[88] <http://www.publications.parliament.uk/pa/ld201012/ldselect/ldconst/272/272.pdf> accessed 29 August 2016 (House of Lords Select Committee).

criteria specified by this Report have been divided into five categories—intellectual capacity (expertise and appropriate knowledge of the law), personal qualities (integrity, decisiveness, objectivity, among others), ability to understand and deal fairly (commitment to justice and independence, and willingness to listen with patience and courtesy), authority and communication skills (ability to inspire respect and confidence, and maintain authority), and efficiency (ability to work at speed and under pressure). The Select Committee acknowledges that since assessing merit is not a wholly objective exercise the various criteria will have to be weighed up differently according to the importance attached to each one by the individual selector.[13]

There are some indicative measures that can be used as criteria for adjudging the suitability of a potential appointee. Further, in an Indian context, certain other criteria are crucial. One of these is the minimum educational qualifications of the potential appointee. Different criteria can be devised for the different categories of appointees to the Supreme Court under Article 124: for instance, while a master's degree in law should be made mandatory in case of a judge of a High Court, a doctorate degree can be contemplated as mandatory in case a potential appointee belongs to the category of 'distinguished jurist'. Additionally, other indicators of academic merit should be considered, such as the number of academic publications to an appointee's credit, teaching experience, and academic lectures delivered. For people who are elevated to the bench from the bar, a certain minimum number of cases argued and appearances recorded should be considered. This would be indicative of the standing of the person as an advocate, and at the same time, assist in judging the legal acumen of such person. Another important indicator of the standing of a person at the bar is the number of junior advocates such person has had under him/her whom he/she has trained. This would give a general idea of the extent of contribution made by such advocate to the legal profession by bringing junior advocates (sometimes, fresh law graduates) under their tutelage and mentoring them about the nuances of the legal profession.

These criteria can be used as a bare minimum threshold to be met by potential appointees for them to be considered for appointment. Since these criteria are to be indicators of the merit of particular candidates,

---

[13] House of Lords Select Committee (n. 12).

some subjectivity of opinion on the part of the appointing authority should be expected. Like the UK Select Committee suggests, these suitability criteria can be used while inserting a caveat that these criteria will be weighed up according to the opinion of each individual member of the collegium.

While the above discussion covers suitability criteria, some thought should also be given to 'eligibility criteria' for the selection of candidates.[14] In terms of Article 124, while an upper limit in terms of the age is given, no minimum age is given (below which a person cannot be appointed as judge). While there was no written rule for this purpose, it is well known that no judge usually has a tenure longer than ten years in the Supreme Court. At the same time, seniority in terms of age appears not to give a judge any entitlement to be considered before junior judges. Criteria regarding age of a judge, both the minimum age, as well as the role of seniority should be clearly laid down.

Laying down objective criteria before appointing a judge can address two pertinent issues—first, ensuring the quality of the judges appointed, and second, bringing transparency into the process by making appointments on the basis of pre-determined criteria. In the long run, this will reduce arbitrariness in the manner of appointments, an aspect that currently plagues the working of the collegium.

The Ideal Appointing Body—Who Appoints

The judicial appointments process in India has undergone a transformation in keeping with key developments that have taken place in the years after the coming into force of the Constitution. The number of members who form part of the appointing body, and the nature and extent of their participation has also changed considerably. What should not escape anyone's attention is that the NJAC attempted to strike a harmonious balance between the six persons who were to be

---

[14] There is a distinction between 'eligibility' and 'suitability', which has been discussed by the Supreme Court in *Mahesh Chandra Gupta v. Union of India* (2009) 8 SCC 273. The Court explains, in para 39, that while the process of judging the fitness of a person to be appointed as a High Court Judge falls in the realm of suitability, the aspect of eligibility comes at the threshold stage under Article 217(2)(b).

part of it. In doing so, the predominance of the judicial branch was preserved, with three out of the six members on the Commission being judges. At the same time, participation of the executive was secured by inclusion of the Law Minister. Lastly, the NJAC contemplated the inclusion of two eminent persons, who were to be representatives of the citizenry of the country, the ultimate consumers of justice.

In my opinion, a harmonious balance can be struck in an appointing body if it comprises a few judges and, at the same time, has some participation from the executive as well as from members of the public (akin to the eminent persons on the NJAC). The presence of judicial members is essential so as to prevent the kind of situation which existed at the time of the Emergency. The executive branch made serious inroads into judicial independence, and appointments were tainted by executive interference. Judicial members on the appointing authority will act as a buffer against any such executive interference in appointments in the future, as was sought to be done by the NJAC.

However, at the same time, executive participation in the appointing body cannot be wished away, or worse still, startlingly held unconstitutional (as in the *NJAC Case*). The executive performs the important function of providing information on the antecedents of potential appointees. During the time I was Law Minister, a certain candidate was recommended as a judge by the collegium to the Madras High Court. The recommendation was returned by the Central Government because of adverse inputs. Despite such inputs, the recommendation was reiterated. In the second round, President A.P.J. Abdul Kalam returned the recommendation giving detailed reasons. The President was overruled by the collegium and the recommendation was reiterated for a second time. The nominee was appointed as an Additional Judge. His performance as a judge raised many eyebrows confirming the government inputs and the President's concerns. He was not confirmed as a permanent judge.

In another case, the Central Government raised serious security concerns about a candidate recommended for judgeship in the Jammu and Kashmir High Court. The concerns were overruled and he was confirmed as a Judge. A series of orders passed by him in a sensitive High Court helped the cause of separatists.

Equally crucially, the presence of the executive also grants democratic legitimacy to the appointments process due to the accountability of the executive to the citizens of the country. This is why the world over, as well as in the debates in our Constituent Assembly, appointment of judges is considered a core executive function.[15]

Lastly, the presence of members of the public, or lay persons, would ensure that citizens who are the ultimate consumers of justice also have a voice in the judicial appointments process. Several countries across the world have opened their judicial appointments processes to participation from the citizens. There is no reason, except our own hubris and a frog-in-the-well attitude, as to why India should continue its antiquated, opaque, and semi-feudal practices, keeping its own citizens out of key decision-making functions.

Conclusion

The process of judicial appointments in India is at the cusp of major developments and reform. Even though the NJAC as an appointing body did not see the light of day, the principled changes that it sought to usher in can still be embraced. The collegium system, as formulated by the judgments in the *Second* and *Third Judges' Cases*, has been mired in controversy for manifold reasons. It is time that the collegium system opens itself to real reform if it is going to deliver the judges that India deserves.

[15] Kate Malleson and Peter H. Russel (eds), *Appointing Judges in an Age of Judicial Power: Critical Perspectives from Around the World* (University of Toronto Press 2006).

A Plague on Both Your Houses

NJAC and the Crisis of Trust

5

PRATAP BHANU MEHTA

In this essay, I offer some sceptical reflections on the politics surrounding the proposed establishment of the NJAC. The debate over the NJAC is a *political* debate all the way down. It is a political debate in a very specific sense that I explain below. On the surface there should be no disagreement in a democracy on some basic principles that should govern the selection, promotion, and accountability mechanisms for judges. These mechanisms should preserve the independence of the judiciary. They should also inspire trust that the selection mechanisms are not arbitrary, and judges are selected based on the right attributes. There should also be some credible mechanism for holding the judiciary accountable for any possible misconduct or wrongdoing. But again, this process should not be one that compromises the independence of the judiciary.[1] These are high-level platitudes on which almost all parties to the debate agree. The trouble is that there seems to be deep disagreement over what these important platitudes imply for institutional design. And this is where politics begins. The dispute is *political*, not in the sense that it involves party or ideological politics. But it is political in the sense that the matter cannot be easily settled either by recourse to constitutional text, philosophical principle, or legitimacy of a process. What it requires

---

[1] For one account of this see Justice (Retd.) B.N. Srikrishna, 'Judicial Independence' in Sujit Choudhry, Madhav Khosla and Pratap Bhanu Mehta (eds), *The Oxford Handbook of the Indian Constitution* (Oxford University Press 2016) 349–66.

is a good faith *negotiation*, a drawing up of a new institutional contract that is an exercise of 'all things considered' good judgment.

In order to see the inherently political character of the dispute, let us begin with a thumbnail sketch of the institutional scenario unfolding before us. Both the executive and judiciary are locked in a seemingly intractable battle, where only one maxim seems to apply to each institutional move. In some ways the contest between judges and elected representatives is constitutionally meant to be *undecidable*. It is precisely the *tension* between the two branches that is meant to secure our liberty and democracy. Dr Ambedkar was very clear, for example, that no single branch of government could claim to uniquely embody popular sovereignty. In fact, the entire sensibility of Indian constitutionalism is suspicious of the idea that popular sovereignty can be given a singular meaning. Hence no institution can claim final authority in the name of the people. This very sensibility also inflects the question: Who is the final custodian of the Constitution? The short answer is that this question is also undecidable: Parliament can pass law, the Supreme Court can test its constitutionality; Parliament can, in response, amend the Constitution; in response, the Court can even scrutinize the constitutionality of a constitutionally enacted amendment, and strike it down. In principle Parliament could still retaliate by re-enacting an amendment, and a full blown constitutional crisis would ensue. But there is *prima facie* no warrant to think that either the Supreme Court or the Parliament should have final word over the Constitution. In a sense a Constitution is co-produced by both branches of government, and it should not be otherwise.[2]

It is also a bit of false comfort to say that both Parliament and the Court operate under the Constitution. In a trivial sense that proposition is true. But in a deeper philosophical sense it begs the question. If the dispute is precisely over what the Constitution *means* or what it *requires*, it is not of much help to invoke the very thing that is under

---

[2] For an argument that it is a mistake to think that normatively only judges can be final custodians of constitutional interpretation, *see* Jeremy Waldron, *Law and Disagreement* (Oxford University Press 1999). For reflections on constitutional morality and sovereignty in Ambedkar, *see* Pratap Bhanu Mehta, 'What is Constitutional Morality?' (2010) 615 *Seminar* 17 <http://www.india-seminar.com/2010/615/615_pratap_bhanu_mehta.htm> accessed 27 September 2016.

dispute. The constitutional text is often open-ended, full of inner tensions and ambiguities, and appealing to it, as if it had some indubitable meaning, is misleading. It is a ruse to invoke authority when what is going on is an active choice of interpretations. In a historical sense also, it is a little misleading because the Supreme Court has itself given quite a semantic elasticity to constitutional interpretation. In fact, the judgments in the *Second* and *Third Judges' Cases* that in effect gave the judiciary more control over judicial appointments, had almost no textual warrant. But for almost two decades it came to define the institutional contours of judicial appointments. In short the Court *made* the Constitution; it did not operate under it. Parliament can in turn, make and unmake the Constitution, as it has done through more than a hundred amendments. It is not clear if it has been constrained by the Constitution itself.[3]

These rather plain truths need to be stated, perhaps a little gracelessly and pointedly for this reason. All branches of government will formally argue that they want a judiciary that is both independent and accountable. But what form of accountability secures independence is the question open for debate. Who should get to decide this question? Neither is it clear whether either the executive or the judiciary can claim exclusive or final authority on this matter, nor that any one branch of government can claim exclusive wisdom on the subject. So the matter becomes inherently political. Ideally, what should have happened is a *dialogic constitutionalism*, where the process of amendment of the Constitution by the legislature and review by the Court resulted in a credible process where *reasonable* concerns of all parties were taken into consideration. The judiciary and the legislature should have been responsive to each other's principled concerns. But instead what has emerged is nothing less than an open turf war, with each branch of government implicitly assuming that public opinion is on their side.

The inherently political and unprincipled character of the tussle over the NJAC is apparent in the sequence of events, where both branches

---

[3] For an elaboration of this *see* Pratap Bhanu Mehta, 'The Indian Supreme Court and the Art of Democratic Positioning' in Mark Tushnet and Madhav Khosla (eds), *Unstable Constitutionalism: Law and Politics in South Asia* (Cambridge University Press 2015) 231–2.

of government seem to be operating with the adage: 'Thou shalt meet overreach with more overreach'. To see this point let us recount a brief history of the issue at stake.

A History of Conflict

The judiciary–legislature tussle in India has never been based on first principles. The tussle between the judiciary and the legislature over the custodianship of the Constitution began right after Independence. But till the late 1960s, Parliament legislated, the judiciary exercised its prerogative over reviewing legislation, and if need be, Parliament could, in response, amend the Constitution. It was following the judgment in *Golak Nath v. State of Punjab*[4] in the late 1960s that the possible conflict between the judiciary and legislature became sharper. The judiciary was ostensibly worried that fundamental rights under the Constitution might come under more direct attack. With Nehru gone, and the halo of legitimacy around the Congress party weakening, the judiciary also found more space to assert its authority over the Constitution. The *Golak Nath* judgment enshrined the idea that Part III of the Constitution, the section on fundamental rights, had a special place in the constitutional scheme: the Constitution could not retain its identity as a Constitution if fundamental rights were tampered with. The legislature saw such a strong reading of fundamental rights, particularly on property matters, as a possible constraint on its policymaking freedoms. *Kesavanada Bharati v. State of Kerala*[5] overturned *Golak Nath*, but in some senses formally enshrined judicial authority even more, since it articulated the idea that the Constitution had a basic structure that Parliament could not amend, even if it followed the process of amendment laid down by the Constitution. Formally the judiciary's custodianship of the Constitution was ascending.[6]

The executive worried about this ascendancy. The fear of judicial obstructionism had always been present, since the early land reform

[4] AIR 1967 SC 1643 (*Golak Nath*).

[5] (1973) 4 SCC 225.

[6] *See* Madhav Khosla, 'Constitutional Amendment' in Sujit Choudhry, Madhav Khosla and Pratap Bhanu Mehta (eds), *The Oxford Handbook of the Indian Constitution* (Oxford University Press 2016) 232–53.

cases.[7] But now the judiciary, on surface, seemed to have armed itself with even more constitutional ammunition, particularly to strike down the radical economic reforms the government was proposing. Second, Indira Gandhi's election was invalidated by the Allahabad High Court. The Supreme Court, in a moment that did not cover itself with glory, stayed the verdict for long enough to allow Mrs Gandhi to declare Emergency.[8] It was in this context that the executive started looking for what was known as a 'committed judiciary': one that would be more in tune with the executive's overall socialist goals, and less likely to politically challenge it. A dominant and authoritarian executive sought to undermine the independence of the judiciary in the 1970s.

Post-Emergency, the Court tried to reclaim the ground it had lost. It did so in two ways. The Court promiscuously expanded the scope of its jurisdiction considerably, by articulating a new set of social and economic rights, positioning itself not just as a Court of Law but a Court of Governance. Through the mechanism of public interest litigation, the Court also positioned itself as a populist Court—a branch of government responsive to the needs of the people when the executive was failing to do its job. The effects of the Court's judicial, semantic, and jurisdictional promiscuity are debated: we have rule by the Courts; whether that is the same thing as rule of law is an open question. But the fact that the Supreme Court has now reached a point where it can literally pronounce on any matter, where its role in policy, accountability, and governance has expanded beyond any constitutional warrant, is part of the current backdrop to the legislature's attempts to rein in the judiciary a bit.

Second, after the experience of the 1970s the judges tried to protect the judiciary by asserting its control over appointments. Judges created an appointments process where they could, as Justice Chelameswar writes, 'exult and frolic in our emancipation from the other two organs of the state.'[9] The legitimacy of this arrangement, where the judiciary

---

[7] For a brief background of the Supreme Court's response to these land reform cases, *see* Lavanya Rajamani and Arghya Sengupta, 'The Supreme Court' in Niraja Gopal Jayal and Pratap Bhanu Mehta (eds), *The Oxford Companion to Politics in India* (Oxford University Press 2016) 82, 83.

[8] *Indira Nehru Gandhi v. Raj Narain* (1975) 2 SCC 159.

[9] *NJAC Case* [1113].

effectively shut out other branches of government, was always dubious on constitutional grounds. But we put up with these two developments because there was a sense that the executive was corrupt and unresponsive. The idea that judicial independence could be secured if the appointments process was *depoliticized* by giving the judiciary more control seemed reasonable. In the early 1990s, in an era of coalition politics and fragmented mandates, it was also not easy for Parliament to muster coalitions to take on the judiciary. The important thing to note in this brief history is this: the tussle between the judiciary and legislature has been shaped by larger developments in politics. These developments in turn have allowed one or other branches of government to establish themselves as having *comparatively* more credibility. So the judiciary got away with a kind of constitutional usurpation.

Rule by Courts

So, radical independence of the judiciary, understood as control over appointments, and an acceptance of the Court's expanded jurisdiction, became the norms because both were seen as, in some senses, serving the public interest. But in a significant sense the legitimacy of the judiciary also increasingly began to come into question in two different ways. First, there were increasing allegations of corruption and misconduct within the judiciary.[10] This posed a particular problem for designing the NJAC. It could be argued that our constitutional scheme has placed greater emphasis on independence rather than accountability. In our constitutional scheme the only punishment that could be meted out for errant judges is impeachment, which is an extraordinarily difficult process and has been used only once. The collegium, created by the judiciary, had to often rely on 'minor' sanctions like transfers to send a signal to errant judges. Informal processes are difficult to study formally.

[10] The most glaring instance was the allegations of corruption, possession of wealth disproportionate to known sources of income, and illegal encroachment on public property levelled against Justice P.D. Dinakaran. *See* 'Panel Slaps Corruption Charges against Justice Dinakaran', *The Hindu Business Line* (New Delhi, 19 March 2011) <http://www.thehindubusinessline.com/economy/panel-slaps-corruption-charges-against-justice-dinakaran/article1552956.ece> accessed 28 September 2016.

In interviews, several judges have said that senior judges would exercise 'moral leadership' to impose a modicum of discipline, the effectiveness of which depended upon the Chief Justice's credibility. However, formally, there were few efficient sanctioning mechanisms for judges who engaged in misconduct. This was not considered a significant problem so long as the higher judiciary retained a generally good reputation. But as the overall reputation of the judiciary declined, the need for creating a mechanism that could examine the conduct of judges grew stronger.

Second, the test of a judiciary's credibility is, ultimately, the quality of judgments. On reasonable interpretation, are these judgments exercises in the rule of law? Or when the Court is operating in its expanded jurisdiction, do these judgments embody public reason? Even at the risk of offending the judiciary it has to be said that there is great concern over quality and consistency of judging. This, in turn, has raised questions about the selection procedures for judges. And frankly, for most of the public, this procedure remains shrouded in mystery. And when the results are not manifestly compelling, there will be a clamour to make the judiciary more transparent and accountable. The collegium system's credibility broke down because the judiciary did not exercise leadership on its own matters, *when it was given full freedom to do so*. The judiciary is refusing to face up to a serious crisis of credibility. There is a perception that the process of appointments is not yielding the desired quality. Internal discipline within the hierarchy of courts is broken. Witness the extraordinary spectacle in Madras of a High Court Judge bringing contempt proceedings against a Chief Justice, and the Supreme Court responding to it through legal rather than administrative measures.[11] In public perception, the judiciary carries the odour of both incompetence and corruption. One effect of the Jayalalitha case, whatever the facts of the matter, will be to send a signal to judges

---

[11] Justice C.S. Karnan of the Madras High Court initiated contempt proceedings and a case under the Scheduled Castes and Scheduled Tribes (Prevention of Atrocities) Act, 1989 against the High Court Chief Justice Sanjay Kishan Kaul. The Supreme Court stayed the contempt proceedings sought to be initiated by Justice Karnan. *See* Utkarsh Anand, 'Supreme Court Stays Madras High Court Judge's Order against Chief Justice Sanjay Kaul', *The Indian Express* (New Delhi, 12 May 2015) <http://indianexpress.com/article/india/india-others/supreme-court-stays-contempt-proceeding-against-hc-chief-justice-kaul/> accessed 28 September 2016.

of lower courts that guilty verdicts in high profile political cases are unlikely to be backed up by superior courts.[12] We deride lower courts a lot. And much is wrong at that level. But it is hard to argue that judicial courage, or credibility goes up, the higher up the system you go. The judiciary's claims of 'trust us' are less credible than they were a decade ago. Seven star lawyers can make the judiciary starry-eyed about its own virtues and, therefore, its entitlement to be exempt from outside scrutiny. No one else is convinced. This is the crisis of credibility which occasioned the NJAC.

NJAC: A Question of Institutional Design

The implicit constitutional accusation and counter-accusation implicit in the debate over the NJAC is this—the judiciary had, through improvisation, created a method of appointing judges that effectively sidelined other branches of government. This arrangement was tolerated, not because it conformed to a constitutional text or some hallowed principle. It was tolerated because it seemed to maintain the independence of the judiciary. The experience of the 1970s made the prospect of political packing of the judiciary a live fear. This arrangement is being challenged, not because we have discovered a new principle, but because the credibility of the judiciary has declined. We are, in effect saying, that any arrangement which relies solely on the judiciary itself has proved to be untrustworthy. Those who are challenging the NJAC are relying on the ghost of the 1970s: do you really want the political class to have a greater say in appointments? Both branches of government are accusing each other of not being worthy of trust. In the process they have dragged each other down. The problem is that both are right. But the deeper problem is that neither is conceding ground to the other. The judiciary is not recognizing that it is facing a deep crisis of credibility. 'Trust the judges and trust the judges alone' is looking more like an adage for the protection of judicial impunity, lack of transparency, and breakdown of internal discipline. The judiciary, by its own conduct, simply does not carry the public authority to invoke this trust. Parliament, on the other hand, was perhaps a little less sensitive

---

[12] *Selvi J. Jayalalitha v. Superintendent of Police, Chennai* (2015) SCC Online Kar 124 (Karnataka High Court).

to the idea that there is a genuine fear of political power being used to manipulate judicial appointments more than has been the case in the past. So between a judiciary that has undermined its own credibility and a legislature with a single majority party in government that evokes fear of politicization, whom do you trust?

Parliament, with a rare political unity, passed the 99th Amendment and the NJAC Act. It was right on two grounds: first, it had the power to pass such a law; second, the appointments process also needed to be broadened. It is vital that the appointments process be broadened to include some non-judicial inputs into the process. Judges, operating under their own protective cloaks, have become increasingly impervious to the wider range of considerations that goes into the making of public reason. Upon the advent of the NJAC, it was expected that individuals who are not part of the regular and insulated hierarchies of judges would at least be able to ask questions and would introduce a new measure of accountability in judicial appointments.

It is also important that the process of selection ensures some transparency, as well as institutional support, in the form of a secretariat, to back that process. But we should not have illusions about what transparency can achieve. In civil society circles there is often a very crude conception of transparency that does more harm than good. The formal design of the system, whether old or new has little bearing on quality: it is the persons not the principles that will determine the quality of selections. We want more 'criteria' specified for the selection. Selection involves judgment, it cannot be robotically reduced to some transparent criteria. This is the false comfort of formalism lawyers often peddle.

Let us face it—this issue has come to a head because there is a deep crisis of character and trust. And we think a formal process can be a fix. It can help, but only up to a point. A political debate that India needs to have is this—across a range of institutions we came to the conclusion that some publicly observable, objective assessment is necessary to do away with the discretion selection committees often exercise in selections. The judiciary itself has fuelled this sloppy thinking that is inherently suspicious of judgment. But this quest for a 'false' objectivity has proved to be a chimera. Ultimately, in several kinds of selections, there is no getting around the fact that a group of *peers will have to exercise judgment*. Ultimately the credibility of the process will depend upon the

quality of the judgment exercised by those in position of making judgments. Formal processes can help to the extent that they can ensure that
all the relevant considerations are being taken into account in making
appointments. But we should not be under an illusion that transparent,
publicly-stated criteria will solve the problem.

Is This the NJAC We Needed?

So Parliament was right in its basic premises. We needed something
like the NJAC. The crucial question is: Did the NJAC Act overreach in a
design and institutional sense? The trouble is that there is no straight-
forward answer to this question. Where you come out on this question
depends on a *judgment* call you make about how the process is actually
going to work. There is nothing in the constitutional text that allows
you to settle this question. Nor is there any knock-down empirical evidence which suggests one way or the other. The Supreme Court took the
view that the presence of non-judicial members and the Law Minister
would result in an appointing body which, in all probability, would
undermine the independence of the judiciary, even if it possibly made
it more amenable to outside inputs. There are two questions in relation
to having the Law Minister on the judicial appointing body. First, is
there a potential conflict in that the government is a major litigator,
and this puts the Chief Justice directly in a 'negotiating' position with
the government on a day-to-day basis? Possibly, though more informed
jurists can enlighten us on this issue.

But more importantly, apprehensions on this come more from our
lack of faith in our Chief Justices. The question 'Is the presence of the
Law Minister likely to tilt the balance of power in favour of the executive?' is not an easy question to answer. Anthropological observation of
the dynamics of committees and the general power the Law Minister
exercises suggests that the risks that the executive will dominate are
high. And implicitly, the Supreme Court has taken this view. The claim
can be debated. But what makes it plausible is a political judgment on
how executive–judiciary dynamics are likely to work if the Law Minister
is part of the mix.

Perhaps Parliament should have been more careful in drafting legislation. The NJAC was a sound mechanism. It was right to bring outsid-
ers into the appointments process. But it should not have been done in

a way that raised the spectre of political dominance. Many had hoped that the judiciary would give due deference to what Parliament was trying to do, would acknowledge that there is a serious problem with the current arrangement, but possibly introduce safeguards by reading down the legislation in some ways. This is always a tricky thing to do, because it also involves an overreach of sorts—rewriting legislation. But the Supreme Court went the whole way by declaring the NJAC unconstitutional with a 4–1 majority.

The judiciary came to the conclusion that the NJAC, as currently constituted, would be a threat to judicial independence. There is some merit in this sentiment. The judgment and reasoning is quite careful. There are several technical details that need separate discussion. These include the matter of recusal of a judge and referral to a Constitution bench.

But the core argument is this. The judiciary has established the principle of the independence and primacy of the judiciary on several occasions, not just once.[13] Since this matter was settled, there was no need for reference to a higher bench; and Parliament should have taken that settled doctrine as a frame of reference. The judiciary believes that judicial independence cannot be maintained without two things—first is the *primacy* of the judiciary in the appointments process. The second, more controversial claim which is embedded in the judgment is that judicial primacy is challenged and independence impugned if the views of the judges can be rejected by non-judges on grounds other than 'dubious antecedents'. This is overreach. Justice Khehar does as clever a job as you can do of saying that under the current process there is also executive participation.[14] In a delightful historical aside he turns the tables on those who invoke Dr Ambedkar's authority to suggest that judges are to be mistrusted more than the executive. Where he overreaches is in the inference that inputs from non-judicial branches should be confined to such things as character and antecedents, not judicial quality. It is not clear why only judges can give inputs on judicial quality.

---

[13] See *Subhash Sharma v. Union of India*, 1991 Supp (1) SCC 574 [44]; *Second Judges' Case* [432]; *Third Judges' Case* [12].

[14] *NJAC Case* [545].

Judging is too important to be left only to judges. In this light the proposed NJAC was right to think that non-judicial inputs would be important for the process. The mere presence of non-judicial members on a committee to appoint judges does not compromise independence. If that were so, then no court ever would have been considered independent.

The second interesting issue surrounds the invocation of basic structure. Justice Chelameswar in his dissent seems to make the interesting observation that the basic structure does not apply here because this matter concerns institutional design not individual rights.[15] If judicial independence is a core value, so is an efficient and well-functioning judiciary. And his starting point is that the current system does not meet the latter objective. He also questions the assumption that the primacy of the judiciary would necessarily mean better protection of constitutional values. He is correct in chiding his fellow judges for creating a discourse where politicians cannot be trusted, and trust in judges should be self-evident. In short, there is no empirical reason to trust the judiciary more than the executive.

How should one think of this issue? The historical narrative that both the majority and dissent rely on can cut both ways. But Justice Joseph gets the basic institutional logic right. The issue is not whether in the past judges or politicians have better served the cause of liberty. The issue as he puts it, is whether the current NJAC institutional design would lead to a kind of adverse 'structured bargaining'.[16] Given the voting rules of the NJAC and the presence of the Law Minster, this was a likely outcome.

The majority judges in the *NJAC Case* have basically opted for institutional caution. The present system has grave deficiencies, in terms of efficiency, accountability, and even competence. But it compromises the *structural* independence of the judiciary much less. A change over to a non-judicial or executive dominance could jeopardize that structural independence even more. And the judiciary also has a point that it is not clear that appointments processes with greater executive input are giving better results either.

---

[15] *NJAC Case* [1201]–[1202].

[16] *NJAC Case* [988].

But in the judgment in the *NJAC Case*, the judiciary has been forced to acknowledge its own faults. Even Justice Joseph, who formed part of the majority, is scathing on this.[17] This suggests a ruefully missed opportunity. The politics of excess, the lack of full application of mind even in bipartisan legislation, makes institutional resolutions harder. Parliament missed an opportunity to reform the system in a convincing manner. If it had been more modest, not challenged judicial primacy, and shown how its reforms would be an improvement, it could perhaps have achieved a more participatory process. The tenor of arguments would have been different. Instead, it heightened the risks. The Court's exercise of near exclusive prerogative in response is not ideal either; there are reasons to doubt its capacity for reform. But it tells you something about the mess Indian institutional life is in, that preserving institutions requires deforming them—we choose a lesser evil to prevent a greater evil. The judiciary was hoping that citizens will see this judgment that way.

The Politics of NJAC II

One issue in the politics of the *NJAC Case* that has not been discussed is this. The NJAC was passed with near consensus in Parliament. It was challenged and the hearings were more or less over by June 2015. The judgment itself was delivered in October 2015. Now here is a counterfactual to think about. The NJAC Act was passed near unanimously. The Supreme Court struck it down. What would have happened if Parliament had again passed a more or less similar version of the NJAC Act, or perhaps a slightly watered-down version, to take care of the residual concerns of the Supreme Court? Parliament would have been within its rights to do so, and in my view, that is what it should have done. Done in good faith, as an attempt to find a solution to a genuine problem, Parliament would have been asserting its rights as a co-producer of the Constitution. But it did not do so, largely perhaps because of a political exigency. If the judgment had come in June, it is possible that politics would have taken this turn. The new Bharatiya Janata Party (BJP) government was still in a honeymoon period, and

17 *NJAC Case* [990].

the opposition could not risk non-cooperation with the government. In any case the interests of the political class are aligned on this issue. But by October, it is arguable, that the BJP government had lost a little bit of that overwhelming political aura it had right after election. This was partly a function of the passage of time; partly because a whole series of ideological controversies around 'toleration' had broken out. So the prospects of opposition–government cooperation had dimmed somewhat, and the fears that the government's intentions could not be trusted had increased. This is one background fact that explains why Parliament's outrage at a near unanimous legislation being struck down was not more stirring. Once again, background political developments had a bearing on the prospect of opposition–government cooperation. But it also had a bearing on which *fears* dominated—the fear of an unaccountable judiciary or the fear of government packing the Courts?

As things have worked out, the crisis of overreaching has only deepened because of two developments. The Court, recognizing that it had to put its house in order, agreed to come up with a more tangible process for the functioning of the collegium. Could the government's point of view be brought into this process? If so, what form should it take? If reports are to be believed, one of the sticking points in the conversation seems to be about how decisive should the 'intelligence' and 'national security' inputs be in deciding the suitability of judges? The judiciary apparently wants to deny that these considerations, as presented by government, can constitute a kind of veto. The government wants to say that there has to be some mechanism of ensuring that the judiciary does not ignore them. Now this is a matter that would have been more easily resolved if there were a minimal degree of trust, common sense, and good judgment in both the executive and judiciary. Both are looking for guarantees for each other's conduct that are hard to formalize.

The second development has been open discontent within the judiciary itself. The dissenting judge, Justice Chelameswar, stopped attending the meetings of the collegium demanding a more transparent process.[18] We are not privy to all the issues. But the fact that this conflict

[18] Krishnadas Rajagopal, 'Justice Chelameswar opts out of collegium', *The Hindu* (New Delhi, 2 September 2016) <http://www.thehindu.com/news/national/justice-chelameswar-opts-out-of-collegium/article9066616.ece> accessed 26 September 2016.

has become public once again erodes the credibility of the judiciary. Having usurped the powers of appointment, the only way it could have sustained public trust is by inspiring faith in its own proceedings and processes. But it is far from clear that this is about to happen. The judiciary may come to some compromise with its own dissenters and with the government, but there is no question that the public's faith in the judiciary's leadership and credibility has been dented.

The obvious solution would be for Parliament to take a crack at getting an NJAC Act II legislated. The revised NJAC might tweak the voting rules of the old NJAC to ensure that non-judicial members do not exercise veto. In my view, the Law Minister's membership could also be dispensed with, since that is such a visible bone of contention. But the political prospects of such a resolution are diminishing. Till then, the larger crisis of constitutionalism continues. This battle, between the executive and the judiciary, was always a contest over the question 'Whom do you trust more?' The answer, increasingly, appears to be 'A plague on both your houses'.

II

THE ANALYSIS OF THE NJAC JUDGMENT

Judicial Review and Parliamentary Power

6

Reorienting the Balance

K.T. THOMAS

I rejoiced with the rest of India when a thirteen-judge bench of the Supreme Court ruled in *Kesavananda Bharati v. State of Kerala*,[1] though only with a wafer-thin majority, that Parliament's power to amend the Constitution does not include the power to destroy its basic structure. I was then a practising advocate. I felt that henceforth the Constitution will ever remain unimpaired. However, the verdict of the majority on the five-judge bench of the Supreme Court in the *NJAC Case*, to my dismay, has ominously portended the dangerous extent to which the sword of *Kesavananda Bharati* could be swung; the swinging being by means of semantic exercises even against seemingly harmless mechanisms to appoint judges to the Supreme Court of India and the High Courts.

Judicial Independence and the NJAC Judgment

The 99th Amendment and the NJAC Act collectively aimed to usher in a new system for appointment of judges to the Supreme Court and the High Courts by establishing a six-member NJAC. Due deference must be given to the fact that the 99th Amendment, which was introduced as the Constitution (One-Hundred Twenty-first Amendment) Bill, 2014 was passed by both Houses of Parliament with an overwhelming

---

[1] (1973) 4 SCC 225 (*Kesavananda Bharati*).

majority. The numbers speak for themselves as the 99th Amendment was passed in the Lok Sabha with 367 members voting in favour and none voting against it.[2] In the Rajya Sabha, it was passed by 179 members voting in favour, while one member abstained from voting.[3] However, the majority judgment in the *NJAC Case* administered a warning that even four judges are enough to strike down a law not palatable to the judges of the Supreme Court, no matter that such amending law had the backing of the Parliament, was ratified by 20 States,[4] and in essence, was symbolic of the will of the people manifested by their representatives in Parliament.

The striking down of the 99th Amendment also bears testimony to Parliament's inability to exercise its constituent power to amend the Constitution and adopt an alternative to the collegium system of appointing judges to the higher judiciary. As is known, the collegium system is a creation of the judges themselves, being the outcome of judgments delivered by the Supreme Court in the *Second* and *Third Judges' Cases.* Interestingly, while striking down the 99th Amendment and nipping in the bud the system of judicial appointments that it sought to establish, the bench in the *NJAC Case* did acknowledge the frailties of the collegium system. The perils highlighted by Justice Joseph are almost a testimonial pointing to the nadir to which the collegium system has plummeted over the years. Justice Joseph acknowledged the fact that 'the present Collegium system lacks transparency, accountability, and objectivity' and 'very serious allegations and many a time not unfounded too, have been raised that its approach has been highly subjective'.[5] Yet, the learned judge joined his brother judges in striking down the 99th Amendment on the premise that independence

---

[2] *Lok Sabha Debates*, vol. 4, no. 2 (Parliament Secretariat) 12–13 August 2014 <rajyasabha.nic.in/Debate%20LS-121.doc> accessed 28 September 2016.

[3] *Rajya Sabha Debates* (Parliament Secretariat) 13–14 August 2014 <http://rajyasabha.nic.in/rsnew/bill/rs_bill_debate/RS%20debate%20121%20Bill.pdf> accessed 28 September 2016.

[4] Editorial, 'An Assertion of Primacy', *The Hindu* (New Delhi, 17 October 2015) <http://www.thehindu.com/opinion/editorial/supreme-court-bench-order-on-national-judicial-appointments-commission-act-an-assertion-of-primacy/article7770892.ece> accessed 28 September 2016.

[5] *NJAC Case* [990].

of the judiciary is safe in the collegium system but will be destroyed by the new alternative adumbrated in the 99th Amendment.

The silver lining discernible from all five opinions in the *NJAC Case* is the finding that independence of the judiciary is part of the basic structure of our Constitution. But on the question whether the 99th Amendment has destroyed it, Justice Chelameswar in his dissent advanced strong reasons to hold that it has not. In expounding upon judicial independence, Justice Chelameswar observed that 'Articles 124 and 217 deal with one of the elements necessary to establish an independent judiciary—the appointment process.'[6] At the same time, he noted that the following are the most essential safeguards to protect the independence of the judiciary:

> ... certainty of tenure, protection from removal from office except by a stringent process in the cases of Judges found unfit to continue as members of the judiciary, protection of salaries and other privileges from interference by the executive and the legislature, immunity from scrutiny either by the Executive or the Legislature of the conduct of Judges with respect to the discharge of judicial functions except in cases of alleged misbehaviour, immunity from civil and criminal liability for acts committed in discharge of duties, protection against criticism to a great degree...[7]

Having made these pertinent observations on what constitutes judicial independence, and upon a detailed analysis of its individual provisions, Justice Chelameswar upheld the constitutionality of the 99th Amendment. In having done this, he stood apart from the majority, which categorically held that the 99th Amendment and the NJAC Act were violative of the independence of the judiciary. The inevitable result then was the revival of the collegium system, despite all its criticisms and flaws.

A Conspicuous Refusal to Read Down the 99th Amendment

The fact that the 99th Amendment secured overwhelming support from the Parliament and the State Legislatures did not suffice to protect it

---

[6] *NJAC Case* [1177].

[7] *NJAC Case* [1132].

from judicial invalidation at the hands of the majority. I have no dissent over this approach, provided the Supreme Court could discover that the 99th Amendment was indeed destructive of the basic structure of the Constitution. Unfortunately, no effort was made to chisel/expand/ restrict the dangerous potentialities of the 99th Amendment, assuming it had any. It would have been a splendid display of judicial statesmanship to show creativity by protecting the 99th Amendment instead of whipping the weapon of destruction, i.e., judicial invalidation.

The majority judges could have attempted to emulate previous instances of judicial reading down, or striking down in part, of constitutional amendments. A seven-judge bench in *L. Chandra Kumar v. Union of India*,[8] of which I was a part, struck down only specific clauses of Article 323-A and Article 323-B.[9] *L. Chandra Kumar* witnessed a challenge to sub-clause (d) of clause (2) of Article 323-A and sub-clause (d) of clause (3) of Article 323-B, which totally excluded the jurisdiction of 'all courts', except that of the Supreme Court under Article 136, with respect to all or any of the matters falling within the jurisdiction of the tribunals constituted to deal with matters enumerated under these two articles. Thus, the impugned clauses excluded the jurisdiction of the High Courts to review decisions rendered by tribunals. Consequently, the question of whether tribunals constituted under Article 323-A and Article 323-B possess the competence to test the constitutional validity of a statutory provision/rule, was raised. In response to these contentions, the Supreme Court held Article 323-A(2)(d) and Article 323-B(3)(d) to be unconstitutional to the extent that they excluded the jurisdiction of the High Courts under Articles 226 and 227 of the Constitution.[10] Simultaneously, the Court held that the tribunals created under these two articles are possessed of the competence to test the constitutional validity of statutory provisions/rules, with their decisions

---

[8] (1997) 3 SCC 261 (*L. Chandra Kumar*).

[9] Articles 323-A and 323-B fall under Part XIVA of the Constitution, which was inserted by the Constitution (Forty-second) Amendment Act, 1976. Article 323-A lays down that Parliament may, by law, provide for the adjudication and trial by administrative tribunals of disputes with regard to persons appointed to public services. Article 323-B provides for establishment of tribunals by appropriate Legislature, by law, with respect to other matters.

[10] *L. Chandra Kumar* (n. 8) [99].

being subject to scrutiny before a Division Bench of the High Court within whose jurisdiction the concerned tribunal falls. Therefore, by giving a constrained reading to the provisions impugned, administrative tribunals were protected as courts of first instance in respect of the areas of law for which they have been constituted, and the provision for approaching the High Court was also safeguarded.

There were powerful arguments in *L. Chandra Kumar* to the effect that the entire scheme of Articles 323-A and 323-B had the effect of ousting the jurisdiction of High Courts under Articles 226 and 227. However, the judges adopted creative judicial skills to avert a drastic turn of events by saving the two provisions and only striking down certain sub-clauses. There are several other instances where the Supreme Court has read down, restricted, or only partly struck down provisions of constitutional amendments. For instance, in *Kesavananda Bharati*, the Supreme Court declared part of Article 31C (which was inserted by the Constitution [Twenty-fifth Amendment] Act, 1971) invalid for giving immunity to laws giving effect to the Directive Principles of State Policy from being challenged on the ground of abridging the rights under Articles 14 and 19. Similarly, in *Minerva Mills v. Union of India*,[11] Section 55 of the Constitution (Forty-second Amendment) Act, 1976 was declared unconstitutional and void for inserting clauses (4) and (5) in Article 368 which removed judicial review over amendments to the Constitution and declared that the constituent power of Parliament to amend the Constitution will be unlimited. Evidently, both these are instances of striking down constitutional amendments in part.[12] In

---

[11] (1980) 3 SCC 625.

[12] The only other instances of the Supreme Court having struck down constitutional amendments (again, only in part) include *Indira Gandhi v. Raj Narain*, 1975 Supp SCC 1, where Article 329 A(4), inserted by the Constitution (Thirty-ninth) Amendment Act, 1975, was struck down for abolishing the forum for adjudicating upon a dispute relating to the validity of the elections of the Prime Minister and Speaker; *P. Sambamurthy v. State of Andhra Pradesh* (1987) 1 SCC 362 where Article 371-D(5), inserted by the Constitution (Thirty-second) Amendment Act, 1973, was declared unconstitutional for empowering the Government of Andhra Pradesh to modify or annul final orders passed by administrative tribunals before their implementation; and *Kihoto Hollohan v. Zachillhu*, 1992 Supp 2 SCC 651, where Para 7 of the Tenth Schedule, inserted by the Constitution (Fifty-second) Amendment Act, 1985 was declared invalid

fact, in India's constitutional history there has never been an instance of a wholesale quashing of a constitutional amendment. This distinction squarely falls upon the 99th Amendment. The Supreme Court has sparingly used the power to strike down constitutional amendments, and has done so only with utmost caution.

Presence of Eminent Persons on the NJAC

One of the several thorny issues which invited the wrath of the majority in the *NJAC Case* was Article 124A(1)(d) which envisaged the presence of two 'eminent persons' on the NJAC. Eminent persons were meant to be representatives of the civil society in the judicial appointments process with a view to make it more participatory and consultative. However, the majority adversely viewed the presence of eminent persons on the NJAC on two grounds: first, the concept of 'eminent persons' was vague and not defined; second, in light of the first proviso to Section 5(2), and Section 6(6) of the NJAC Act,[13] the concurrent view of any two members of the NJAC could effectively veto a proposed candidature for appointment; thus, the two eminent persons by themselves could veto a proposed appointment, which was otherwise favourable to the other members of the NJAC.[14] The issue of nomination of eminent persons presented an opportunity to creatively read down Article 124A(1)(d) to provide for qualifications for eminent persons, instead of striking it down in the first instance. However, the seemingly determined stance of the majority to strike down the provision on eminent persons was evident when Justice Khehar spoke of the 'absurdity of including two "eminent persons" on the NJAC', and also termed the Attorney

---

insofar as it affected the power of judicial review in respect of matters connected with disqualification of a member of a House, and because it was inserted into the Constitution without ratification from at least half of the State Legislatures.

[13] The first proviso of s 5(2) mandated that the NJAC shall not recommend a person for appointment as a Judge of the Supreme Court if any two members of the Commission do not agree for such recommendation. Similarly, s 6(6) provided that the NJAC shall not recommend a person for appointment as a Judge of a High Court if any two members of the NJAC do not agree for such recommendation.

[14] *NJAC Case* [333].

General's arguments defending the eminent persons as 'a submission with all loose ends, and no clear meaning'.[15] In fact, submissions citing instances of foreign jurisdictions which envisage the presence of 'lay persons' on judicial appointment commissions were rebuffed with the remark that 'it is imprudent to ape a system prevalent in an advanced country, with an evolved civil society' in India.[16]

At the same time, the bench seemed to have assumed that the eminent persons, in collaboration with the Law Minister, would act as a structured bloc. Justice Goel observed, 'It cannot be wished away by presuming that the Law Minister and the two distributors will not be influenced by any extraneous considerations'.[17] This observation signified a prevailing distrust of the non-judicial members on the NJAC, and the assumption that they would necessarily act in a manner so as to prevail over the judicial members. An alternative interpretation to justify the inclusion of eminent persons could have been that they are truly independent from any branch of government. In a way, they could have acted as a check against any purportedly arbitrary exercise of power by the other members of the NJAC to steer through an undeserving candidate by exercise of their veto power. However, the intended exercise of power by eminent persons was viewed only adversely by the majority, resulting in the invalidation of Article 124A(1)(d).

Participation of the Executive

The presence of one member of the executive branch of government—the Law Minister—also did not pass muster with the Court. The presence of the Law Minister was seen as violative of the independence of the judiciary, primarily on the ground that there would be a 'conflict of interest' since the government, which is a major litigant in the courts, cannot be part of the body responsible for appointing judges. Justice Khehar categorically said that keeping in mind the significant participation of the executive in judicial adjudication, 'reciprocity and feelings of pay-back to the political-executive' may arise, which would be

[15] *NJAC Case* [334].

[16] *NJAC Case* [334].

[17] *NJAC Case* [1090].

'disastrous to "independence of the judiciary"'.[18] However, the reasoning offered by the majority judges that the presence of even a single member of the executive would erode all the independence of the judiciary is far from convincing. As cited by the Attorney General during the course of the proceedings, the independence of high constitutional functionaries, such as members of the Election Commission (EC) and the Comptroller and Auditor General (CAG) is not impinged due to participation of the executive in the matter of their appointments. The power of appointment of the Chief Election Commissioner (CEC) and the Election Commissioners under Article 324(2) and the CAG under Article 148(1) is vested exclusively with the President. However, the fact that these functionaries are appointed by the executive alone was not considered by the drafters of the Constitution as capable of impairing the independence of these institutions. This is evident from the Constituent Assembly Debates where the specific issue of the establishment of the EC was discussed. In the context of the CEC, K.M. Munshi observed:

> The Chief Election Commissioner, as the House will find, is practically independent. No doubt he is appointed by the President, that is, the Central Government. There can be no other authority, no higher authority in India than the President for appointing this Tribunal. You cannot omit this important thing.[19]

The fact that once appointed, the CEC is not removable at the will of the President also weighed with the drafters of the Constitution when they discussed draft Article 289 (which ultimately became Article 324). The proviso to Article 324(5) mandates that the CEC shall not be removed from his office except in like manner and on the like grounds as a Judge of the Supreme Court, and his/her conditions of service shall not be varied to his disadvantage after his appointment. Similarly, Article 148(1) provides that the CAG shall only be removed from office in like manner and on the like grounds as a Judge of the Supreme Court, and under the proviso to Article 148(3), his salary and his rights in respect of leave of absence, pension, or age of retirement shall not be varied to his disadvantage after his appointment.

---

[18] *NJAC Case* [315].

[19] *Constituent Assembly of India Debates*, vol. 8, no. 3 (Lok Sabha Secretariat) 16 June 1949, 924.

Evidently, the protection provided for judges in the context of removal from office, payment of salary, among others, are also provided for other institutions, such as the EC and CAG, and in this regard, they stand on a similar footing. Thus, the reasoning proffered by the Court that the EC and CAG are different from the judiciary is quite unconvincing. The question whether such instrumentalities too could function independently in spite of the role played by the executive in their appointment was not addressed by the judges. In his observation on the appointment of the members of the EC and CAG, and that the President is not required to consult anyone in this process, Justice Lokur cursorily said:

> Since the consultation provision was incorporated only for the appointment of judges, surely, the Constituent Assembly had good reasons for making this distinction.[20]

Justice Khehar voiced a similar opinion by saying:

> The process of 'consultation' contemplated therein [in Article 124], has to be meaningfully understood. If it was not to be so, the above provision would have been similarly worded as those relating to the appointment of the Comptroller and Auditor-General of India, Governors of States, Chairman and Members of the Finance Commission, Chairman and Members of the Union Public Service Commission, Chief Election Commissioner and Election Commissioners, Chairperson and Vice Chairperson and Members of the National Commission for Scheduled Castes, as also, those of the National Commission for Scheduled Tribes.[21]

Clearly, while the judges cite the differences between the manner of appointment envisaged for each of these constitutional functionaries, they stop short of elaborating upon these differences, and the reason why the judiciary stands on a pedestal as compared to them. In this regard, an important aspect that Justice Chelameswar acknowledged (and which was previously acknowledged by Justice E.S. Venkataramiah in the *First Judges' Case*) is that independence of judiciary is also in the sphere of functional performance, and its requirement is in the post-appointment years.[22] Thus, independence of the judiciary is also contingent on matters such as protection against arbitrary removal,

---

[20] *NJAC Case* [772].

[21] *NJAC Case* [131].

[22] *See NJAC Case* [1132] and *First Judges' Case* [1268].

protection of salaries, and other privileges. Mere presence of a non-judicial member on the appointing body, even if that member is the Law Minister, will not be violative of judicial independence if there are constitutional protections for post-appointment aspects.

The validity of the presence of the Law Minister was also questioned by the judges in light of the first proviso to Section 5(2), and Section 6(6) of the NJAC Act. The apprehension that the Law Minister, in unity with one of the eminent persons, would prevail over the judicial members of the NJAC (by exercising a veto as envisaged by the aforesaid provisions) was not acceptable to the majority on the bench. However, even in this regard, the reasons offered in the majority opinions were too fragile and tenuous to overturn constitutional provisions. It should not be overlooked that the unity of two persons on the NJAC could only have prevented the selection of a person from becoming a judge. Such a unity could not have enabled an ill-suited person for appointment. Would that not have been a safety measure to prevent an unfit person from reaching the Supreme Court bench, even at the risk of its maximum demerit that a suitable person would not have been selected? The presence of one representative of the executive, none other than the Law Minister, should have been welcomed wholeheartedly, particularly when the role of the executive in the selection of judges in all other democratic countries is of a much higher dimension.

Conclusion

It is an enigma why the five-judge bench did not refer this momentous issue to be decided by a much larger bench, at least larger than the nine-judge bench in the *Second Judges' Case* that created the collegium system. A plea was raised by the Union Government for adopting such a course, and referring the matter to a larger bench for revisiting the judgments in the *Second* and *Third Judges' Cases*, before going into the merits of the case. However, by an order of 12 May 2015, the Supreme Court declined this plea and refused to decide the issue of reference as a preliminary issue before hearing the main case on merits.[23] The

---

[23] *NJAC Case*, order dated 12 May 2015 in W.P. (C) No. 13/ 2015.

judgment in the *NJAC Case* also carried a detailed order on reference, which witnessed an eventual refusal by the Court to revisit or review the *Second* and *Third Judges' Cases*, and refer the matter to a larger bench.[24] Of course, if the 99th Amendment was upheld, it would be a different matter; but when it appeared to the judges otherwise, it was only proper that such an issue of immense importance ought to have been decided by a larger bench.

Nevertheless, what should not have happened has happened. We can learn a lesson for the future. Is it safe for parliamentary democracy to persist with the power of even a unity of just four judges striking down a constitutional provision on the premise that it violates the ratio of *Kesavananda Bharati*? In this regard, I will make a suggestion which may be considered: Whenever it appears to the Supreme Court in future that the validity of any constitutional provision requires to be decided on the touchstone of the basic structure doctrine, the same shall be decided by a bench of at least the size which decided *Kesavananda Bharati*. This can be achieved through amendment of the relevant rule by the Supreme Court itself in the exercise of its powers under Article 145(2) of the Constitution. This will not only ensure judicial discipline but also give constitutional amendments the respect that they deserve from the higher judiciary.

---

[24] *NJAC Case* [134].

Checks and Balances Revisited

The Role of the Executive in Judicial Appointments

7

MUKUL ROHATGI

In what will be called the *Fourth Judges' Case* in the history of constitutional law in India, the judgment of the Supreme Court in the *NJAC Case* will have far-reaching implications on several facets relating to judicial appointments. Both the 99th Amendment and the NJAC Act were held unconstitutional by the Supreme Court. My two fundamental criticisms of the judgment are: First, the judgment flows from a deep distrust of the executive—the judgment holds that the Law Minister who is a part of the executive will completely vitiate the selecting body even though he is only one out of a total of six members, even when the remaining five are not remotely connected with the executive. This is difficult to justify, for reasons I provide below. Second, it proceeds on the unquestioned belief that judges are best suited for selecting and appointing judges—this belief has no legal, factual, historical, or comparative basis. From 1950 till 1993, judges were appointed by the executive in consultation with the Chief Justice of India. This era produced some of the finest judges in the history of independent India. Further, no other comparable system in the world provides for judges appointing judges. So for the majority judges in the *NJAC Case* to determine otherwise, is mistaken.

Article 124A, which established the NJAC, was inserted into the Constitution by the 99th Amendment and it provided for the Union Minister of Law and Justice (Law Minister) to be one of the members in this commission of six people.[1] The majority on the bench frowned upon the presence of the Law Minister in the NJAC since it impinged upon the independence of the judiciary and, by necessary implication, affected the basic structure of the Constitution.

The purported role of the Law Minister in the NJAC was much contested on the ground that the presence of a member of the executive would have the effect of shifting the power dynamics in the appointments process and undermine judicial independence.[2] Against the backdrop of this contention, this essay argues that the Law Minister's presence on the NJAC, instead of violating the independence of the judiciary would, in fact, have led to valuable inputs in the selection process, apart from giving effect to the principle of checks and balances. To this end, this essay will commence with a short discussion of the role of the executive in appointments to the higher judiciary as was envisaged by the framers of the Constitution, and how executive participation eventually turned out in the matter of judicial appointments. This will be followed by a discussion of what was held by each of the judges who were part of the majority on the NJAC bench on the role of the executive. Thereafter, this essay will analyse the concerns raised by the majority in the *NJAC Case*, and whether the presence of the executive on the NJAC constituted a potent threat to the independence of the judiciary.

Executive Role in Appointments over Time

The need for ensuring judicial independence formed the background when the framers of the Constitution debated the process for appointment of judges to the higher judiciary. Protecting judicial independence was deemed necessary in light of the fact that appointment of judges at the sole whims of the executive led to the appointment of several judges

---

[1] Under Article 124A(1), the NJAC was to comprise the Chief Justice of India, two other senior Judges of the Supreme Court next to the Chief Justice, the Law Minister, and two eminent persons.

[2] Argument made by the petitioners, as noted in Justice Chelameswar's dissent, *NJAC Case* [1218].

favourable to the colonial government.[3] To take appointments outside of the unfettered discretion of the executive, the Sapru Committee Report proposed a consultative method where judges of the Supreme Court were to be appointed by the Head of the State (President) in consultation with the Chief Justice of India while judges of the High Court were to be appointed in consultation with the Head of the Unit, the Chief Justice of the High Court, and the Chief Justice of India.[4]

The various stages of drafting of the precursors to Articles 124 and 217 strengthened the impending need to preserve an inter-institutional balance in the matter of appointments. This is evident from the chief architect of the Constitution, Dr Ambedkar's speech on 24 May 1949 where he was categorical that the power to appoint judges to the Supreme Court and the High Courts could neither be left to be exercised by the President merely on the advice of the executive, nor was it considered feasible to make every appointment according to the wishes of the executive subject to the concurrence of the Chief Justice. Speaking in the Constituent Assembly, he said,

> With regard to the question of the concurrence of the Chief Justice, it seems to me that those who advocate that proposition seem to rely implicitly both on the impartiality of the Chief Justice and the sound-ness of his judgment. I personally feel no doubt that the Chief Justice is a very eminent person. But after all the Chief Justice is a man with all the failings, all the sentiments and all the prejudices which we as com-mon people have; and I think, to allow the Chief Justice practically a veto upon the appointment of judges is really to transfer the authority to the Chief Justice which we are not prepared to vest in the President or the Government of the day. I therefore, think that is also a dangerous proposition.[5]

The underlying idea was not to allow any one organ veto over appoint-ments, and have a consultative process between the President and the

---

[3] Law Commission of India, *A New Forum for Judicial Appointments* (121st Report, Ministry of Law and Justice, Government of India 1987) paras 1.1–1.2 (121st Report).

[4] Tej Bahadur Sapru (ed.), *Constitutional Proposals of the Sapru Committee* (Padma Publications 1945) 193.

[5] *Constituent Assembly of India Debates*, vol. 8, no. 3 (Lok Sabha Secretariat) 24 May 1949, 258.

Chief Justice of India. The Constituent Assembly thus contemplated a multiplicity of authorities for appointing judges to the higher judiciary, with each of these authorities mutually checking and balancing their function. Mutual checks and balances were preserved with the power of appointment being invested focally with the President who was required to consult the Chief Justice of India for all the appointments.[6]

However, the envisioned procedure underwent a sea change due to several events that took place during the working of the Constitution. Interference by the executive in appointments during the 1970s—the supersession of three justices for the post of Chief Justice of India by the executive in 1973, in contravention of the convention of seniority in appointment of the Chief Justice of India, and again the supersession of yet another justice in 1977 led to the unmistakable apprehension that the politicization of the judiciary was in process.[7] The response to this perceived politicization was the judgment in the *Second Judges' Case*, which fundamentally altered the nature of the appointments process in Article 124(2) and Article 217(1) of the Constitution. Among other things, the *Second Judges' Case* held that in the event of disagreement between constitutional functionaries involved in the consultation process prior to a judicial appointment under Articles 124 and 217, the opinion of the Chief Justice of India would have primacy. This opinion would not be his personal opinion but rather the opinion of the judiciary 'symbolised by the Chief Justice of India', and in reaching this opinion, the Chief Justice of India would have to consult two of his senior-most colleagues.[8] A similar process was envisaged for appointment of judges to the High Courts. After the *Third Judges' Case*, the collegium was expanded to include the five senior-most judges of the Supreme Court for Supreme Court appointments, and three senior-most judges of the Supreme Court and the respective High Court for appointments to High Courts.

However the operation of the collegium system in the last two decades has created much disaffection. One of the major concerns is

[6] *See* also, Arghya Sengupta, 'Independence and Accountability of the Higher Indian Judiciary' (unpublished DPhil thesis, University of Oxford 2015)17.

[7] N.A. Palkhivala, *Our Constitution: Defaced and Defiled* (MacMillan 1974) 93.

[8] *Second Judges' Case* [68].

that the reasons for substantive appointments and non-appointments made by the collegium were not known because of the completely opaque nature of the process.[9] Also, certain egregious appointments raised serious apprehensions about its suitability.[10] Further, the collegium was founded in an invalid interpretation of the Constitution, since the institution of the collegium has no constitutional warrant and was a creation of the Court pursuant to the *Second Judges' Case*. These principled and practical deficiencies in the operation of the collegium led to several reform proposals across the years[11] which materialized in the form of the 99th Amendment and the NJAC Act.

Views of the Majority

The majority on the NJAC bench held Article 124A(1)(c) *ultra vires* the provisions of the Constitution on the ground that the inclusion of the Law Minister, as an *ex officio* member of the NJAC impinged upon the independence of the judiciary as well as separation of powers, and hence, was violative of the basic structure of the Constitution.[12] This is notwithstanding the fact that the Law Minister was one in a commission of six persons, which means he/she did not constitute a numerical majority on the Commission and was not in a position to single-handedly block any recommendation made by the other members.

An overarching issue flagged by the judges pertained to the conflict of interest that would arise due to the participation of the executive in the selection process when it is also one of the major litigants before the courts (both the Supreme Court and the High Courts). Justice Khehar, the lead author of the majority judgment, denied the possibility of the political executive having a role in the final selection and appointment

---

[9]   V.R. Krishna Iyer, 'The Syndrome of Judicial Arrears' *The Hindu* (New Delhi 2 December 2009) <http://www.thehindu.com/opinion/lead/the-syndrome-of-judicial-arrears/article58416.ece> accessed 1 August 2016 (Krishna Iyer).

[10]   Krishna Iyer (n. 9).

[11]   Legislative reform proposals emerged in the form of the Constitution (Sixty-seventh Amendment) Bill, 1990, the Constitution (Ninety-eighth Amendment) Bill, 2003, and the Judicial Appointments Commission Bill, 2013, which proposed the establishment of commissions for broad-basing the appointments process.

of judges to the higher judiciary in light of the 'enormity of the participation of the political-executive, in actions of judicial adjudication.'[13]
He felt that participation of the executive in the appointments process
would generate among the judges feelings of reciprocity and pay back
to their appointing authority, which would be disastrous for judicial
independence.[14] Justice Khehar summed up his views on executive
participation in judicial appointments as follows:

> In the NJAC, the Union Minister in charge of Law and Justice would be
> a party to all final selections and appointments of Judges to the higher
> judiciary. It may be difficult for Judges approved by the NJAC, to resist a
> plea of conflict of interest (if such a plea was to be raised, and pressed),
> where the political-executive is a party to the lis. The above, would have
> the inevitable effect of undermining the 'independence of the judiciary',
> even where such a plea is repulsed. Therefore, the role assigned to the
> political-executive, can at best be limited to a collaborative participation,
> excluding any role in the final determination.[15]

The other majority judges also shared adverse views on the participation of the executive in the NJAC. Even while acknowledging that the
Law Minister is one in a body of six, Justice Lokur apprehended that he
has the influence of clouding the vision of every other member on the
NJAC. He says that 'being a Cabinet Minister representing the entire
Cabinet and the Government of India in the NJAC, the Law Minister
is undoubtedly a very important and politically powerful figure whose
views can, potentially, have a major impact on the views that other
members of the NJAC may hold'.[16] The irony of this statement should
not be lost on the reader: Does this suggest that one Law Minister
would have had the potential to influence three judges on the NJAC,
one of whom was the Chief Justice of India?

Justice Lokur also acknowledged the system of checks and balances
inherent in the matter of judicial appointments albeit in the context
of the unfavourable appointments made by the collegium. He said
that even though the executive has an important consultative role, 'it

---

[12] *See NJAC Case* [416].

[13] *NJAC Case* [315].

[14] *NJAC Case* [315].

[15] *NJAC Case* [319].

[16] *NJAC Case* [914].

mortgaged its constitutional responsibility of maintaining a check on what may be described as the erroneous decisions of the collegium'.[17] While summing up his opinion, Justice Lokur said that 'the struggle for the independence of the judiciary has always been pivoted around the exclusion of the executive in decision-taking, but the inclusion of the Law Minister in the NJAC is counterproductive',[18] and that the presence of the Law Minister in the NJAC is 'ill-advised' and 'casts a doubt on the principle of Cabinet responsibility'.

Justice Joseph also remained generally averse to the participation of the executive or any non-judicial members in the appointments process on the ground that '[d]irect participation of the Executive or other non-judicial elements would ultimately lead to structured bargaining in appointments, if not, anything worse'.[19] Such bargaining in the appointments process, he believed, would possibly dilute the basic structure to create a committed judiciary and should be nipped in the bud.[20] Justice Goel added in by saying that 'the power of appointment of judges cannot be exercised by the Executive as the same will affect independence of the judiciary'.[21] He also went on to say that 'primacy of judiciary and limited role of the Executive in appointment of judges is part of the basic structure of the Constitution'.[22]

Two prevailing sentiments emerge from the observations of the majority with regard to participation of the executive in judicial appointments. First, two judges (Justices Khehar and Lokur) were unwilling to give the executive a determinative role or a voice in the final decision-making as to the selection and appointment of judges, but open to receiving 'inputs' from the executive on potential candidates. Second, the mere participation of the executive in the appointments process is construed as leading to its probable politicization and, consequently, impinging upon judicial independence.

[17] *NJAC Case* [599].
[18] *NJAC Case* [923].
[19] *NJAC Case* [988].
[20] *NJAC Case* [988].
[21] *NJAC Case* [1067].
[22] *NJAC Case* [1071].

A Critical Analysis

The majority on the NJAC bench shows conspicuous concern for the issue of conflict of interest if the executive were to be given a determinative voice in the appointment of judges to the higher judiciary. However it gives rise to the perception that certain countervailing propositions pertaining to why the conflict of interest apprehension is not a significant one, why it is not unique to India, and why it cannot be assumed that the Law Minister might act against the interest of an independent judiciary may not have been adequately considered.

First, participation of the Law Minister in the NJAC would have addressed an important practical requirement that the executive fulfils in the appointment process. While the judicial members of the NJAC would have assessed the judicial knowledge and acumen of potential candidates, the Law Minister would have provided vital inputs about his/her character and conduct. Justice J.S. Verma envisaged this exact function for the executive in the appointments process, when he observed in the *Second Judges' Case* that

> There may, however, be some personal trait of an individual lawyer or Judge, which may be better known to the executive and may be unknown to the Chief Justice of India and the Chief Justice of the High Court, and which may be relevant for assessing his potential to become a good Judge. It is for this reason, that the executive is also one of the consultees in the process of appointment....[23]

In the context of this function, Justice Lokur makes a rather interesting observation. He says,

> There is a distinction, as mentioned above, between the Law Minister providing inputs to the Chief Justice of India and the Law Minister having a say in the final decision regarding the appointment of a judge of a High Court or the Supreme Court. While the former certainly cannot be objected to and in fact would be necessary, it is the participation in the decision-taking process that is objectionable. In other words, the Law Minister might be a part of the decision-making process (as the position was prior to the 99th Constitution Amendment Act) but ought not to be a part of the decision-taking process. This distinction is quite crucial. The voting participation of

[23] *Second Judges' Case* [462].

the Law Minister in the decision-taking process goes against the grain of the debates in the Constituent Assembly and clearly amounts to an alteration of the basic structure of the Constitution.[24]

Clearly, Justice Lokur is not averse to the Law Minister providing inputs on a potential candidate to the Chief Justice. In fact, this seems to be the dominant opinion with Justice Khehar also willing to give at best a limited 'collaborative participation' to the executive, which is short of any role in the final determination.[25]

However, it can be nobody's case that the presence of the Law Minister on the NJAC gives him/her, or the government, a 'determinative' role in the selection process.[26] The NJAC, as it was proposed, was expected to function as a collaborative body where decisions were to be taken after due consultation amongst all functionaries. Having one vote in a body of six members can hardly be termed as having a determinative voice, and certainly not a ground for invalidating Article 124A(1)(c) as violative of the independence of the judiciary. As mentioned above, the executive was not in a numerical majority, and the Law Minister could neither veto nor push through any appointment based on the one vote given to him/her. For all practical purposes, the casting of the one vote by the Law Minister is the manifestation of the function of providing inputs on the antecedents of candidates, something which Justices Lokur and Khehar expressly allow the Law Minister to do. Suggesting that inputs may be provided from the outside but not as a participating member of the appointment process is a distinction without a difference.

Second, the majority raises the plea of conflict of interest due to the presence of the Law Minister on the NJAC, on the ground that the Central Government is the largest litigant before the courts in India. This, the majority says, is violative of the independence of the judiciary. However, if the plea of conflict of interest were to be readily accepted, it would lead to the conclusion that most judiciaries in the world, where appointments are made at the behest of or pursuant to a dominant role played by the executive, are not independent. The Union made this

---

[24] *NJAC Case* [921].

[25] *NJAC Case* [319].

[26] Arghya Sengupta, 'Judicial Primacy and the Basic Structure: A Legal Analysis of the NJAC Judgment' (November 2015) L (48) *Economic and Political Weekly* 27, 29.

ardent plea by citing instances of other jurisdictions, such as the United States of America, Australia, and Canada where the executive has an overriding power to make appointments, much greater than what was envisaged for the executive in India under the NJAC Act.

However, the crux of this submission did not find favour with the bench. In their treatment of the examples from other jurisdictions, all three judges—Justices Khehar, Lokur, and Goel—have taken resort to the assertion that the considerations in other countries are different from those in India and the models prevalent elsewhere cannot be replicated here.[27] Justice Lokur's sentiment sums up the position taken by all three judges when he says, 'The considerations in different countries are, to put it simply, different. We need to have our own indigenous system suited to our environment and our own requirements.'[28] There is no attempt to bring out the differences which justify the manner in which appointments are made in India, why it is different from other jurisdictions which equally prize independence of the judiciary. Without this analysis, it is fair to say that comparative practices were shunned without adequate consideration.

Third, it appears that the core of the majority's beliefs with regard to executive participation rests on presumptions and surmises, and a prevailing apprehension of the executive wing of the government. The trepidation regarding the abuse of power is evident even from the submissions of the petitioners who witnessed the presence of the Law Minister on the NJAC as 'surrendering one-sixth of the power of appointment, to the Government',[29] a contention which has been accepted on face value by the Hon'ble Court. Much of the Court's consternation arose due to two specific provisions of the NJAC Act—the second proviso to Section 5(2),[30] and Section 6(6)[31]—which allowed

---

[27] *See NJAC Case* [320]–[329] (Justice Khehar); [916], [918] (Justice Lokur); [1061], [1081], [1103] (Justice Goel).

[28] *NJAC Case* [319].

[29] Contention of the petitioners as noted in Justice Khehar's opinion, *NJAC Case* [45].

[30] NJAC Act, second proviso to s 5(2)—Provided further that the Commission shall not recommend a person for appointment if any two members of the Commission do not agree for such recommendation.

[31] NJAC Act, s 6(6)—The Commission shall not recommend a person for appointment under this section if any two members of the Commission do not agree for such recommendation.

two members of the NJAC to veto a proposed candidature for judicial appointment. The likelihood of the Law Minister acting with the support of one of the two eminent persons to stall an appointment, which would otherwise fall in favour with the judges, did not pass muster with the majority.

Such an observation displays a general distrust of the executive in the matter of judicial appointments. In fact, the depth of this apprehension is stark in Justice Goel's assertion when he says that the presumption that the Law Minister and the nominated members will conduct themselves independently in selecting judges cannot be accepted.[32] Can it not be said, with equal assertiveness, that the apprehension that the Law Minister will act in a partisan manner and attempt to influence the other members on the NJAC is unacceptable? This is a difference in perception of the possibility of a hypothetical event taking place—such perception cannot ordinarily be the foundation for a proposition of law. It is also opposed to the settled position in law that the mere possibility of the abuse of power by an authority cannot be sufficient to deny the vesting of power in that authority.[33]

It is rather unfortunate that the presumption of abuse of power is selectively applied against the Law Minister, to the exclusion of all other members. An attempt to stem the tide of apprehensions against the executive comes from the bench itself, in Justice Chelameswar's dissent, when he says, 'The Executive Branch of Government cannot push through an "undeserving candidate" so long as at least two members representing the Judicial Branch are united in their view as to unsuitability of that candidate. Even one eminent person and a single judicial member of NJAC could effectively stall entry of an unworthy appointment.'[34] Evidently, Justice Chelameswar attempts to objectively apply the rigour of the proviso to Section 5(2) and Section 6(6) to all the members of the NJAC by unearthing the true import of these provisions (which is to stall the appointment of unworthy candidates).

---

[32] *NJAC Case* [1081].

[33] *See Mafatlal Industries Ltd. v. Union of India* (1997) 5 SCC 536 [88].

[34] *NJAC Case* [1214].

Conclusion

The Union of India argued that the mere presence of the executive in the NJAC did not *per se* affect independence of the judiciary. There was no basis to claim that the composition of the NJAC would have adversely affected the impartial and effective adjudication of disputes. In fact, the composition demonstrated a harmonious mixture of branches of government—a predominant role for the judiciary, with executive presence in the form of the Law Minister and leading representatives of the legislature being part of the committee to select the eminent persons on the NJAC—that would have furthered mutual checks and balances between various organs. One can go so far as to say that the composition of the NJAC realigned the process of appointments in accordance with the general principle of separation of powers as it operates in India, and with what the framers of the Constitution envisaged.

The NJAC rectified this imbalance by giving greater say to the executive than it had previously. Merely doing so, and not securing judicial primacy cannot *per se* be said to have violated judicial independence. However the Supreme Court in its wisdom determined otherwise. One can only hope that this episode will lead to serious reform of the process of appointment of judges in India today. As vacancies mount and deserving candidates dwindle, a fair, merit-based, transparent method of appointments that involves all key stakeholders is the need of the hour. The NJAC might have been a near-optimum amalgamation of the aforesaid desiderata. It is my ardent hope that that the reworked collegium system that replaces it too achieves the same in a manner that passes constitutional muster and enjoys popular confidence of the people of India.

Opening up Appointments

8

Civil Society Participation in the NJAC

MADHAVI DIVAN

The higher courts in India, that is the Supreme Court and the High Courts, are regularly in the news, not so much in their traditional avatar as adjudicators of private disputes between citizens or between the State and the citizen. They make far more news in their activist avatar.[1] About three decades ago, the higher courts in India opened their doors to entertain public interest (or social action) litigation. Traditional barriers to approaching the higher courts were lowered, the principle of *locus standi* relaxed, and access to justice democratized by entertaining petitions by public spirited persons. To start with, public interest litigation (PIL) petitions were entertained on behalf of the poor, downtrodden, and marginalized sections of society. Their popularity grew and over the years, courts began to entertain PIL petitions on myriad issues, not only on behalf of the poor or those without access to justice but also on important, often cutting-edge socio-economic issues. The outcomes of such PIL cases have had far-reaching consequences on the society, the economy, and the day-to-day lives of ordinary citizens.

Cases such as those relating to the allocation of coal blocks,[2] allotment of telecom licenses,[3] stashing away of black money in secret

---

[1] *See* Lavanya Rajamani, 'Public Interest Environmental Litigation in India: Exploring Issues of Access, Participation, Equity, Effectiveness and Sustainability' (2007) 19 *Journal of Environmental Law* 293–321.

[2] *Manohar Lal Sharma v. Union of India* (2014) 3 SCC 170.

[3] *Centre for Public Interest Litigation v. Union of India* (2012) 3 SCC 1.

overseas accounts,[4] air and water pollution,[5] rights of the lesbian, gay, bisexual, and transgender (LGBT) community,[6] and sexual harassment of women in the work place[7] are indicative of the phenomenal range of issues that higher courts in India are called upon to determine. There are also PIL petitions on issues such as whether Yoga and Sanskrit should be made part of school curriculum,[8] the criteria on which children should be admitted to primary school,[9] whether riders of two wheelers should be compelled to wear helmets,[10] tackling the monkey menace in the capital city,[11] and whether *sardar* jokes should be banned.[12]

There is hardly any facet of life that is left untouched by PIL jurisdiction. In several cases, the Court has played a positive activist role and has been applauded for taking on inert, apathetic, and often, corrupt governments. However, it must not be forgotten that a single order passed in a PIL can have a cascading impact on livelihoods, development, the economy, and, in some cases, India's international obligations. This is not to suggest that courts ought not to act as they do—that analysis necessarily differs from case-to-case—but to emphasize the enormity and sensitivity of the role of our higher courts, arguably the most powerful in the world. That power stems not only from the expanded role that courts play, but also on account of the sheer number of people

[4] *Ram Jethmalani v. Union of India* (2011) 8 SCC 10.

[5] *M.C. Mehta v. Union of India* (2009) 17 SCC 59 (on vehicular pollution); *M.C. Mehta v. Union of India* (2010) 14 SCC 625 (on relocation of polluting industries).

[6] *Suresh Kumar Koushal v. Naz Foundation* (2014) 1 SCC 1; *National Legal Services Authority v. Union of India* (2014) 5 SCC 438.

[7] *Vishakha v. State of Rajasthan* (1997) 6 SCC 241.

[8] *J.C. Seth v. Union of India*, SLP (C) No. 3987/2011 (on Yoga, currently pending in the Supreme Court); *Santosh Kumar v. Secretary, Ministry of HRD* (1994) 6 SCC 579 (on Sanskrit).

[9] *Major Saurabh Charan v. NCT of Delhi* (2014) 6 SCC 798.

[10] *R. Mallika v. A. Babu* (2015) 3 LW 435 (Mad); *Accident Victims Association v. State of Tamil Nadu* (2008) 1 LW LW 667 (Mad).

[11] *New Friends Colony Residents v. Union of India*, W.P. (C) No. 2600/2001 (Delhi High Court, decided on 14 March 2007); *Master Aayush Tripathi v. State of Uttarakhand*, WPPIL 17/2015 (pending in the Uttarakhand High Court).

[12] *Harvinder Chowdhury v. Union of India*, W.P. (Crl) No. 160/2015 (pending in the Supreme Court).

impacted by their orders, considering the fact that India is home to one-sixth of the world's population.

The judicial system is an equal and crucial partner in India's economic growth and social progress. As India takes its place on the global firmament, the courts will have to ready themselves, to take on not only the burden of pending litigation, but also the new social, economic, and technological challenges that confront us. Efficiency in governance may be no good without public confidence in the justice system. How do we achieve public confidence in the administration of justice? Can civil society play a role in achieving that confidence?

It is in the backdrop of the significantly expanded role of the higher judiciary in India that the process of appointment of judges must be examined. What makes a good judge? Does legal competence suffice or do social consciousness and sensitivity also determine the eligibility of a candidate? Quite apart from this—How public should the process of appointment be? Who should have a say in this process? Are judges best equipped to determine who makes a good judge? Or should civil society have a voice in the process? Should the judiciary reflect social diversity or is merit the sole consideration? These are some of the questions which need to be considered while examining the process for appointment of judges to the higher judiciary.

The NJAC Verdict

The 99th Amendment and the NJAC Act sought to substitute the judicially evolved collegium system of appointment of judges with a more broad-based appointments system—the NJAC. The Commission was to comprise six members of which three were to be judges (with the Chief Justice of India as Chairperson), one was the Law Minister, and the remaining two were to be 'eminent persons' who were to be appointed by a committee comprising the Chief Justice of India, the Prime Minister, and the Leader of the Opposition in the Lok Sabha (in case there was no such Leader of Opposition, then the Leader of the single largest Opposition Party in the House of the People). The 99th Amendment and the NJAC Act were both silent on the qualifications of the eminent persons. There was no indication that they were required to be qualified in law. The first proviso to Article 124A(1)(d) prescribed that one of these two eminent persons was to be a member of a Scheduled Caste or Scheduled Tribe, Other Backward Classes, a minority community or a woman. Under the NJAC Act (but significantly, not under the 99th Amendment), any two members on the NJAC could veto the proposal for appointment of a potential candidate. This meant that the two eminent persons acting together could override the decision of the judicial members on the suitability of a candidate. Alternately, one eminent person and the Law Minister could outvote a candidate of the judges' choice.

Although the power of veto did not find mention in it, the 99th Amendment was struck down on the ground that the primacy accorded to the Chief Justice of India under Article 124 was eroded by the presence of eminent persons who might have been entirely unconnected with law or the legal profession but who, nonetheless, could outvote the judicial members in decision-making. Justice Khehar regarded this intrusion into judicial primacy as 'outrightly obnoxious', and 'an easy breach of the "independence of the judiciary"'.[13] Another ground in support of striking down Article 124A(1)(d) was the absence of qualifications of eminent persons. Justice Khehar felt that the nomination of 'eminent persons…cannot be left to the free will and choice of the nominating authorities, irrespective of the high constitutional positions held by them'.[14] While concluding that the role of eminent persons as envisaged by the 99th Amendment and the NJAC Act could be 'disastrous', Justice Khehar was however, willing to provide an 'advisory/consultative role' to civil society representatives provided they had a connection with or insight into the functioning of the judicial system.[15]

The concurring judgment of Justice Lokur supports Justice Khehar on this issue:

> Two eminent persons who had no role to play in the appointment process prior to the 99th Amendment Act have suddenly assumed Kafkaesque proportions and together they can paralyze the appointment process, reducing the President and the Chief Justice of India to ciphers for reasons that might have nothing to do with the judicial potential or fitness and suitability of a person considered for appointment as a judge.[16]

---

[13] *NJAC Case* [306]–[307].
[14] *NJAC Case* [333].
[15] *NJAC Case* [334]–[335].
[16] *NJAC Case* [907].

Justice Lokur was however, not averse to allowing persons from outside the legal fraternity ('eminent persons from all walks of life')[17] a consultative role in the appointment process, so long as they did not have the power to altogether jettison appointments.

In comparison, the minority judgment of Justice Chelameswar voices a very different view:

> To believe that members of the judiciary alone could bring valuable inputs to the appointment process requires great conceit and disrespect for the civil society.[18]

The opinion of Justice Goel is important on the aspect of civil society participation. Apart from concurring with the majority opinion that affording 'eminent persons' not just a 'supporting role' but a 'predominant' one would seriously compromise judicial primacy in appointments, he found the 'reservation' in respect of one of the two 'eminent persons' objectionable. He said:

> There is no justification for reservation for one of the nominated members being from specified categories. Such provision is against the scheme of the Constitution and contrary to the object of selecting judges purely by merit. The nature of appointment does not justify any affirmative action for advancement of any socially and educationally backward classes or the Scheduled Castes; or Scheduled Tribes or women. The appointment of judges has to be on evaluation of merits and suitability of the candidates. Religion, caste or sex of the evaluator has no relevance.[19]

Justice Goel put merit above all other affiliations. In other words, merit must override diversity, and considerations of regional representation, gender, caste, and religion should be less relevant than merit. In practice, is that the case?

Diversity under the Collegium System

Under the prevailing collegium system of judicial appointments, there are no written criteria of eligibility. Instead, there are informal, unstated norms that govern eligibility for judicial office. The Constitution does

---

[17] *NJAC Case* [908].

[18] *NJAC Case* [1222].

[19] *NJAC Case* [1082].

not specify norms for eligibility, beyond requiring that a candidate be a citizen of India, have a minimum number of years of practice or have held judicial office for a minimum number of years, or be qualified as a distinguished jurist.[20] It does not provide for reservation—formal or informal—for any caste or class of persons.

However, in actual practice, unstated diversity criteria for appointments to the Supreme Court and the High Courts do exist. In the Supreme Court, these include regional representation and the representation of religious minorities. Since India is a federal Republic, it is considered necessary to have judges from different geographic regions of the country, even if all states are not represented in the Court.[21] Attempts are also made to appoint members from religious minorities. There is an informal attempt to represent backward castes although this has not been uniformly practised across the country.[22] Therefore, diversity is acknowledged as an important criterion in judicial appointments even under the present system. However, what weight is accorded to diversity and how far the net is cast to attract diverse applicants is not known.

Gender representation on the bench remains particularly weak, especially when compared with other parts of the developing world, including several African countries. When the Chief Justice of Kenya visited the Supreme Court in 2015, he expressed great surprise (presumably disappointment), that there was only one woman judge in the Supreme Court despite a sanctioned strength of 31 judges. Incidentally, Kenya's former Deputy Chief Justice was a woman and, speaking of diversity, is of Indian origin.[23] In the sixty-seven years of the history of the Indian Supreme Court, however, there have only been six women judges.

Diversity as a Facet of Judicial Independence

The collegium system crafted by the Supreme Court in the *Second* and *Third Judges' Cases* was an assertion of judicial independence intended

[20] Constitution of India, art. 124 and art. 217.

[21] Abhinav Chandrachud, *The Informal Constitution: Unwritten Criteria in Selecting Judges for the Supreme Court of India* (Oxford University Press 2014) 216.

[22] Chandrachud (n. 21) 218.

[23] Ms Kalpana Rawal, former Deputy Chief Justice of Kenya, retired on 14 June 2016.

at insulating the process of judicial appointments from executive influence. But the notion of judicial independence is acknowledged as a broader concept that entails freedom from pressure not only from outside of the judiciary but also from within. The *First Judges' Case* emphasized that the notion of independence of the judiciary connotes independence from wide ranging forms of pressure—not merely political or executive control, but freedom even from 'the class to which Judges belong'.[24] Diversity in appointments is necessary to liberate the judiciary from the impression that they belong to a 'class'. In *Registrar General, High Court of Madras v. R. Gandhi*,[25] the Supreme Court acknowledged that

> appointments cannot be exclusively made from any isolated group nor should it be pre-dominated by representing a narrow group. Diversity therefore in judicial appointments to pick up the best legally trained minds coupled with a qualitative personality, are the guiding factors that deserve to be observed uninfluenced by mere considerations of individual opinions. It is for this reason that collective consultative process as enunciated in the aforesaid decisions has been held to be an inbuilt mechanism against any arbitrariness.[26]

Diversity is an important facet of judicial independence inasmuch as it means that judges come from backgrounds which represent different sections of society and are not dominated by one section (for example, predominantly male or upper caste) so that diverse worldviews are brought to bear on decisions. Diversity liberates the judiciary from a possible public impression that the vast majority of judges will think in a particular way or not be adequately sensitive to the needs of certain sections of society. If judges are to do justice to all, 'without fear or favour, affection or ill will',[27] they should not come from a particular class, much less be perceived as having come from such class. Diversity enhances public confidence in the judiciary. Justice McHugh, former judge of the High Court of Australia says: 'When a court is socially and

---

[24] *First Judges' Case* [27].

[25] (2014) 11 SCC 547 (*R. Gandhi*).

[26] *R. Gandhi* (n. 25) [16].

[27] Constitution of India, Third Schedule, Oath of Office for Chief Justice and Judges.

culturally homogeneous, it is less likely to command public confidence in the impartiality of the institution.[28]

The manner and process of judicial appointments has a direct nexus with the extent of diversity that can be achieved in appointments. Diversity can be achieved only if the pool from which selections are made is wide enough, by a publicly declared process which involves some participation from civil society. A complaint often made in the United Kingdom (UK) is that due to their excessive involvement in the appointments process judges, howsoever well meaning, tend to look for candidates in their own image thus perpetuating self-replication rather than encouraging diversity. The rationale behind involving lay persons or persons who do not belong to the legal fraternity is that they will encourage diversity in appointments and act as a buffer against self-replication. A passage from the Twenty-Fifth Report of the House of Lords Select Committee on Judicial Appointments[29] reads:

> 66. Many of our witnesses argued that having greater lay involvement in the selection process was the most appropriate way of avoiding the problem of self-replication within the judiciary. Whilst some queried whether lay members could properly assess candidates for a judicial role, others stressed that the lay members of the JAC 'are very powerful people with strong backgrounds in business, politics or what have you' who are 'of extremely high calibre and [who bring] different qualities ... and a broader perspective'. [...]
>
> 67. For the judiciary to be solely responsible for the appointments process would risk undermining the promotion of diversity and, ultimately, public confidence in the judiciary. Furthermore, the appointments process is enhanced by the involvement of lay persons who can bring a different perspective to the assessment of candidates' abilities. It is therefore important that selection panels include a mixture of judicial and lay representation.

The Selection Commission created under the UK Constitutional Reform Act 2005 (CRA 2005) for appointment of judges to the Supreme Court

---

[28] As quoted in Simon Evans and John Williams, 'Appointing Australian Judges: A New Model' (2008) 30 *Sidney Law Review* 295, 300.

[29] Select Committee on the Constitution, *Judicial Appointments* (House of Lords 2012, 272) <http://www.publications.parliament.uk/pa/ld201012/ldselect/ldconst/272/272.pdf> accessed 21 September 2016.

of the UK, is composed of at least five members, at least one of whom should be non-legally qualified.

Furthermore, the Judicial Appointments Commission (JAC) in the UK, also created under the CRA 2005 comprises fifteen persons, of whom at least five must be 'lay' or non-judicial members. The JAC appoints judges to all courts and tribunals except the Supreme Court and a few specified posts. The CRA 2005 was amended by the Crime and Courts Act 2013 which mandated that 'the number of Commissioners who are holders of judicial office must be less than the number of Commissioners (including the chairman) who are not holders of judicial office' (Schedule 13, Paragraph 19 of the CCA 2013). Thus there are more non-judicial members than judicial members on the JAC at present.

Lay members are regarded as bringing a broader perspective to the process which is instrumental in the appointment of people from diverse backgrounds. They also introduce an element of detachment to the selection process. As Brian Gill, former Lord President and Lord Justice General of Scotland, remarks:

> We must ensure that the appointments boards include people of significant legal experience, as well as lay membership that will provide a check on the process from a detached standpoint. Lay members from a variety of backgrounds possessing different life experiences can evaluate non-legal competencies from the ordinary citizen's perspective. Temperament and commitment are attributes that require no legal skill for their assessment.[30]

Merit versus Diversity

A common misconception is that diversity can come only at the cost of merit. It is true that merit might be compromised if one were to insist on representation of a certain region, gender, minority or caste in proportion to the demographic composition of society.[31] If, for example,

---

[30] Brian Gill, 'Independence of the Judiciary and the Profession' (19th Commonwealth Law Conference, Glasgow, 13 April 2015) <http://www.pressreader.com/zambia/the-post1401/20150501/281925951568976> accessed 24 September 2016 (Brian Gill).

[31] In South Africa, for example, the Constitution provides for 'the judiciary to reflect broadly the racial and gender composition of South Africa'. See Constitution of the Republic of South Africa, art. 174(2).

there were a mandate to fill in half the number of judicial vacancies in India with women appointees, it is possible that given the current state of things it would come at the cost of merit at least in some parts of the country—the exercise may result in having to overlook a very large number of meritorious male candidates and quite apart from that, given the historical disadvantages that women have faced in the legal profession, it may also be difficult identifying such a large number of meritorious women candidates all at once to fit the bill. However, diversity can be encouraged, even insisted upon, without specific regard to gender, minority, or caste composition in society in terms of actual numbers.

Substantial representation of traditionally disadvantaged sections can be achieved without compromising on merit. For instance, in High Courts located in cosmopolitan cities such as Mumbai, Delhi, Chennai, Kolkata, or Bengaluru where, relatively speaking, a larger number of women are active practitioners, it would not be very difficult to identify a substantial number of women candidates who are at par with male candidates. Yet, the number of women judges even in these courts is abysmally low. In 2012, out of a total of 605 High Court judges across the country, only 52 were women, which is less than 8.6 per cent. In 2016, the figure had risen to 62 out of 611.[32] In 2012, the Delhi High Court had the highest number of women judges (7 out of 34), the Calcutta High Court had 4 out of 45, the Gujarat High Court had 2 out of 27, the Madras High Court had 7 out of 54 and the Bombay High Court, 6 out of 58.[33] These figures show that even in metropolitan cities the number of women judges is extremely low. Far from representing the gender composition of society, the figures fall miserably short of proportionately representing even the number of women in active practice. Interestingly, in the subordinate judiciary where appointments are made on the basis of an open selection system through the judicial service examinations, the proportion of women judges is much higher

[32] Prabha Sridevan, 'Judiciary, An Old Boys' Club', *The Hindu* (New Delhi, 30 March 2016) <http://www.thehindu.com/opinion/op-ed/judiciary-an-old-boys-club/article8410065.ece> accessed 26 September 2016 (Prabha Sridevan).

[33] National Social Watch, *Position of Women in Indian Judiciary: An Analysis* (2012) <http://www.socialwatchindia.net/images/documents/285/women%20in%20judiciary%20an%20analysis.pdf> accessed 26 September 2016.

than the High Courts.[34] This would indicate that under an open and objective merit-based selection process, women fare much better than under a system of appointments which is based on unstated criteria.

As a woman in practice for a little over two decades, I see the importance of role models for younger women practitioners. There is a need to know that others have gone there, done that, and been able to secure positions of recognition or importance. That knowledge is invaluable for it engenders confidence, self-belief, and tenacity, qualities essential for under-represented sections of the legal profession. To achieve this, women do not necessarily need appointments in proportion to the gender composition of society, nor to the gender composition within the profession. Nonetheless, they need a very substantial representation from among meritorious women candidates in the legal fraternity. Even that is sadly wanting. The purpose of allowing an eminent person, one of whom might have been a woman, to have a say in the appointments process in the stillborn NJAC, was to steer the direction of appointments in favour of meritorious but underrepresented sections of society.

There is another misconception about what is meant by 'representation', whether based on region, gender, caste, or minority. Representation does not mean that a member of a particular section of society becomes the voice of that particular section that they seek to 'represent'. It would be preposterous to suggest that a member of a Scheduled Caste or a minority would necessarily decide in favour of his/her community when faced with questions involving the community. That is a grossly blinkered approach to diversity in judicial appointments. For instance, Judge Clarence Thomas, an Associate Justice of the Supreme Court of the United States did not accept the views of the African-American Community in certain civil liberties cases even though he belonged to that community and 'represented' that community on the bench.[35] Justice Prabha Sridevan, a retired judge of the Madras High Court writes that when she was appointed a judge, and a reporter asked her: 'Madam, will you be deciding cases in favour of women?', she responded by directing him to the three male judges

---

[34] National Social Watch (n. 33).

[35] Sherrilyn A. Ifill, 'Racial Diversity on the Bench: Beyond Role Models and Pubic Confidence' (2000) 57(2) *Washington and Lee Law Review* 405, 487.

elevated on the same day: 'Ask them if they will decide cases in favour of men.'[36]

The idea of 'representation' is not to be confused with mouthpieces on the bench for the community represented. It is intended to achieve a powerful symbolic statement of a judiciary that will do justice to all. That apart, it improves the quality of decision-making by bringing in a diversity of perspectives. The very presence on the bench of a judge from a traditionally under-represented or excluded community may have the effect of sensitizing fellow judges and removing their preconceptions or prejudices.

While addressing the argument that diversity connotes a dilution of merit, it must be acknowledged that 'merit' itself is a nebulous virtue when it comes to the task of judging. What is the amalgam of qualities that goes into making a good judge? It cannot be academic brilliance by itself, nor can success or lack of it at the bar be indicative of a candidate's potential as a judge. Unsuccessful practitioners have gone on to make great judges, as have successful lawyers made poor judges. As Lord Brian Gill remarked:

> In 48 years in the business of the law I have known judges of outstanding academic brilliance who found it difficult to make a decision for fear of being wrong; or who pursued relentless logic without due regard to common sense. I have known lawyers who were not forceful pleaders at the Bar yet flourished in the judicial life when they had time for reflection. So when a judicial appointment is made and the profession—as always—passes its confident verdict, remember this: you never can tell.[37]

Several diverse qualities go into making a good judge and legal competence is only one of them. Belonging to a disadvantaged or under-represented section of society can by itself be a virtue. That experience brings new insights and perspectives, whether subconscious or otherwise. Compassion and sensitivity are two vital qualities that make a good judge and often surpass legal brilliance. Social cloisters are anathema to the task of rendering justice, more so in a country that is so dramatically diverse—socially, culturally, economically, and developmentally. Civil society deserves a voice in the process of appointment, for it offers

---

[36] Prabha Sridevan (n. 32).

[37] Brian Gill (n. 30).

the multiple benefits of diversity, detachment, accountability, and transparency.

Conclusion

At the end of the day, judges dispense justice to real people with real life problems. To be able to do justice, judges must be as conversant with the real world around us as with the letter of law. All the more so in the PIL age where our higher courts are routinely called upon to determine a range of issues often beyond their core competence—matters of policy, expertise, and delicate social sensitivity, on which civil society are the largest and most vital stakeholders. That is substantial reason why civil society must have a voice on judicial appointments, one that is heard loud and clear.

The Obvious Foundation Test

Re-inventing the Basic Structure Doctrine

9 RAJU RAMACHANDRAN AND
MYTHILI VIJAY KUMAR THALLAM*

On 24 April 1973, the Supreme Court of India introduced the 'basic structure' doctrine in the paradigm-shifting case of *Kesavananda Bharati v. State of Kerala*,[1] altering the very basis on which constitutional power is divided between the plenary amendatory bodies and the judiciary. The basic structure doctrine placed judicially created limits on the power of the legislature to amend the Constitution, and made it clear that the judiciary (in which the power to interpret the Constitution is vested) will have the final say. *Kesavananda Bharati* granted the Court the power to scrutinize amendments to the Constitution to see if they violated the 'basic structure.'[2] Therefore, the Court now has the power to strike down amendments when they are found to violate the *essence* of the Constitution.

The decision, consisting of eleven individual judgments, does not lay down an exhaustive list of what would constitute basic structure. However, different perceptions of what would constitute the basic

---

* The authors are grateful to Vikram Aditya Narayan for his invaluable help with this essay.

[1] (1973) 4 SCC 225 (*Kesavananda Bharati*).

[2] Raju Ramachandran, 'The Supreme Court and the Basic Structure Doctrine' in B.N. Kirpal, Ashok H. Desai, Gopal Subramanium, Rajeev Dhavan, and Raju Ramachandran (eds), *Supreme but not Infallible: Essays in Honour of the Supreme Court of India* (Oxford University Press, 2000) 107–33 (Ramachandran).

structure are illustrated in some of the majority judgments, which are summarized here.[3]

In his judgment, Chief Justice S.M. Sikri, held that the following features would comprise the 'basic structure':

> The basic structure may be said to consist of the following features: (i) Supremacy of the Constitution, (ii) Republican and democratic form of government, (iii) Secular character of the Constitution, (iv) Separation of powers between the legislature, the executive and the Judiciary, (v) Federal structure of the Constitution. The above structure is built on the basic foundation, i.e., the dignity and freedom of the individual. This is of supreme importance. This cannot by any form of amendment be destroyed.[4]

Justice J.M. Shelat and Justice A.N. Grover,[5] who termed their lists as illustrative, added sovereignty of the country, unity and integrity of the nation, the dignity of the individual secured by the various basic rights in Part III, and the mandate to form a welfare state as contained in Part IV to Chief Justice Sikri's list.

Justice K.S. Hegde and Justice A.K. Mukherjea observed that the basic features or fundamental elements of our Constitution can be discerned from the Preamble.[6] Justice P. Jaganmohan Reddy held that 'A sovereign democratic republic, Parliamentary democracy, the three organs of the State, certainly, in my view, constitute the basic structure'[7] Justice H.R. Khanna, who did not specify individual components of the basic structure, held that what was to be observed was that the power to amend the Constitution did not include the power to abrogate it and replace it with an entirely new one.[8] From this standpoint he observed that the basic structure or the *framework* of the Constitution could not be destroyed.

It is interesting to note, however, that the Court did not specifically mention 'independence of the judiciary' as a part of the basic structure, which it undoubtedly is.

[3] Ramachandran (n. 2) 114–15.

[4] *Kesavananda Bharati* (n. 1) [292].

[5] *Kesavananda Bharati* (n. 1) [582].

[6] *Kesavananda Bharati* (n. 1) [651].

[7] *Kesavananda Bharati* (n. 1) [1159].

[8] *Kesavananda Bharati* (n. 1) [1426].

In the recent decision in the *NJAC Case*, the primacy of the judiciary in the appointment of judges to the constitutional courts of India, and separately, compulsory consultation with the Chief Justice in the matter of appointments, have been held to be aspects of the 'basic structure'. In this essay, we will first discuss the evolution of the doctrine since it was first posited, and then go on to analyse the understanding of the basic structure that stems from the judgment in the *NJAC Case*. The final part of this essay will present the future implications of the principles upheld in the *NJAC Case*.

The Evolution of the Basic Structure Doctrine

Between *Kesavananda Bharati* and the *NJAC Case*, in the instances where the Supreme Court has dealt with the basic structure doctrine, the Court has viewed the same as an underlying theme, i.e., it has looked at the essence of the principles of the basic structure, and not at the components of the individual principles themselves. This essay will expound on this approach, called the 'overarching principles test' for brevity, after a summary of the cases where the Supreme Court has applied the basic structure doctrine to invalidate or read down constitutional amendments. It is to be noted that the Court has invoked the basic structure doctrine in just a handful of cases to strike down or read down constitutional amendments. A summary of these cases is as follows:

- In *Indira Nehru Gandhi v. Raj Narain*,[9] a five-judge bench applied the basic structure doctrine to invalidate a part of Article 329(A) which was inserted to the Constitution to validate an invalid election. The provision was inserted in the Constitution solely to keep one individual in office. This was struck down invoking various principles, such as democracy, equality, and free and fair elections. Justice K.K. Mathew observed that the amendment 'would toll the death knell of the democratic Constitution'.[10]
- In *Minerva Mills v. Union of India*,[11] the Constitution (Forty-second Amendment) Act, 1976, by which the Directive Principles of State

---

[9] (1975) Supp SCC 1 (*Indira Gandhi*)

[10] *Indira Gandhi* (n. 9) [308].

[11] (1980) 3 SCC 625 (*Minerva Mills*)

Policy were sought to be given primacy over Articles 14, 19, and 31 (all of which are fundamental rights), was struck down holding that the Constitution was based on a 'bedrock of balance'[12] between the Directive Principles and Fundamental Rights, and that by granting one absolute primacy over the other, this essential feature of the basic structure would be disturbed.

• In *P. Sambamurthy v. State of Andhra Pradesh*,[13] clause (5) of Article 371-D, which provided that a State Government could modify or annul a decision given by the Administrative Tribunal (for the State of Andhra Pradesh), was struck down as being violative of the basic structure, since it violated the rule of law (the clause essentially gave the Government the power to amend/nullify a decision *against* it). The Court posited that it was the existence of the power of judicial review which made the maintenance of the rule of law possible.[14]

• In *L. Chandra Kumar v. Union of India*,[15] the validity of Article 323-A came to be examined. Article 323-A envisaged setting up of administrative tribunals, and enabled the ouster of the jurisdiction of High Courts (under Article 226) in matters where an effective alternate institution could exercise jurisdiction. The power of the Supreme Court was untouched. The Court, however, held that the principle of judicial review, which was a basic feature of the Constitution, was violated by the exclusion of the jurisdiction of the High Courts, since the constitutional safeguards that existed to protect the independence of the judges of the constitutional courts did not exist for judges manning tribunals.[16] The Court interpreted Article 323-A in a manner which preserved the jurisdiction of the High Courts to examine decisions of the tribunals.[17]

After the pronouncement of *Kesavananda Bharati* in 1973 which gave courts the power to scrutinize constitutional amendments against the basic structure, up until the 99th Amendment to the Constitution, which established the NJAC in 2014, the Constitution has been

---

12 *Minerva Mills* (n. 11)[56].

13 (1987) 1 SCC 632 (*P. Sambamurthy*).

14 *P. Sambamurthy* (n. 13) [4].

15 (1997) 3 SCC 261 (*L. Chandra Kumar*).

16 *L. Chandra Kumar* (n. 15) [78].

17 *L. Chandra Kumar* (n. 15) [99].

amended a total of seventy times. The Court has struck down or read down constitutional amendments as violating the basic structure only in five instances since (including the present case), demonstrating a 'basic structure conservatism' approach, i.e., having armed itself with the basic structure doctrine, the Court was clear that it would use it sparingly to strike down amendments to the Constitution.

Interpretation of the Basic Structure: The 'Overarching Principles' Test

While testing constitutional amendments against the basic structure, the approach of the Court has been to see if some *fundamental essence* of the Constitution has been violated. Very often such a principle is not to be found only in the text of the Constitution, but on a collective reading of various principles underlying the Constitution.

The 'overarching principles' test applied by the Court is best exemplified in three decisions—in M. *Nagaraj v. State of Karnataka*,[18] the Court made it clear that it is 'overarching principles' which are beyond the amending power of Parliament. In explaining why it was the 'overarching principles' test which had to be applied, the Court pointed out that 'the theory of basic structure is based on the principle that a change in a thing does not involve its destruction and destruction of a thing is a matter of substance and not of form'.[19]

This was reiterated in the case of *I.R. Coelho v. State of Tamil Nadu*,[20] where the Court interpreted *Kesavananda Bharati* to mean that it is the 'principles' underlying fundamental rights or their essence which are part of the basic structure of the Constitution, and not the individual rights themselves.[21]

Next, in the context of alleged violation of the principle of equality (embodied in Article 14 of the Constitution), the Court in *Glanrock Estate (P) Ltd. v. State of Tamil Nadu*[22] clearly held that for a constitutional amendment to have violated the principle of equality, it was not

---

[18] (2006) 8 SCC 212 (*M. Nagaraj*).

[19] *M. Nagaraj* (n. 18) [35].

[20] (2007) 2 SCC 1 (*I.R. Coelho*).

[21] *I.R. Coelho* (n. 20) [151(iii)].

[22] (2010) 10 SCC 96 (*Glanrock Estate*).

sufficient to violate the principle of equality enshrined in Article 14 or a formal equality, but should be found to abrogate a much wider platform of egalitarian equality which, in this case, comprised the doctrine of sustainable development and inter-generational equity under Article 21 with Article 14.[23] When legislation violates the principle of equality under Article 14, the same would be 'a case of violation of ordinary principle of equality before law' and would therefore not require 're-writing of the Constitution'.[24] However, when it comes to the validity of a constitutional amendment, the question to be asked was whether it violated any overarching principle of the Constitution.

The judgment in the *NJAC Case* holds that primacy of the judiciary in the appointment of judges is essential to ensure independence of the judiciary, which is a part of the basic structure. For the first time, the Court has applied the 'derivative test', i.e., where a *component* of a feature of the basic structure is elevated to the basic structure itself in order to invalidate the impugned amendment. This marks a stark departure from the Court's earlier approach of looking at whether the overarching principles or the *essence* of the basic structure has been violated by the impugned amendment, not whether composite elements of the individual features had been violated.

NJAC Case and the Basic Structure

The focus of the present essay with respect to the *NJAC Case* is two-fold—first, it analyses the judgment to highlight what *precisely* has been held to be part of the basic structure, and second, it proceeds to critically examine whether such findings are normatively defensible. The essay ends with a look at the implications of the judgment on future interpretations of the basic structure.

The 99th Amendment to the Constitution, which was challenged in the present case, introduced a federal body (the NJAC) which was hereafter to be responsible for the appointment of the judges of the constitutional courts. The NJAC was to comprise three sitting judges of the Supreme Court, a representative of the political executive, and two members of the civil society. It intended to replace the collegium

---

[23] *Glanrock Estate* (n. 22) [24]–[31].

[24] *Glanrock Estate* (n. 22) [26].

system of appointments, by which the Chief Justice of India and senior judges of the Supreme Court are responsible for these appointments, a system which was introduced in the *Second Judges' Case* and re-affirmed in the *Third Judges' Case*. The 99th Amendment was struck down by a majority of 4:1.

It is instructive to begin by summarizing the majority judgments in the case, and then looking at each of them in greater detail. It is important to note that while all the majority judgments have struck down the 99th Amendment to the Constitution for violating the principle of independence of the judiciary, Justice Khehar and Justice Goel have explicitly held that the 99th Amendment to the Constitution violates the basic structure, since it violates *judicial primacy* in the process of appointments. Justice Lokur's judgment strikes down the 99th Amendment and the NJAC Act as violative of the basic structure, since it does not provide for mandatory consultation of the Chief Justice of India, and therefore violates the intention of the provision (Article 124)[25] as it originally stood. Justice Joseph, who concurs with the reasoning of Justice Khehar and Justice Lokur, holds that the 99th Amendment, by diluting the role of the judiciary in the process of appointments, impairs the process of checks and balances between the three organs of democracy, and is therefore violative of the basic structure. Since Justice Khehar and Justice Goel come to similar conclusions and broadly follow the same line of reasoning, their findings have been discussed together. Justice Joseph's findings are discussed thereafter. Justice Lokur's judgment has not been discussed here, since it has been discussed in detail elsewhere in this volume.[26]

To justify his finding that the NJAC violates the basic structure, Justice Khehar first interprets that what constitutes basic structure is not

[25] The relevant part of Article 124 as it was originally enacted reads

(2) Every Judge of the Supreme Court shall be appointed by the President by warrant under his hand and seal after *consultation* with such of the Judges of the Supreme Court and of the High Courts in the States as the President may deem necessary for the purpose and shall hold office until he attains the age of sixty-five years.

[26] Justice Lokur's opinion has been discussed at Alok Prasanna Kumar, 'Justice Lokur's Concurring View: The Future of Appointments Reform', 146–157 in this volume.

determined from a plain reading of the provisions, but from a 'holistic understanding' of the same; he adds that the cause, effect, and width of the provision will have to be ascertained from an overall reading of the text of the provision along with 'vital silences hidden therein', since the effect of the provision may not be apparent from a plain reading.[27] He also says that the interpretation of the provision would be based on a harmonious reading of the surrounding provisions.[28]

Following this, Justice Khehar clarifies that any procedure that does not ensure primacy of the judiciary in matters of appointment would affect the independence of the judiciary (a component of the basic structure), and would hence be unacceptable. To justify that judicial primacy in the appointing process is essential, Justice Khehar gives four reasons: first, that primacy of the Chief Justice's view had been accorded in judgments dating back to the 1970s; second, that the Constituent Assembly Debates revealed that the framers wanted to keep the judiciary independent from the political executive; third, that it was convention that the judiciary have the final say in appointments; and fourth, that the terms of the Memorandum of Procedure drawn up for appointment of judges shows that the executive conceded that the appointment of judges would be made on the advice of the Chief Justice. It is stated that accepting an alternate procedure which does not ensure primacy of the judiciary is out of the question. Ultimately, the 99th Amendment is struck down since the newly inserted Articles 124A(1)(a) and (b) do not give the judiciary an *overwhelming majority*, and are therefore *ultra vires* the basic structure of the Constitution.[29]

Justice Goel examines the ratio in the *Second* and *Third Judges' Cases* to hold that the opinion of the judiciary, as symbolized by the view of the Chief Justice of India, would have primacy, and therefore primacy of the judiciary in the appointment process is binding precedent on a bench of five judges (like in the present case). Further, he holds that the Chief Justice (speaking for the judiciary) will have the first and last word on the subject of appointment. He holds that any role that the executive might play must be minimal, so as to eliminate political influence.

---

[27] *NJAC Case* [299].

[28] *NJAC Case* [299].

[29] *NJAC Case* [308].

With these findings, Justice Goel concludes that the primacy of the role of the judiciary and a limited role of the executive in the appointment process is part of the basic structure of the Constitution.[30]

Such an interpretation of the principle of 'independence of the judiciary' hedging entirely on the primacy of the judiciary in the appointment process elucidated in Justice Khehar and Justice Goel's opinions is problematic due to the following reasons.

First, the concept of judicial primacy in the appointment process is held to be the *only* way to secure judicial independence, a finding which is not adequately justified. The Court proceeds on the assumption that judicial primacy in the appointment process is essential, but neither demonstrates how this sole feature ensures independence of the functioning of the judiciary nor expands on the meaning of independence of the judiciary to demonstrate how else such independence can be achieved. Unlike the reasoning of the Court in *P. Sambamurthy*, where the Court held that it was the power of judicial review that made the maintenance of the rule of law (a feature of the basic structure) possible since it ensured that law is observed, no such reasoning as to how the primacy of the judiciary ensures judicial independence is forthcoming here.

A common thread in all the majority judgments is to hold that primacy to the Chief Justice's view in appointments is convention, as gauged from judgments since the 1970s, culminating with the interpretation of Article 124 in the *Second* and *Third Judges' Cases*, as well as parliamentary debates. However, a long-established practice alone is not a constitutionally permissible determinant as to whether a particular feature will be considered a part of the basic structure.

Judicial primacy is also sought to be gauged from Dr Ambedkar's[31] views in the Constituent Assembly while the draft provision (which

---

[30] *NJAC Case* [1071].

[31] 'The draft article, therefore, steers a middle course. It does not make the President the supreme and the absolute authority in the matter of making appointments. It does not also import the influence of the Legislature. The provision in the article is that there should be consultation of persons who are *ex hypothesi*, well qualified to give proper advice in matters of this sort, and my judgment is that this sort of provision may be regarded as sufficient for the moment. With regard to the question of the concurrence of the Chief Justice, it seems to me that those who advocate that proposition seem to rely implicitly

was to later become Article 124 as it was originally enacted) was being discussed. The judgment conveniently interprets Dr Ambedkar's intention to assign primacy to the judiciary. However, a plain reading of the speech reveals that what the framers had in mind was a well-balanced system, with both the judiciary and the executive having a say. What was sought to be excluded was executive *dominance*, and not the exclusion of the executive entirely from the process. To give an overwhelming say to the judiciary in the appointment process is neither contemplated in the text of unamended Article 124, nor was it the intention of the framers of the Constitution.

Conflating judicial independence with primacy of the judiciary in the appointment process, this judgment for the first time, creates the theory of 'derived basic structure'. Under this theory, called the 'derivate approach' for convenience, an unjustified offshoot of the basic structure is elevated to the basic structure itself. In doing so, this judgment significantly, and unjustifiably, expands judicial power and succeeds in liberalizing the basic structure doctrine. The Court has now made it difficult to stick to the overarching principle test in future challenges to constitutional amendments. This approach is likely to provide scope for a lot of forensic creativity, especially in matters concerning the judiciary.

Second, the judgment does not engage with arguments that the judiciary being entirely responsible for the appointment process, without any formal system of accountability for the decisions of the collegium, is more aptly judicial essentialism rather than judicial independence. While an independent judiciary is part of the basic structure, so too is the principle of checks and balances. Such an interpretation of independence of the judiciary, which privileges the primacy of the judiciary

---

both on the impartiality of the Chief Justice and the soundness of his judgment. I personally feel no doubt that the Chief Justice is a very eminent, person. But after all the Chief Justice is a man with all the failings, all the sentiments and all the prejudices which we as common people have; and I think, to allow the Chief Justice practically a veto upon the appointment of judges is really to transfer the authority to the Chief Justice which we are not prepared to vest in the President or the Government of the day. I therefore, think that that is also a dangerous proposition.' *See Constituent Assembly of India Debates*, vol. 8, no. 3 (Lok Sabha Secretariat) 24 May 1949, 258.

over all other facets of the basic structure, is normatively indefensible. Judicial primacy in the appointment process aside, the collegium is an opaque body, with no transparency with respect to its functioning.[32] In no circumstances can the grant of such un-checked power to any organ of democracy be said to be constitutionally valid.

The debate around the process of appointments ought not to be viewed as a partisan battle between the executive and legislature on the one hand and the judiciary on the other. The debate is one which concerns the whole culture of constitutionalism in our country. If 'we the people' have given vast powers of judicial review to the constitutional courts, and the judges have given themselves the power to annul amendments to the Constitution by inventing the basic structure theory, do 'we the people' have the right to participate in the process of appointment of judges, or should judges self-select? Outside participation in the process of judicial appointments, whether it be the other organs of democracy or civil society, is necessary in the system of checks and balances, which itself is a part of the basic structure of the Constitution.

Even assuming that the primacy of judiciary is a necessary condition for ensuring an independent judiciary, a form of primacy was certainly incorporated in the 99th Amendment, because the judiciary, as an institution, was in a majority (with three out of six members) in the NJAC, while the political executive was in a minority of one-sixth and civil society (in the form of two eminent persons) was in a minority of one-third. Therefore, the clear implication of the judgment is that the judiciary must have an overwhelming say in the appointment of judges.

Justice Joseph's judgment states that the bench in the present case is bound by the principles of the *Second Judges' Case*, which holds that the independence of the judiciary is part of the basic structure, and that the process of appointment of judges is an integral part of the independence of the judiciary. Justice Joseph reiterates that the *Second Judges' Case* restored the structural supremacy of the judiciary in the constitutionally allotted sphere in the process of appointment of judges, and is binding precedent. Therefore, the NJAC, which takes away such structural supremacy, violates the principle of checks, and balances and violates the basic structure.

Justice Joseph's direct finding that the bench is bound by the interpretation of the *Second Judges' Case*, which held that primacy in appointments is part of the basic structure, is a running theme in the other majority judgments and is rather telling. A reading of the judgment in its entirety makes it quite clear that the question of primacy of the judiciary in the appointment process was a *fait accompli*, and the only question that was going to receive any meaningful consideration was whether the NJAC in its present form violated that formulation of primacy.

While it is evident that the doctrine of precedent applies to constitutional courts of common law jurisdictions, on the question of reconsideration of the earlier judgments, it is important to remember that the Court has often reversed an earlier held view. For instance, in the *Second Judges' Case* itself, by interpreting the word 'consultation' in Article 124 to mean giving the final word to the Chief Justice in the matter of appointments, the Court overruled its judgment in the *First Judges' Case*, where 'consultation' was interpreted to mean giving 'due weight' to such opinion. If the Court has this power, no fault could have been found with the Union of India for asking for a reconsideration of the earlier judgments since 'primacy was taken as a given', in view of those earlier cases. The Court ought to have examined this contention on merits and not shut out an argument merely on the ground that the Union of India had taken a particular position seventeen years ago, or on an equally untenable ground based on the unanimity or near unanimity of the previous judgments. After all, the Court could also have been unanimously wrong.

Conclusion

In the judgment in the *NJAC Case*, the Supreme Court has effortlessly moved from the overarching principle test to the 'obvious foundation' test. The Court presumes that because it has held primacy to be essential to judicial independence, a removal of its own perception of what that primacy entails must necessarily destroy the basic structure. Justice Khehar and Justice Goel have, at least, tried to identify primacy as part of the basic structure but Justice Lokur does not clearly indicate why the basic structure is violated. He prefers to say, 'If this does not alter the basic structure of the Constitution, what does?'[33]

A perceptive scholar[34] rightly points out that the approach adopted by the Supreme Court, if taken to its logical conclusion, must mean that the right to sleep is part of the basic structure, since the Supreme Court has held that the right to sleep without undue disturbance from the State has been held to be a part of the right to life under Article 21.[35]

It is also clear that whenever there is a need to reconcile different basic features, one of which is the independence of the judiciary, judicial perception of what constitutes judicial independence will remain the first among equals or the 'basic of basics'.

---

[33] *NJAC Case* [892].

[34] Arghya Sengupta, 'Judicial Primacy and the Basic Structure: A Legal Analysis of the NJAC judgment' (November 2015) 40 (48) *Economic and Political Weekly* 27, 28.

[35] *In re: Ramlila Incident* (2012) 5 SCC 1 [Para 318].

Eight Fatal Flaws

The Failings of the National Judicial Appointments Commission

10

ARVIND DATAR

The framers of the Constitution intended that appointment of judges of the Supreme Court and the High Courts was to be made by the President under Article 124(2) and Article 217(1). However, the manner in which the appointments process unfolded in the years after the coming into force of the Constitution meant that appointments were not made necessarily from the best and brightest of the potential appointees. The process was vitiated by the fact that considerations other than merit also contributed in the manner of making appointments. A spate of appointments in the 1970s and 1980s, which symbolized severe executive interference, led to the origin of the 'collegium system', which by itself was severely criticized as not having been contemplated by the text of the Constitution, and for being an act of judicial legislation. The 99th Amendment and the NJAC Act collectively attempted to replace the collegium system of appointments with the NJAC. However, before the NJAC could be operationalized, the Supreme Court struck down both the 99th Amendment and the NJAC Act as unconstitutional.

This essay focuses on what I call the eight 'fatal flaws' in the NJAC as envisaged by the 99th Amendment and the NJAC Act, with primary emphasis on the provisions of the Act. The essay commences with a short description of what necessitated a commission model for appointments to the higher judiciary, while also taking note of other legislative attempts to amend the provisions of the Constitution dealing with judicial appointments. The essay then lists the flaws in the

NJAC Act and how, if operationalized, the NJAC would have made a severe dent on the independence of the judiciary.

From 1947 to 2015—Tracing the Seeds of the NJAC

Independence of the judiciary, separation of powers, and rule of law are a few of the basic features of the Constitution. The Constituent Assembly realized the need and importance of an independent judiciary and, as Professor Granville Austin pointed out, devoted more time discussing this issue than any other:

> The subjects that loomed largest in the minds of Assembly members in framing the judicial provisions were the independence of the courts and closely related issues, the powers of the Supreme Court and judicial review. The Assembly went to great lengths to ensure that the courts would be independent, devoting more hours of debate to the subject than to almost any other aspect of the provisions. If the beacon of the judiciary was to remain bright, courts must be above reproach, free from coercion and political influence.[1]

An excellent summary of the appointments process from the Government of India Act, 1919 to the 99th Amendment is contained in Justice Lokur's opinion in the *NJAC Case*.[2] Briefly, Section 101 of the Government of India Act, 1919 enabled His Majesty to appoint judges who held office during his pleasure. In the Government of India Act, 1935, the executive had the power to appoint judges of the Federal Court and the High Courts. In theory, the appointments were to be made by the Crown and there was no formal consultation process. At the same time, the record shows that the appointments of judges were invariably made on the basis of the recommendations of the Chief Justices of various High Courts.[3] Unfortunately, the report made by the Conference of Chief Justices in 1948 shows that almost immediately after Independence, in 1947, there was interference by the executive and it was found that recommendations of the Chief Justices were not followed, and some appointments were made without even consulting

---

[1] Granville Austin, *Working a Democratic Constitution: A History of the Indian Experience* (Oxford University Press 1999) 164 (Austin).

[2] *NJAC Case* [475]–[543].

[3] Austin (n. 1).

the Chief Justice of India.[4] Evidently, the appointment of judges became controversial even before the draft Constitution was finalized.

The Law Commission of India, on several occasions, took note of the defects in the appointments process and also made reform recommendations. After Independence, serious defects in the appointment process were pointed out by the first Law Commission—which was chaired by the first Attorney-General for India, Motilal Setalvad—in its 14th Report.[5] This Report, made in 1958, pointed out that communal and regional considerations had prevailed in the appointment of High Court judges and that executive influence was being exerted in respect of some appointments to the bench.[6] It also found that the best talents from amongst the High Court judges were not appointed to the Supreme Court.

Twenty years later, in its 80th Report, the Law Commission again delved into what constituted an independent judiciary.[7] Under the Chairmanship of Justice H.R. Khanna, the Commission recommended adoption of a consultative procedure whereby the Chief Justice of India would consult his three senior-most colleagues before making any recommendation so as to minimize the chance of arbitrariness or favouritism.[8] The next important report by the Law Commission was the 121st Report in 1987 which gained significance because it was made after the controversial decision in the *First Judges' Case*. The Law Commission noticed that the prevailing model conferred overriding power on the executive in selecting and appointing judges and recommended the setting up of a multi-member National Judicial Service Commission wherein the judiciary would have a pre-eminent position.[9] It also

---

[4] Austin (n. 1).

[5] Law Commission of India, *Reform of Judicial Administration: Vol. I* (14th Report, Ministry of Law and Justice, Government of India 1958) (14th Report).

[6] 14th Report (n. 5) 69–70. An account of how the executive began to gradually interfere in the process of judicial appointments and the various ways in which such interference manifested itself is also discussed by Justice Lokur in the *NJAC Case* [510]–[511].

[7] Law Commission of India, *The Method of Appointment of Judges* (80th Report, Ministry of Law and Justice, Government of India 1979) (80th Report).

[8] 80th Report (n. 7) 32–6.

[9] Law Commission of India, *A New Forum for Judicial Appointments* (121st Report, Ministry of Law and Justice, Government of India 1987) [7.7] (121st Report).

suggested that it would be advisable to suitably amend the Constitution to implement this proposal.[10]

Legislative Attempts to Transform the Process of Judicial Appointments

Even before the 99th Amendment, on at least three occasions, the Constitution was proposed to be amended to alter the procedure for appointment of judges to the Supreme Court and the High Courts. The first attempt was the Constitution (Sixty-seventh Amendment) Bill, 1990 which proposed setting up a National Judicial Commission (NJC), which was to consist of the Chief Justice of India and two senior-most judges of the Supreme Court for appointment to the Supreme Court. For appointment of judges to the High Courts, the NJC was to consist of the Chief Justice of India and the second senior-most judge of the Supreme Court, the Chief Minister or Governor of the State concerned, and the Chief Justice and second senior-most judge of the concerned High Court. This Bill could not be taken up for consideration because of the dissolution of the Lok Sabha in May 1991, and lapsed.

After more than a decade, the Constitution (Ninety-eighth Amendment) Bill, 2003 was introduced after important recommendations had been made by the National Commission to Review the Working of the Constitution (NCRWC). The NCRWC was headed by former Chief Justice M.N. Venkatachaliah, and it suggested the formation of a National Judicial Commission that was to consist of:

1. the Chief Justice of India (Chairman);
2. two senior-most Supreme Court judges;
3. the Union Minister for Law and Justice;
4. one eminent person nominated by the President of India after consulting the Chief Justice of India.[11]

This Bill adopted the recommendation of the NCRWC with the modification that the eminent citizen was to be nominated by the President of India in consultation with the Prime Minister of India

[10] 121st Report (n. 9) [7.15].

[11] National Commission to Review the Working of the Constitution, *Report of the National Commission to Review the Working of the Constitution: Vol. I* (Ministry of Law and Justice, Government of India 2002) [7.3.7].

(instead of the Chief Justice of India), for a period of three years. Unfortunately, this Bill could also not be passed due to the dissolution of the Lok Sabha.

The third attempt to amend the Constitution was made by the Constitution (One Hundred and Twentieth Amendment) Bill, 2013 which also recommended the establishment of a 'National Judicial Appointments Commission' to enable the 'equal participation' of the judiciary and the executive in the appointment process. The Bill clearly intended to get rid of the collegium system established by the *Second Judges'* and *Third Judges' Cases*. This Bill was passed in the Rajya Sabha, but remained stillborn as the Lok Sabha was dissolved.

By a coincidence, all the three Bills could not be passed because of dissolution of the Lok Sabha—perhaps a divine indication that legislative attempts to alter the appointment process should not be made. Finally, it was the fourth legislative attempt that was successful and the Constitution (One Hundred and Twenty-first Amendment) Bill, 2014[12] was passed unanimously in the Lok Sabha; in the Rajya Sabha, there was only one member—Ram Jethmalani—who opposed the Bill and abstained from voting. It is significant that this was a rare display of unanimity amongst all members of Parliament to pass this Bill. Indeed, the only other occasion when members are usually unanimous is when there is a Bill to increase their pay and allowances.

Fatal Flaws in the NJAC Legislation

The NJAC Act was passed along with the 99th Amendment. As will be seen later, the constitutional amendment and the NJAC Act were part of a 'package deal.'[13] It is sad that such an important legislation was not referred to a Select Committee for deliberation. In the end, even if the 99th Amendment was upheld, the Act would have been struck down

---

[12] To avoid any confusion, it must be clarified that while the amendment inserting Article 124A was introduced as the 121st Constitution Amendment Bill, 2014, it was ultimately passed as the 99th Constitution Amendment Act, 2014.

[13] *NJAC Case* [851] where Justice Lokur adverts to the Attorney General referring to the 99th Amendment and the NJAC Act as a 'package deal', and terms such description to be correct.

as several provisions were badly drafted and would have rendered the NJAC to a pathetic, farcical body.

The Court struck down Sections 5(i), 5(ii), 6(i), 6(ii), 6(iv), 7, and 8 as unconstitutional. Significantly, the majority followed the view taken in *Madras Bar Association v. Union of India*[14] and struck down an ordinary law, which was the result of legislation by the Parliament, on the ground of infringement of the basic structure. Due to constraints of space, it is not possible to examine in detail each section of the NJAC Act individually, like the NJAC bench did. However, the fatal flaws in the 99th Amendment as well as the NJAC Act that led to their invalidation merit discussion in this section.

The NJAC Comprised an Even Number of Members

The first flaw in the proposed NJAC was that it was composed of an even number of members. It is elementary that the number of members in a committee should always be an odd number so that a clear majority can be ascertained. If it is intended that a body is to comprise an even number of members, the Chairman normally has a casting vote, so that any deadlock can be resolved. However, this issue was not considered in the context of the NJAC.

Eminent Persons

Secondly, while prescribing that the NJAC would have two eminent persons in it, neither the 99th Amendment nor the NJAC Act laid down any guideline or yardstick for nominating such eminent persons. Most references in other Central and State Acts are to 'eminent person in the field of...', with the field being determined by the nature of the statute. There are 70 statutes and rules that use the term 'eminent person(s)'. In 67 of these, there is a specification as to the field in which such person(s) must be eminent. For instance:

- In Lokpal and Lokayuktas Act, 2013, Section 3(3)(b) states that an eminent person must be a person with impeccable integrity and outstanding ability, having special knowledge and expertise of not less than twenty-five years in matters relating to anti-corruption policy,

---

[14] (2014) 10 SCC 1 [109].

public administration, vigilance, finance, including insurance and banking, law, and management. Similar provisions are present under Section 3(2) of the Odisha Lokayukta Act, 2014.

- In the National Law School of India Act, 1986, Section 13 states that a person on the Academic Committee must be eminent in 'law'.
- Under Section 22(4) of the Biological Diversity Act, 2002, the Chairperson of the State Biodiversity Board must be an eminent person having adequate knowledge and experience in the 'conservation and sustainable use of biological diversity'.

In only three statutes—the Madhya Pradesh Niji Vishwavidyalaya (Sthapana Avam Sanchalan) Adhiniyam, 2007, the Orissa Universities Act, 1989, and the Assam Police Act, 2007—the term 'eminent person' finds mention without any further qualification. In the Madhya Pradesh statute, the eminent person in question is one member amongst a large body of persons. While in the Orissa Act, the eminent person is appointed to the Executive Committee of a University, in the Assam Act, such eminent person is appointed to a District Accountability Authority. A detailed note on the presence of eminent persons in various statutes and their prescribed qualifications was submitted to the bench in the *NJAC Case*. It was also pointed how the absence of qualifications was the exception and not the rule. It was utterly irresponsible to leave the expression eminent person undefined in the 99th Amendment as well as the NJAC Act. To add insult to injury, the Union tried to justify this lapse by arguing that one had to trust that the appointments would be properly made.

In the case of the NJAC Act, apart from the failure to prescribe the domain expertise of these eminent persons, another serious difficulty would have been in their appointment from amongst the Schedule Castes, Schedule Tribes, Other Backward Classes, minorities or women, as mentioned in the first proviso to Article 124A. Once there is a requirement of nominating two eminent persons, there is no justification of making further sub-classification in the proviso.

Appointment by Statutory Legislation

Article 124C delegated to the Parliament the power to regulate the procedure for the appointment of Supreme Court and High Court judges. Thus, the appointment of these judges could be regulated by an ordinary legislation which was capable of being amended at any time. Section 12 of the NJAC Act further delegated, to the NJAC, the power to make regulations providing for suitability criteria for appointment of judges, manner of their selection, as well as for matters crucial for discharge of the NJAC's functions. Regrettably, it never occurred to the Parliament that the appointment of judges was an extremely important function and the procedure and method of selection as well as the eligibility and suitability criteria must be contained in the Constitution itself. These aspects could not be left to the whims of a simple majority in Parliament. Perhaps, there was indeed a plan to ensure that the power and role of the judiciary is cut to size by altering the process of appointment itself. When the determination of disqualification of its members is not left to Parliament but is contained in the Tenth Schedule to the Constitution, the method of appointment of judges and the manner of their selection should have been part of a separate Chapter or Schedule in the Constitution, itself and not subject to regulation by the Parliament.

Simply put, the operation of essential constitutional provisions cannot be left to the will of the Parliament. Article 124C, it is submitted, is violative of the basic structure of the Constitution as it renders a fatal blow to the independence of the judiciary. What was worse was that the NJAC Act further delegated the power to prescribe qualifications by means of notifications in the Official Gazette! This important point was unfortunately not discussed in the judgment although it was noted by Justice Khehar.

NJAC Regulations Were Susceptible to Modification by Parliament

No part of the NJAC Act demonstrated a greater non-application of mind than Section 13. Under Article 124C, NJAC was conferred the power to make regulations and lay down the procedure for discharge of its functions, prescribe the method of selection of persons for appointment of judges in the Supreme Court and High Courts, and for such other matters as may be considered necessary by it. Section 13 prescribed that every regulation framed by the NJAC was to be laid before each House of Parliament. What is shocking is that these regulations could be modified and even annulled by Parliament and the regulations as modified would then have the force of law. If any regulation made by the NJAC were to be annulled, would there have been no procedure for judicial appointments at all?

A standard 'laying' provision like Section 13 is contained in most statutes that delegate legislative power to the executive. But the NJAC was a constitutional body and regulations framed by it should not have been made subject to modification by Parliament. The autonomy of a constitutional body is greatly imperiled if the Parliament reserves the power to override or modify the regulations framed by such body.

Veto Power

Section 5 of the NJAC Act prescribed the procedure for selection of judges of the Supreme Court. A shocking provision was the second proviso to Section 5(2) which read:

> Provided further that the Commission shall not recommend a person for appointment if any two members of the Commission do not agree for such recommendation.

In effect, any two members could veto the appointment of a proposed appointee. The members did not have to give any reason as to why a particular candidate was not being recommended. A similar veto provision was also contained in Section 6(6) in the context of appointments to the High Court. Now, under Section 5(2), the Commission could make recommendations only on the basis of ability, merit, and any other criteria of suitability as may be specified by the regulation. If a candidate had the necessary ability, merit, and met all the requirements of suitability, on what basis could the two members veto the recommendation? In the absence of any guidance as to its exercise, it is not difficult to foresee the gross misuse of the veto power to promote vested interests of different sections of society. It would have resulted in an unhealthy practice amongst the NJAC members whereby the chosen candidates, irrespective of ability and merit, could be appointed by mutual bargaining. The veto power in Section 5 was thus liable to be struck down and indeed it was. The veto power was also a ground to hold the constitution of NJAC as invalid as it would have potentially compromised the independence of the judiciary.

Incomprehensible Appointment Procedure

Section 6 of the NJAC Act contained a complex and unworkable procedure for appointment of High Court judges. The more one reads the section, the more incomprehensible it appears to be. The NJAC was first required to seek nomination from the Chief Justice of each High Court for the purpose of recommending persons to be appointed as judges of that court. Section 6(4) mandated that the Chief Justice can make his nomination only after consulting two senior-most judges of that High Court and such other judges and eminent advocates of that High Court as may be specified by the regulations. There was no clarity as to whether the word 'consult' in Section 6(4) meant 'concurrence'. There was also no indication as to whether the opinion of the other senior judges and eminent advocates will be binding on the Chief Justice. There was no specification of the number of judges who would have had to be consulted and whether a view would have been taken by majority or otherwise. Let us assume that the Chief Justice made a nomination after consultation with the other judges and eminent advocates and such nomination was unanimous. The next step, under Section 6(3), was even more puzzling because apart from the nomination from the Chief Justice of the High Court, the NJAC also had the simultaneous power to nominate names of persons for appointment as judges of a High Court from persons who are eligible under Article 217(2). The NJAC had to send its nomination to the Chief Justice of the concerned High Court for 'its views'.[15] The Chief Justice had to discuss the suggested nominations from the NJAC with two senior-most judges along with other judges and eminent advocates before giving his views.

Thus, you would have had the shabby spectacle of one group of names who were nominated by a Chief Justice of the High Court in consultation with his brother and sister judges and eminent advocates and another group of candidates nominated by the NJAC. After receiving requests from these two groups, the NJAC had to make its recommendation of the persons who were found suitable on the basis of ability, merit, and other criteria. There is no indication on what basis the Commission could confirm its own nominees or accept nominations of the High Court. What would have happened if the views of the High Court were adverse to their nomination? What would have been the binding nature of such views on the Commission?

[15] This appears to be a typographical error and the correct provision should have read '...forward such names to the Chief Justice of the concerned High Court for "his" views.'

Since the NJAC was to consist of the Chief Justice and the two senior-most judges of the Supreme Court, it is difficult to imagine Chief Justices giving any adverse comments on the names recommended by the NJAC. The net result would have been that the nomination made by the Chief Justices of the High Courts (after due consultation with other judges of the High Courts and his brother and sister judges and eminent advocates) would have been redundant. The problem would have been acute if the names nominated by the Chief Justice and those recommended by the NJAC were completely different. The Chief Justice of the High Court and his brother and sister judges are perhaps best suited to recommend suitable persons to be appointed as judges of that High Court. It is not clear on what basis the NJAC had been given the power to nominate or how it would have made its nominations. It is a fundamental principle of natural justice that a body should not be a judge in its own cause. Although the NJAC was not a quasi-judicial tribunal, it was being called upon to decide either to select its own nominees or the nominations that came from the High Court. The logic in having these complex and parallel procedures of recommendation is unfathomable. Section 6, if implemented, would have rendered the appointment process not only unworkable but would have reduced the High Courts to mere rubber stamps for the appointment of judges.

The problem was compounded by Section 6(7) whereby the NJAC had to elicit the views of the Governor and the Chief Minister of the State concerned. What was the binding nature of these views? Were the views to be made public? What would have happened if the Governor and Chief Minister objected to the nominations made by the NJAC as well as the High Courts? Finally, the regulations had to provide for not only the criteria of suitability but also such other procedures and conditions for selection and appointment of Chief Justices and judges of the High Courts as may be prescribed. None of these were laid down in the NJAC Act, as should have been the case.

NJAC Regulations by Notification

Another shocking provision was Section 12 which empowered the NJAC to frame regulations which were to be notified in the Official Gazette. The NJAC had the power to frame regulations on extremely critical matters, such the suitability criteria for appointment of Supreme

Court and High Court judges, the procedure for selection and appointment, and for transfers. These were to be 'notified' and would have taken the character of delegated legislation. Effectively, these criteria could be changed by another executive notification. The unfortunate consequence would have been that the regulations framed by the NJAC had no higher status than a central excise notification that grants an exemption or a concession in the payment of excise duty.

Quorum

Another dangerous provision was Section 12(2)(i) which enabled the NJAC to prescribe a 'quorum' for its meetings. The NJAC consisted of six persons and nothing prevented the Commission from prescribing a quorum of just the members. What happens to the veto power if such a quorum is prescribed? Suppose the quorum is of two members and a meeting is held without any of the judges present, and appointments are made at such a meeting. Such appointments would have remained beyond question because of Article 124A(2) which prescribed that the proceedings of the NJAC could not be invalidated merely on the ground of the existence of any vacancy or defect in its constitution.

Conclusion

Keeping in view the above flaws and shortcomings, the majority in the *NJAC Case* rightly invalidated the NJAC Act. Far from reforming the process of appointments, the NJAC would have unleashed utter confusion while also infringing on the independence of the judiciary. This is not to say that the collegium system was free from blemish. Lack of transparency and objective criteria for assessing merit, and allegations of favouritism are said to have vitiated the collegium system. Appointments to the Supreme Court and the High Courts were, in some instances, baffling, for there was no reason why one Chief Justice was elevated to the Supreme Court or why another eligible Chief Justice was not. Similar issues arose with respect to appointments to the High Courts. Unfortunately, the Supreme Court did little to eliminate these concerns.

In such circumstances, the appropriate remedy would have been, perhaps, to have a Judicial Commission with a simple majority of judicial members. Better still, there should have been a determined attempt to remove the ills that plagued the collegium system. It is my view that a single Judicial Commission would have been unable to effectively appoint judges for all twenty-nine states of the country. Keeping this in mind, the collegium system is a better mechanism for appointments, since it enables the High Courts to recommend potential candidates who can then be appointed by the Supreme Court after further examination.

While rendering its judgment in the *NJAC Case*, the Supreme Court also invited representations and suggestions on how the collegium system could be improved. Hundreds of suggestions were received and these were divided into specific recommendations by me and the learned Additional Solicitor General, Pinky Anand. The Supreme Court has not incorporated any of these suggestions till date and the finalization of a new Memorandum of Procedure to be followed by the collegium is awaited. Unfortunately, the Memorandum is again stuck in controversy while the vacancies in the High Courts persist and contribute to an increase in the backlog of cases. In the end, the person for whom the courts have been constituted—the litigant, remains badly affected. The 99th Amendment as well as the NJAC Act were an opportunity lost to usher in reforms in the judicial appointments process, and more thoughtful drafting could have plugged the loopholes that plagued these two legislative instruments. However, all is not lost and reforms to the collegium system give hope for a robust as well as independent judiciary.

The Sole Route to an Independent Judiciary?

The Primacy of Judges in Appointment

11

GAUTAM BHATIA*

In its judgment in the *NJAC Case*, the Supreme Court of India struck down the 99th Amendment as well as the NJAC Act, and revived the pre-existing collegium system of judicial appointments. The collegium system is based upon the primacy of judges. To fix ideas, let us accept the definition of the term 'primacy of judges' as provided by one of the opinions in the *NJAC Case*: the judiciary makes the *initial selection*, and has the *final* or *ultimate voice*, in the appointments of judges to the High Court and the Supreme Court.[1] Under the collegium system, the five senior-most judges of the Supreme Court ('the collegium') make the initial selections. The executive then provides its own set of comments with regard to the putative appointments, which the collegium can choose to accept or reject. Once the collegium finalizes the names, the executive (acting through the President) formally confirms the appointments.[2] Clearly, the collegium—that is, the judiciary, acting through

* The author would like to thank Arvind Datar for the opportunity to work on the *NJAC Case* in its final phase, and for many stimulating discussions on the topic of this essay. He would also like to thank Suhrith Parthasarathy and Vishwajith Sadananda for helping him to clarify and deepen his views on the subject. The author assisted the petitioners challenging the constitutional validity of the 99th Amendment and the NJAC Act.

[1] *NJAC Case* [1071].

[2] *See*, e.g., Department of Justice, Ministry of Law and Justice, Government of India, *Memorandum Showing the Procedure for Appointment of the Chief Justice*

the five senior-most judges of the Supreme Court—has a dominant role as well as the first and ultimate voice in judicial appointments.

In concrete terms, the collegium was a creation of the 1993 judgment in the *Second Judges' Case*. Therefore, in the basic structure challenge to the 99th Amendment, which replaced the collegium with the NJAC, the first question that the Court had to answer was what, precisely, did the *Second Judges' Case* hold on the question of the primacy of judges. The importance of this question will be dealt with in the first part of this essay and the *NJAC Case*'s treatment of it will be examined in the second section. In the final part, I will examine what the judgment in the *NJAC Case* itself, through its multiple opinions, concluded about the primacy of judges in judicial appointments, in the constitutional scheme. I will argue that the multiple opinions in the *NJAC Case* failed to satisfactorily engage with this question, thus undermining the majority's central conclusions.

What the *Second Judges' Case* Held (and Why It Mattered)

Article 124 of the Constitution, as it stood before the 99th Amendment, stated that 'every Judge of the Supreme Court shall be appointed by the President... after consultation with such of the Judges of the Supreme Court and of the High Courts in the States as the President may deem necessary for the purpose'.[3] In the *Second Judges' Case*, the Supreme Court—broadly speaking—interpreted the word 'consultation' to mean 'concurrence', and accordingly established the collegium system under the authority of Article 124. If this was *all* that the *Second Judges' Case* did, then the 99th Amendment was rather unproblematic. As the Union of India correctly argued, Parliament is entitled to amend the terms of a constitutional provision with a view to removing the basis of a court judgment.[4] Via the 99th Amendment, the Parliament had done

---

of India and Judges of the Supreme Court of India <http://doj.gov.in/appointment-of-judges/memorandum-procedure-appointment-supreme-court-judges> accessed 8 March 2016.

[3] Constitution of India, art. 124.

[4] Union of India, *Written Submissions in the NJAC Case*, Part II [80]–[91] (on file with the author). *See* for instance, *Indira Nehru Gandhi v. Raj Narain* (1975) 2 SCC 159.

just that, by *replacing* Article 124, along with the word 'consultation' (as interpreted by the Court in *the Second Judges' Case*), with the NJAC.

However, the petitioners' argument went beyond that. The petitioners claimed that the basis of the *Second Judges' Case* was not simply the linguistic move of reading 'consultation' as 'concurrence', but the finding that judicial primacy in appointments was an indispensable feature of judicial independence, which, in turn, was part of the *basic structure of the Constitution*. The 99th Amendment was invalid because, by doing away with the collegium, it violated the basic feature of judicial independence. And to counter this argument, the Union of India also addressed detailed submissions asking for the case to be referred to an eleven-judge bench, so that the correctness of the *Second Judges' Case* could be reconsidered— and, if necessary, the *Second Judges' Case* could be overruled.[5]

The issue required substantial analysis, because the majority opinion in the *Second Judges' Case* is itself ambiguous on the point.[6] Paragraph 72 of the opinion appears to link judicial independence and primacy,[7] and paragraphs 40 and 41[8] suggest that in cases of deadlock, or stalemate, between the executive and the judiciary, the primacy of the Chief Justice is necessitated by the *constitutional scheme* (and not simply the text of Article 124). At the same time, at no point does the *Second Judges' Case* expressly hold that judicial primacy is *necessarily* required to secure judicial independence.[9] The paragraphs extracted above, apart from not

---

[5] Union of India, *Written Submissions in the NJAC Case*, Part II [75]–[79].

[6] Lord Cooke of Thorndon, 'Where Angels Fear to Tread' in B.N. Kirpal, Ashok H. Desai, Gopal Subramanium, Rajeev Dhavan and Raju Ramachandran (eds), *Supreme but Not Infallible: Essays in Honour of the Supreme Court of India*, (Oxford University Press, 2000) 97, 101.

[7] *Second Judges' Case* [72] (majority opinion of Justice Verma).

[8] *Second Judges' Case* [40]–[41] (majority opinion of Justice Verma). For an argument connecting these disparate paragraphs, *see* Gautam Bhatia, 'Judicial Appointments, and the Basic Structure—I' (*Indian Constitutional Law and Philosophy*, 15 July 2015) <https://indconlawphil.wordpress.com/2015/07/15/debating-the-njac-the-second-judges-case-judicial-appointments-and-the-basic-structure-i/> accessed 8 March 2016.

[9] Seervai, for instance, treats the *Second Judges' Case* as only being about the interpretation of the word 'consultation'. In his entire discussion, he makes no mention of the basic structure. *See* H.M. Seervai, *Constitutional Law of India*, vol. 3 (4th edn, Universal Law Publishing 1996) 2927–71 (Seervai).

being dispositive, can also be read as *obiter dicta*,[10] or at best, limited to the specific situation of resolving a stalemate.[11]

The Court in this case, therefore, was required to decide, first, whether the *Second Judges' Case* had established the collegium on the basis that judicial primacy in appointments was part of the basic structure. If the answer to that was yes, then the Court would have to decide whether that conclusion was suspect, and if the answer to *that* question was yes, then to refer it to a bench of eleven judges for reconsideration. However, if the answer to the second question was no, then the Court would have to examine whether the 99th Amendment affected judicial primacy to an extent that it would 'damage or destroy'[12] the basic feature of judicial independence. On the other hand, if the Court was to find that the *Second Judges' Case* had only held that the word 'consultation' in Article 124 meant 'concurrence', it would then have to ask itself whether there was any *other* way in which the 99th Amendment violated the basic structure. In either event, a close reading and interpretation of the *Second Judges' Case*, in order to determine what that case had said about the relationship between the collegium, judicial primacy, Article 124, and the basic structure, ought to have been the first bit of analysis that the bench in the *NJAC Case* would engage in.

The *NJAC Case's* Analysis of the *Second Judges' Case*

Let us begin with the lead opinion of Justice Khehar. Justice Khehar's judgment, ostensibly, made a clean separation between the issue of reference to a larger bench and the issue of merits, and considered them

---

[10] Suhrith Parthasarathy, 'Debating the NJAC: Why Judicial Primacy in Appointments Is Not Part of the Basic Structure' (*Indian Constitutional Law and Philosophy*, 20 July 2015) <https://indconlawphil.wordpress.com/2015/07/20/debating-the-njac-why-judicial-primacy-in-appointments-is-not-part-of-the-basic-structure-guest-post/> accessed 8 March 2016.

[11] Vishwajith Sadananda, 'Debating the NJAC: The Second Judges Case, Judicial Appointments, and the Basic Structure: A Response—I' (*Indian Constitutional Law and Philosophy*, 17 July 2015) <https://indconlawphil.wordpress.com/2015/07/17/guest-post-debating-the-njac-the-second-judges-case-judicial-appointments-and-the-basic-structure-a-response-i/> accessed 8 March 2016.

[12] *Kesavananda Bharati v. State of Kerala*, (1973) 4 SCC 225.

successively. Justice Khehar advanced five arguments supporting the correctness of the *Second Judges' Case*, and declining the request for a referral. First, he held that the primacy of judges in judicial appointments had been upheld by judgments even before the *Second Judges' Case*.[13] Second, the *Second Judges' Case* did not efface the constitutional scheme, since the collegium continued to accord a significant role to the executive, giving primacy to the judiciary only in cases of a stalemate.[14] Third, a close reading of the Constituent Assembly Debates indicated that the framers' paramount concern was to maintain judicial independence in appointments by 'curtailing the will of the executive' and therefore 'shielding' the appointments process from executive dominance.[15] It was in this context that the word 'consultation' would have to be understood, and if so understood, the *Second Judges' Case* was clearly correct in interpreting it beyond its dictionary meaning. Fourth, there had been a near-uniform practice since the framing of the Constitution of the President accepting the 'advice' of the Chief Justice before finalizing an appointment.[16] And last, the principle of separation of powers precluded the executive from having the final word in appointments.[17]

The validity of these arguments, some of which are troublingly impressionistic (in particular, the glib move from 'curtailing executive dominance' to 'shielding the appointments process from the executive'[18]), has been discussed elsewhere in this volume. Here, I want to point out that even if we accept each of the five claims as true, they only establish the very limited proposition that *the collegium is not inconsistent with the constitutional scheme*. That, however, leaves the central question unanswered: does the collegium (and, by extension, judicial primacy in appointments) *merely* arise out of a contextual interpretation of the word 'consultation' in Article 124 (an interpretation that Justice Khehar

---

[13] *NJAC Case* [89]–[91].

[14] *NJAC Case* [94]–[101].

[15] *NJAC Case* [106]–[108].

[16] *NJAC Case* [113].

[17] *NJAC Case* [121].

[18] *See*, e.g., Arghya Sengupta, 'Judicial Primacy and the Basic Structure: A Legal Analysis of the NJAC Judgment' (November 2015) L (48) *Economic and Political Weekly* 27, 28 (Sengupta 2015).

spent considerable effort to defend)—or is it a *necessary* aspect of judicial independence and the basic structure? As I have argued above, without answering that question, the constitutional validity of the 99th Amendment cannot satisfactorily be decided. In his referral opinion, Justice Khehar pronounced on the correctness of the *Second Judges' Case* insofar as the existence of the collegium was concerned, but remained agnostic about the constitutional foundations of the collegium, *as understood by that case.*

This confusion between the two distinct questions—is the collegium *constitutionally valid*, and is judicial primacy *necessarily* entailed by judicial independence and the basic structure – persisted in the merits part of Justice Khehar's opinion. It emerged particularly sharply in paragraph 300, which, in my opinion, is the nub of his entire judgment. Here, Justice Khehar observed:

> ... the word consultation... will have to be read as assigning primacy to the opinion expressed by the Chief Justice of India (based on a decision, arrived at by a collegium of Judges), as has been concluded in the 'Reference Order'. In the Second and Third Judges cases, the above provisions were interpreted by this Court, as they existed in their original format, i.e., in the manner in which the provisions were adopted by the Constituent Assembly, on 26.11.1949 (-which took effect on 26.01.1950). Thus viewed, we reiterate, that in the matter of appointment of Judges to the higher judiciary, and also, in the matter of transfer of Chief Justices and Judges from one High Court to any other High Court, under Articles 124, 217 and 222, primacy conferred on the Chief Justice of India and his collegium of Judges, is liable to be accepted as an integral constituent of the above provisions (as originally enacted). *Therefore,* when a question with reference to the selection and appointment (as also, transfer) of Judges to the higher judiciary is raised, alleging that the 'independence of the judiciary' as a 'basic feature/structure' of the Constitution has been violated, it would have to be ascertained whether the primacy of the judiciary exercised through the Chief Justice of India (based on a collective wisdom of a collegium of Judges), had been breached...[19] (emphasis mine)

Effectively, Justice Khehar got rid of the problem by simply *eliding* the two distinct questions, by the use of the connector 'therefore'. In the first

---

[19] *NJAC Case* [300].

part of the paragraph, he reiterated the *correctness* of the *Second Judges'*
Case insofar as it read the word 'consultation' to mean 'concurrence'.
He then held that 'therefore', primacy of the judiciary was a necessary
component of judicial independence and the basic structure. As we
have seen, however, this entirely begs the question.[20] And once armed
with the proposition that primacy of the judiciary in appointments was
part of the basic structure, it was possible for Justice Khehar to find that
the NJAC, by creating a six-member Commission in which judges were
not in a majority, failed to maintain the primacy of judges.[21]

The crucial preliminary question of what the *Second Judges' Case*
actually held was unfortunately missed by all the other individual
opinions as well. Justice Lokur followed Justice Khehar in ground-
ing the constitutional validity of the collegium in the Constituent
Assembly Debates[22] and long-standing constitutional conventions,[23]
and in protesting that the collegium system continued to maintain the
balance of power between the executive and the judiciary in a manner that was consistent with the constitutional scheme.[24] Justice Goel's
concurrence largely followed this pattern,[25] and added an assertion that
once the *Second* and *Third Judges' Cases* were held to be binding precedents, 'It has to be held that primacy of the judiciary in appointment
of judges is part of the basic structure.'[26] After subsequently recording
the Attorney-General's submission that the basis of the *Second Judges'*
Case had been taken away by the repeal of Article 124,[27] he then merely
reiterated that the submission could not be accepted in light of the fact
that the binding precedents required no reconsideration.[28] And Justice

---

[20] But, *see also* paragraph 380, where Justice Khehar appears to hold that
the *Second Judges' Case* held that judicial primacy was part of the basic structure
on a conjoined reading of all of the above. Again, no substantive argument is
provided to back up this assertion.

[21] *NJAC Case* [306].

[22] *NJAC Case* [451], [467], [469], [543], [545], [569]–[569.4].

[23] *NJAC Case* [474].

[24] *NJAC Case* [695].

[25] *NJAC Case* [1071] (on separation of powers) and [1052] (constitutional
convention).

[26] *NJAC Case* [1054].

[27] *NJAC Case* [1055] (concurring opinion of Justice Goel).

[28] *NJAC Case* [1056].

Joseph simply stated that according to the *Second Judges' Case*, since judicial appointments were a facet of judicial independence, therefore 'the Executive cannot interfere with the primacy of the judiciary in the matter of appointments'.[29]

Surprisingly, even Justice Chelameswar, in his dissenting opinion, expressly recorded that he was expressing no opinion on the correctness of the *Second Judges' Case*[30] or on the correctness of the collegium system.[31] Now, Justice Chelameswar would not have needed to pronounce on the correctness of the *Second Judges' Case* if *and only if* it was his opinion that that case had held that the collegium system arose only out of a textual reading of Article 124 of the Constitution. Had that been the case—as we have seen above—the Parliament was entitled to replace Article 124 and override the judgment, and the correctness of the *Second Judges' Case* did not matter either way. However, if the *Second Judges' Case* had held that judicial primacy, via the collegium, was *required* by the basic structure, then Justice Chelameswar, being bound by that judgment, would have had no choice but to hold that it was incorrectly decided, and dissent on the question of referral. Strangely, however, despite even recording the petitioners' submissions on the *Second Judges' Case* to this effect,[32] he skipped answering the question entirely, apart from a single off-the-cuff remark calling the collegium an 'interpretive gloss on the text of Article 124...'[33] Instead he went straight into an analysis of how, on his reading of the constitutional history and structure, it was only executive *dominance* that went against the grain of judicial independence and the basic structure.[34] On this basis, he then concluded that judicial primacy was not the *only* way of preserving judicial independence,[35] as long as absolute power was not vested with the executive.[36]

It is beyond the scope of this essay to consider, on merits, the *NJAC Case*'s reading of constitutional and political history in support of their

[29] *NJAC Case* [973].
[30] *NJAC Case* [1166].
[31] *NJAC Case* [1179].
[32] *NJAC Case* [1205].
[33] *NJAC Case* [1178].
[34] *NJAC Case* [1177].
[35] *NJAC Case* [1212], [1217].
[36] *NJAC Case* [1213].

conclusions on the correctness of the *Second Judges' Case*.[37] The objective of this part has been, nonetheless, to show that all five opinions miss a crucial piece of analysis that was necessary to decide the constitutionality of the 99th Amendment—i.e., what the *Second Judges' Case* had held with respect to judicial primacy, Article 124 of the Constitution, and the basic structure.

The *NJAC Case* on the Primacy of Judges

Lastly, let us consider what the *NJAC Case* holds with respect to the primacy of judges in judicial appointments. Arghya Sengupta argues that a close reading of the five opinions reveals that only two judges out of five (Justice Khehar and Justice Goel) accepted judicial primacy to be part of the basic structure (and indeed, Justice Lokur expressly held it not to be).[38] Consequently, he contends that the judgment in the *NJAC Case* does not bind the Parliament, or future Courts, to adhere to the proposition that judicial primacy is entailed by the basic structure. Presumably, another constitutional amendment that deprives the judiciary either of the sole first or the last voice in appointments (or both) would have to be considered on its own merits, and would not automatically be rendered unconstitutional by virtue of the *NJAC Case*.

Sengupta is undoubtedly correct that Justice Khehar and Justice Goel unambiguously accepted judicial primacy, and that Justice Lokur and Justice Chelameswar rejected it. The important opinion, therefore, is that of Justice Joseph's. Sengupta argues that since Justice Joseph recorded his agreement with all three of the majority opinions, he cannot be said to have endorsed judicial primacy, since the other opinions are actually split on this point. I disagree. There are three occasions in his concurring opinion where Justice Joseph referenced Justice Lokur. At paragraph 976, he declared himself to be in agreement 'with the analysis and statement of law, in the matter of discussion and summarization of the principles on reconsideration of judgments made by

[37] But, *see* Arghya Sengupta, 'Independence and Accountability of the Higher Indian Judiciary' (DPhil thesis, University of Oxford 2015) 11–23; *see also* Abhinav Chandrachud, *An Independent Colonial Judiciary: A History of the Bombay High Court during the British Raj, 1862–1947* (Oxford University Press 2015); Seervai (n. 9).

[38] Sengupta 2015 (n. 18).

Lokur, J'[39] (i.e., on the question of referral). Again, at paragraph 976, he stated that 'I wholly agree with the view taken by Khehar, Lokur and Goel, JJ., that the [99th] amendment is unconstitutional'.[40] Then, after detailing Philip Bobbitt's categorization of the various modalities of constitutional interpretation, he noted that 'while wholly agreeing with the historic, textual, prudential, and doctrinal approaches made by Khehar and Lokur, JJ., my additional stress is on the structural part'.[41] Justice Lokur was not referenced elsewhere in this short judgment.

Readers will therefore note that the agreement between the two Justices was on three specific points: the question of referral, the final holding of unconstitutionality, and the modalities of constitutional interpretation. Justice Joseph *did not* agree with Justice Lokur's opinion that judicial primacy is not part of the basic structure. On the contrary, at the beginning of his judgment, he noted that 'the Second Judges Case... [held] that appointment of Judges to the High Courts and the Supreme Court forms an integral part of the independence of judiciary, that independence of judiciary is part of the basic structure of the Constitution of India, and *therefore*, the Executive cannot interfere with the primacy of the judiciary in the matter of appointments.'[42] This seems to make it clear that Justice Joseph *held* that judicial primacy is part of the basic structure. That brings us to the requisite majority of three judges, and allows us to conclude that the *NJAC Case* has held that the primacy of judges in appointments (i.e., the initial and final voice) is necessarily entailed in the concept of judicial independence, and is therefore part of the basic structure of the Constitution.

Conclusion

In the judgment in the *NJAC Case*, a majority of three judges out of five held that judicial primacy in appointments—that is, the initial and the final selection of judges—is necessarily entailed by the concept of judicial independence, which is part of the basic structure of the Constitution. Consequently, any future amendment to the Constitution

[39] *NJAC Case* [976].
[40] *NJAC Case* [976].
[41] *NJAC Case* [986].
[42] *NJAC Case* [973].

attempting to do away with the collegium, will either have to persuade another bench that the judgment in the *NJAC Case* is incorrect, or maintain this concept of judicial primacy.

In this essay, I have argued that the reasoning advanced by the majority opinions does not support the claim that judicial primacy is part of the basic structure. It was incumbent upon the bench in the *NJAC Case*, since it was bound by the *Second Judges' Case*, to consider what that judgment held with respect to judicial primacy and the basic structure. However, apart from a few blanket assertions, the Justices failed to engage with this question. On the contrary, they devoted considerable effort towards demonstrating that the *Second Judges' Case* was correctly decided, in light of the constitutional structure, history, and precedent. At best, the majority opinions successfully proved the presence of a constitutional convention mandating executive deference to the Chief Justice's opinion, a line of precedents that held similarly, and the expressed will of the Constituent Assembly to avoid executive dominance of the selection process. This was sufficient to show that the collegium, as established by the *Second Judges' Case*, was constitutionally valid. However, *that* conclusion did nothing to undermine the Parliament's power to amend the Constitution and replace the collegium with another, equally valid system of appointments. To strike down the 99th Amendment, the majority opinions had to show—as Justice Chelameswar correctly observed—that judicial primacy was the *only* way of preserving judicial independence, *or* that there was some other way in which the 99th Amendment violated the basic structure. While the latter attempt was made by Justice Lokur, who consciously avoided the term 'judicial primacy' altogether, Justices Khehar, Goel, and Joseph, who adopted judicial primacy, failed to do either. An attempt, of sorts, was made by Justice Khehar in his move from curtailing executive will to 'shielding' the process of appointments from the executive, but in the absence of anything more, this is insufficient. Consequently, while the findings of the *NJAC Case* on judicial primacy are now law, they rest, I would submit with respect, on intellectually shaky foundations.

Justice Lokur's Concurring View

12 *The Future of Appointments Reform*

ALOK PRASANNA KUMAR

Five separate opinions were delivered in the *NJAC Case* striking down the 99th Amendment and the NJAC Act as unconstitutional, by a majority of 4–1. Of the majority opinions, Justice Lokur's opinion (the second longest after Justice Khehar's) offers a staunch defence of the so-called 'collegium system' for appointment of judges which was to be replaced by the NJAC. It is an opinion that must be engaged with on its own terms since the *NJAC Case* not only tested the constitutional validity of the NJAC, but in some sense also put the collegium system of appointments on trial. One strand of the Union of India's arguments defending the NJAC was clearly aimed at exposing the many deficiencies that were present in the collegium system itself, and the unsatisfactory results in its working.[1] Justice Lokur offers a defence of the system which, in his view, protects judicial independence in India and is a better method than the NJAC in ensuring judicial independence.

Even apart from Justice Lokur's opinion, looking at the Supreme Court's judgment in the *NJAC Case* as a whole, some questions about the future of judicial appointments in India rise for discussion. These are:

1. Assuming that the collegium system is better than the NJAC at protecting judicial independence, does it necessarily make the latter unconstitutional, i.e., contrary to the basic structure?

[1] *NJAC Case* [228].

2. Are the criticisms of the collegium system (acknowledged by Justice Lokur and other judges) one of design or implementation?
3. Is the collegium system of appointment the *only* constitutionally permissible means of judicial appointments under the Constitution of India?

The answers to these questions help us understand the law laid down in the *NJAC Case*—Has the Supreme Court only struck down the NJAC, or has it, wittingly or otherwise, foreclosed the possibility of any reform in the appointment of judges? While Justice Lokur's is one of four concurring opinions forming the majority in the *NJAC Case*, his defence of the collegium gives us a clue as to the answers to these questions. An analysis of his opinion will tell us whether there is any path for future judicial reform when it comes to appointments, and if so, how it may be walked. By going into the history and underlying reasons for the creation of the collegium system of appointment, as we know it today, Justice Lokur's opinion throws light on what a constitutionally permissible alternative to the NJAC may look like. Whether that alternative can only be a 'Collegium 2.1'[2] (that tinkers at the edges of the collegium system as it stands) or something completely different is what will be explored in this essay.

In the first part of this essay, I examine the merits of the collegium system as described by Justice Lokur. The next part will explore the basis on which he has held the 99th Amendment and the NJAC Act to be unconstitutional and see if the legal reasoning holds. The last part will attempt to draw a coherent picture of what a future judicial appointments system might look like on the basis of what has been laid down as the law by the Supreme Court in the *NJAC Case*.

The Basis for Justice Lokur's Defence of the Collegium System

Justice Lokur surveys the history of Article 124 and Article 217 of the Constitution of India[3] extracting from and discussing the key

---

[2] Assuming the *Second Judges' Case* gave us Collegium 1.0 and the *Third Judges' Case*, Collegium 2.0.

[3] *NJAC Case* [423]–[477].

documents which went into the drafting of these provisions concerning appointment of judges to the Supreme Court and the High Courts, respectively. One key concern highlighted by him, and one which the Constitution framers, specifically Dr Ambedkar, did not take into account was the possibility of the political executive[4] being the single largest litigant before the Courts.[5] It is a curious oversight on the part of the Constituent Assembly and one that is slightly baffling given the width of the jurisdiction that they had given the High Courts and the Supreme Court in Article 226 and Article 32, respectively. It is also here that Justice Lokur tentatively draws the link between judicial independence with judicial review, which is also part of the basic structure of the Constitution.[6] However, he does not explore this link further.

The opinion then moves on to the post-Independence operation of Article 124 and Article 217, particularly looking at the Law Commission of India's 14th[7] and 80th Reports[8] which deal with the appointment of judges to the Supreme Court and the High Courts. While the Reports did point to the differences in opinion which had arisen between the various authorities concerned with appointment, namely the Chief Ministers of States and the Chief Justices of the High Courts, Justice Lokur notes that the Chief Justice of India was always given the final word on the matter, at least for the first couple of decades following Independence. Confirmation of this also comes from George H. Gadbois, Jr's book *Judges of the Supreme Court of India, 1950–1989*[9] where

---

[4] To distinguish between the President and the Council of Ministers, I have used 'political executive' to mean the Council of Ministers and the Government, as Justice Lokur has sometimes done in his judgment.

[5] *NJAC Case* [470]–[471].

[6] As held in *Kesavananda Bharati v. State of Kerala* (1973) 4 SCC 225 and re-iterated in *Minerva Mills v. Union of India* (1980) 3 SCC 625 and *L. Chandra Kumar v. Union of India* (1997) 3 SCC 261. Justice Kuldip Singh does draw some links between judicial review and judicial independence in the *Second Judges' Case. See Second Judges' Case* [332]–[335].

[7] Law Commission of India, *Reform of Judicial Administration* (14th Report, Ministry of Law and Justice, Government of India 1958) (14th Report).

[8] Law Commission of India, *The Method of Appointment of Judges* (80th Report, Ministry of Law and Justice, Government of India 1979) (80th Report).

[9] George H. Gadbois, Jr, *Judges of the Supreme Court of India: 1950–1989* (Oxford University Press 2011) (Gadbois).

he extensively discusses the experience of Chief Justices of India in the appointment process of Supreme Court judges.[10] The 80th Report of the Law Commission provides the model for the collegium and is cited with approval by the Supreme Court in the *Second Judges' Case* in creating the collegium of judges who should be consulted by the Chief Justice of India in giving his advice to the President for the purposes of appointment of judges.[11]

In Justice Lokur's view, the period post-Independence and leading up to the *Second Judges' Case* was one of slow but steady incursion into judicial independence because of the greater say that the executive had over appointments.[12] While he cites only the Law Commission Reports to this effect, this is confirmed to quite a degree by Gadbois as well. Gadbois splits the appointment of judges to the Supreme Court into two distinct phases—1950 to 1970 and 1971 to 1989.[13] Based on interviews with surviving ex-judges and then sitting judges of the Supreme Court of India, Gadbois classifies appointments into these two phases depending on the role the then political executive played in the appointment process. Whereas in the first phase, almost all the appointments were made on the basis of the recommendation of the Chief Justice of India alone (with the political executive concurring), in the second phase, it is clear that the political executive sought, and obtained, a greater say in the appointment of judges by recommending its own nominees to the post. This did not mean that the appointment was pushed through even against the opinion of the Chief Justice—rather, though the Chief Justice exercised a veto over appointments he absolutely did not want, in many cases, the judges appointed were initially suggested by the then political executive and not by the Chief Justice himself.[14] The difference is most evident in comparing the tenure of

[10] It is unfortunate that this excellent source with first-hand accounts of the appointments process has not been referred to by Justice Lokur or any of the judges though it does find a very brief mention in Justice Khehar's opinion. It is somewhat puzzling that this book, which has excellent first-hand information on the appointment process in the first four decades after Independence, has not been relied upon by the advocates appearing for the parties either.

[11] *Second Judges' Case* [393].

[12] *NJAC Case* [511].

[13] Gadbois (n. 9) 7–8.

[14] Gadbois (n. 9) 154.

Chief Justice M. Hidayatullah and Chief Justice S.M. Sikri. Whereas the former absolutely refused to consent to the nominees pressed by the political executive,[15] the latter acquiesced to as many as eight judges nominated by the then political executive.[16]

In continuing his historical survey, Justice Lokur hints at 'unsuitable' judges who were appointed as a result of executive interference in the appointments process. What is left unsaid, and up for conjecture, is whether the judges were 'unsuitable' because they were recommended by the political executive or whether their qualifications to be judges left much to be desired. This point is important since it goes to the heart of the appointments debate—Is a judge necessarily 'unsuitable' if she is the nominee of the government of the day? If so, this amounts to calling several of India's finest judges, given their impact on shaping jurisprudence and the role of the judiciary, as 'unsuitable'. If not, then we must rest the notion of judicial independence being affected by the manner on appointments on some other premise. Reading through Justice Lokur's judgment, one gets the sense that he is reaching for the former, without quite stating it, unaware of the consequences of such an overbroad statement. Unfortunately, we get no serious engagement with this issue from any of the judgments in the *NJAC Case* and we are forced to draw our own conclusions on the matter.

Having laid down the historical basis for it, Justice Lokur proceeds to outline the many merits of the collegium system as he sees it. It must be said in fairness that Justice Lokur does not seem to think that mere involvement of the political executive is *per se* unconstitutional or unwarranted. Nor does he agree with the government that the collegium system has 'ousted' the political executive from the process. The place of the political executive in the appointments process is to assist the Chief Justice of India and the collegium in making the right choice by providing the necessary inputs.[17] The collegium, Justice Lokur believes, is more in line with the constitutional intent as expressed by Dr Ambedkar than a system where the executive has primacy.[18] This is a somewhat unsatisfactory basis to rest an argument, as it appeals not

[15] Gadbois (n. 9) 139.
[16] Gadbois (n. 9) 154–5.
[17] *NJAC Case* [545].
[18] *NJAC Case* [543].

to the authority of the Constitution but to the views of one of its key drafters.

Following this line of thought leaves us with a curious Constitution—one which is not in the text itself but in the views of specific members of the Constituent Assembly. As important as taking on board the views of members of the Constituent Assembly, especially someone like Dr Ambedkar who had a key role as the Chairman of the Constitution Drafting Committee, is in interpreting the text of the Constitution, they cannot be a substitute for or entirely replace the text of the Constitution itself.[19]

Justice Lokur's praise of the collegium system is tempered with the acceptance that the system is not perfect—he calls for a 'democratic audit' but in the same line adds that such an audit should be limited to the judiciary and the rule of law.[20] Whether this means that only the judiciary itself is allowed to audit its own performance in light of the rule of law, and no one or nothing else, is not entirely clear but the underlying tone of resentment against external criticism of the judiciary is hard to miss. Also missing in Justice Lokur's defence of the collegium system is a discussion or even an acknowledgement of the importance of criteria such as transparency and efficiency in its functioning.

While the collegium system has undoubtedly protected the independence of the judiciary from executive interference, especially in comparison to the earlier system of executive primacy in appointments, it still falls short in ensuring that those beyond a small and exclusive circle have anything to do with judicial appointments. The appointments process, even under the collegium system, is one with restricted discussion and deliberation between the executive and the judiciary and little, if any place, for inputs from the bar, litigants, or the wider public. It is still unknown and unclear on what basis candidates' credentials for higher judiciary are assessed and what qualifications make a candidate suitable for elevation. The poor representation of women, Scheduled Castes and Tribes, and minorities in the higher judiciary all point to an 'old boys' club' which has taken shape in the form of judicial appointments.[21]

[19] *Indra Sawhney v Union of India*, 1992 Supp (3) SCC 217 [772]–[774].

[20] *NJAC Case* [595].

[21] Alok Prasanna Kumar, 'Absence of Diversity in the Judiciary' (February 2016) 51(8) *Economic and Political Weekly* 10 (Prasanna Kumar).

In effect, we only know that the collegium has protected judicial independence because the judges tell us that it has. The absence of any independent method of scrutiny and verification in the appointments process mean that the claim of protection of independence is one that must be taken only at face value. Still, even accepting the claim that the collegium system of appointments does in fact ensure judicial independence, it does not automatically mean that a different system of appointments which replaces it is likely to disturb judicial independence. With the merits of the collegium system laid out, Justice Lokur proceeds to examine whether the proposed NJAC is an improvement over the collegium system in terms of judicial independence.

On the Unconstitutionality of the NJAC

The manner of appointment of judges, according to Justice Lokur, is not a small or ancillary aspect of judicial independence but foundational.[22] In this he is right at the first step, but he does not move to the next phase of the argument as to why it is so foundational, especially in the Indian context. The importance of the appointment process, especially in the context of the political executive's role in it, lies in the vast powers of judicial review that constitutional courts exercise over the actions of the political executive and the legislature. In the absence of this link between judicial review and judicial independence, it becomes difficult to normatively describe the distinction between 'involvement' (as in the collegium) and 'interference' (as Justice Lokur suggests the NJAC intends). The mere presence of the Law Minister is thus considered an unacceptable and unconstitutional interference with the judicial appointment process and, therefore, a ground to strike down the 99th Amendment. Reasoned thus, it seems like a case of judicial *ipse dixit* resulting in a power grab rather than a principled defence of the concept of judicial independence.

Justice Lokur also does not think the Constitution is a site for experimentation. Judicial independence once lost, he feels, cannot be regained.[23] This contradicts the earlier trajectory of judicial

---

[22] *NJAC Case* [753].
[23] *NJAC Case* [847].

appointments described by Justice Lokur where the collegium system restored the original constitutional intent which was being eroded by increasing interference by the political executive. If judicial independence, weakened no doubt by greater political executive interference in the appointments process, could be regained through judicial interpretation perhaps the judiciary in the future can also be trusted to restore judicial independence if the balance, in reality, were to veer too far off. This contradiction in the opinion can also be attributed to the fact that a serious link is not drawn between judicial independence and judicial review, i.e., executive involvement in the appointments process is acceptable so long as it does not affect or is not likely to affect the power of judicial review. That the NJAC would necessarily lead to the weakening of judicial independence, affecting the manner in which the power of judicial review is exercised is not clear from Justice Lokur's reasoning.

Among the other justifications offered for striking down the NJAC are the reduced scope for the President's role in the appointments process[24] and the possibility of the members of civil society being essentially government nominees.[25] However, the prime reasons for striking down the NJAC seem to be the seemingly diminished role for the judiciary and the involvement of the Law Minister in the process of appointments. Seen along with his conclusion that the NJAC constitutes a violation of the basic structure because it diminishes the role of the Chief Justice of India (which in his view is a part of the basic structure of the Constitution),[26] it would seem that the NJAC's principal defect, in Justice Lokur's eyes, is that it is not the collegium.

A proper discussion of Justice Lokur's opinion in the *NJAC Case* is not possible without a mention of footnote 568 in the judgment which betrays a cringe-inducing lack of self-awareness. It is difficult to imagine how, when commenting upon the views of the National Democratic Alliance Government on homosexuals, he was able to completely blank out the Supreme Court's own egregious judgment in *Suresh Kumar Koushal v. Naz Foundation*[27] which re-criminalized homosexual

---

[24] *NJAC Case* [882]–[886].

[25] *NJAC Case* [883]–[908].

[26] *NJAC Case* [815].

[27] (2014) 3 SCC 220.

acts, dismissing gay rights as 'so-called rights' of a 'miniscule minority'.
In holding up certain prejudices of the executive as a reason to reduce
the role of the political executive in the appointment of judges, Justice
Lokur conveniently ignores the Court's very own and very real prejudices. In some ways this particular line, though it occurs only in a footnote in passing (and inserted possibly without much serious thought)
also unwittingly reflects the deep distrust of the political executive and
concomitant blind faith in the judiciary. It would not be unsurprising
if such prejudice, within the judiciary, seeps into its decision making as
well. In fact, the poor representation of Scheduled Castes, Scheduled
Tribes, and women[28] in the higher judiciary might suggest that such
prejudice is far more ingrained than Justice Lokur thinks it is.

While Justice Lokur is correct in pointing out the many defects of
the NJAC, what his opinion falls short on is the normative basis for
these defects to result in the basic structure of the Constitution itself
being affected. The strongest argument that can be raised, and one
which Justice Lokur addresses to some extent, is that the NJAC gives
the Central Government, the single largest litigant before the Court, a
greater say in the appointments process than the collegium system. It is
not as if the government, represented through the Law Minister in the
NJAC, has a decisive role in recommending names for appointment. In
Justice Lokur's opinion, the Law Minister emerges as a somewhat sin-
ister figure in a committee of six, who possesses a mysterious ability to
influence and dominate the minds of the lesser mortals in his presence.
Even the mere potential for the views of the Law Minister to influence
the other members in the collegium is anathema to Justice Lokur.[29]

What is the appropriate role for the Government in the appointment
process under the Constitution of India? A detailed answer is beyond
the scope of this essay but one possible approach suggests itself. The
appropriate role of the government is to provide inputs to the appointment process and have a say in the suitability of the candidate, without
compromising the independence of the judiciary, specifically, its ability
to carry out a neutral and impartial judicial review of the government's
actions. The latter qualification is in the nature of a boundary to the
scope of the government's involvement in the judicial appointments

---

[28] Prasanna Kumar (n. 21).

[29] Prasanna Kumar (n. 21).

process that I tentatively would like to describe as participation without paramountcy.

What Lies Ahead for the Reform of Judicial Appointments

Assessed only on the metric of judicial independence—of a system that reduces scope for executive 'interference' in judicial appointments, the collegium definitely meets the requirement. Whether it actually ensured that appointments were made without interference from the executive or on entirely relevant criteria is a matter for research for future historians and legal scholars. It is also not true, as alleged, that the political executive has no role to play in the appointment system as Justice Lokur clearly elaborates. An appointment system with absolutely no role for the political executive is neither feasible nor desirable.

Yet, at the same time, Justice Lokur's opinion seriously circumscribes what role the political executive can play in the appointment of judges to the higher judiciary in India. While the political executive is not assumed to be in a position to assess the ability of the judge, Justice Lokur feels that it is in the position to offer inputs on 'antecedents, peculiarities and angularities' of a candidate.[30] Justice Lokur also is of the view that the executive cannot be allowed to have too much of a say in the matter of appointment of judges given that the government is the single largest litigant before the judiciary—not even with the Law Minister as one member out of a committee of six.[31] There is thus a pragmatic reason and a principled reason offered as to why the political executive should be kept out of the appointments process in the way it has been in the collegium system. Any future measure to change the judicial appointments procedure has to keep the political executive at a safe distance from the process on these grounds as I have suggested in the previous part.

The flaws in the reasons notwithstanding, Justice Lokur's opinion does leave sufficient space to imagine (if not create) an alternate to the collegium system of appointment of judges. Some features are non-negotiable and have now been elevated to the level of the basic structure, namely:

[30] *NJAC Case* [692].
[31] *NJAC Case* [914].

1. Involvement of the judiciary in the appointments process.
2. Primacy to the opinion of the Chief Justice (representing the views of the judiciary).
3. Consultation between the President and the Chief Justice in appointments.

In addition, there are certain 'don'ts' which have been laid down, the doing of which will render an appointment procedure unconstitutional. They affect the 'basic structure' of the Constitution inasmuch as the Supreme Court has held that they fundamentally affect the independence of the judiciary. They are:

1. Involvement of the political executive in recommending judges for appointment.
2. Involvement of external parties with any link to the political executive in recommending judges for appointment.

If the weakness of the collegium system was to create a closed-off circle of 'consultants' with no external inputs or accountability, an alternate which addresses this could very well be proposed without seriously affecting any of the above non-negotiables. It is possible to imagine a new appointments process without compromising on, or in any way destabilizing, judicial independence within the strict parameters that the Court has laid down.

This will require the political executive to move beyond the simple concern of greater involvement for itself and token representation of 'civil society'. Rather, the focus needs to be on ensuring greater transparency and inclusiveness in the procedure, without compromising the efficiency of the appointments process.[32] Transparency and efficiency are two areas where the collegium system has failed, and which have not even been attempted to be tackled in the NJAC. No one but a tight-knit coterie knows why a judge is appointed to the Supreme Court or the High Courts, and why another is not. The serious problem of delay and crushing pendency in the High Courts can partially be attributed

---

[32] *See* Alok Prasanna Kumar, 'Judicial Independence, Accountability and Transparency' (*Mint*, 26 October 2015) <http://www.livemint.com/Opinion/jUM5lDd7M0qxRGiBeqi0UO/Judicialindependence-accountability-and-transparency.html> accessed 16 April 2016.

to the fact that the collegium has never been able to fill more than 650 seats on the High Courts, whatever the strength sanctioned by the Government.[33]

The path of reform lies along these lines. What Justice Lokur's opinion does, for all its flaws in reasoning, is to leave sufficient leeway to take this path towards greater transparency and better efficiency, but guided by the need to maintain judicial independence. It may not necessarily be a 'stairway to heaven,'[34] but it shall certainly not be the 'highway to hell'.

[33] Alok Prasanna Kumar, 'Vacant posts remain collegium system's biggest challenge' (*Mint*, 20 October 2015) <http://www.livemint.com/Politics/FZKTZdKUtZRaEcg2msir1J/Vacant-posts-remain-collegium-systems-biggest-challenge.html> accessed 16 April 2016.

[34] Referencing Justice Lokur's judgment in the *NJAC Case* [942]: 'While there might be a need for a more efficient or better system of appointment of judges, the NJAC is not the stairway to Heaven....'

Justice Chelameswar's Dissent

13

Reforming to Preserve

ARGHYA SENGUPTA*

The opinion by Justice Chelameswar in the *NJAC Case* is a gentle reminder of how a judgment on a question of the validity of a constitutional amendment might have been decided were the Supreme Court limited to considering the question as a matter of constitutional law. However, so feisty were the arguments in Court on this matter, and so brittle the relations between the executive and the judiciary at the time that it comes as little surprise that an opinion that separates the wheat from the chaff and limits discussion to the core questions pertaining to constitutional interpretation and amendment is a dissenting one.

This essay primarily focuses on two aspects of the opinion: First, its understanding of the basic structure doctrine together with its methodology of how to assess the validity of a constitutional amendment against the basic structure; second, its understanding of the constitutional relationship between the executive and the judiciary and its implication for separation of powers in India. In both these respects, the opinion is seminal and ripe for a future bench to convert it into binding constitutional law.

* The author would like to thank Jessamine Mathew for her assistance with research for this essay.

Basic Structure and Basic Features: Untying the Strands

A perplexing feature of jurisprudence pertaining to the basic structure doctrine has been the number of expressions that have been used to describe it. 'Basic features',[1] 'essential elements',[2] 'essential features'[3] have all been used at various times to describe the conceptual core of the Constitution that cannot be taken away, even by an amendment to the Constitution itself. It is evident, as a matter of language, that while 'basic' and 'essential' might be quintessential synonyms, 'features', 'structure' and 'elements' are not. However, it is curious that since *Kesavananda Bharati v. State of Kerala*[4] and including it, there have been no judgments that have discussed whether indeed they convey the same or distinct ideas.

In this context, the judgment in the *NJAC Case* provided an ideal opportunity for clarification. The petitioners had argued that the 99th Amendment, by taking away primacy of the judiciary in the matter of appointments, adversely affected judicial independence, held to be part of the basic structure of the Constitution. To establish this claim, four arguments would have to be successfully made: First, that judicial independence is a basic feature of the Constitution; second, primacy of judges in appointment is intrinsic to judicial independence; third, the NJAC in fact takes away such primacy; fourth, the taking away of such primacy damages judicial independence in such a manner that the basic structure of the Constitution is abrogated.

The first question was not contested by either side—that judicial independence is an essential feature of the constitutional framework is both a platitude as well as a settled position of constitutional law.[5] With respect to judicial primacy, Justice Chelameswar quickly comes to the conclusion that primacy is neither itself part of the basic structure nor is it essential

---

[1] *See*, e.g., *Sajjan Singh v. State of Rajasthan*, AIR 1965 SC 845; *S.R. Bommai v. Union of India* (1994) 3 SCC 1.

[2] *See*, e.g., *Minerva Mills Ltd. v. Union of India*, (1980) 3 SCC 625; *I.R. Coelho v. State of Tamil Nadu*, (2007) 2 SCC 1.

[3] *See*, e.g., *Raghunathrao Ganpatrao v. Union of India*, (1993) 1 SCC 363.

[4] (1973) 4 SCC 225 (*Kesavananda Bharati*).

[5] *NJAC Case* [426].

for judicial independence.[6] Though summary in his dismissal of this argument, the reasoning is persuasive. The framing and working of the Constitution both demonstrate that absolute power in any one authority was anathema to the constitutional scheme.[7] Thus the Constitution envisages checks and balances on all organs and in the exercise of all functions. Judicial primacy in appointment of judges might have been a way to restore checks and balances into the system of appointment in light of executive excesses; but that cannot itself make it an essential feature of the Constitution. Other ways to ensure an independent judiciary, short of primacy, but incorporating checks and balances may also suffice.

However, even assuming that judicial primacy is a significant facet of judicial independence, which in turn is an essential feature of the Constitution, the key question of constitutional law lies in the interface between an essential feature and the basic structure of the Constitution. In this context, Justice Chelameswar provides in essence a two-step test to determine the validity of constitutional amendments:

1. Does the amendment affect a basic feature of the Constitution?
2. If yes, does it affect it in a manner that destroys the basic structure of the Constitution?[8]

This two-step test is a coherent reading of precedents that appeared to have used the terms 'basic feature' and 'basic structure' interchangeably. It lays down clearly the remit of basic features such as judicial independence, equality, and the rule of law that are principles that underlie the Constitution. At the same time it clarifies that the basic structure is the 'sum total of the basic features'.[9] Thus simply affecting one basic feature would not be sufficient to hold the amendment unconstitutional; it must violate it in such a manner that the basic structure itself would be destroyed.

A thought experiment can elucidate this—if the procedure for impeachment of judges is simplified to require 20 members and not

---

[6] *NJAC Case* [517].

[7] *Constituent Assembly of India Debates*, vol. 8, no. 3 (Lok Sabha Secretariat) 24 May 1949, 258.

[8] Arghya Sengupta, 'Appointment of Judges and the Basic Structure Doctrine in India' (2016) 132 *Law Quarterly Review* 201, 205.

[9] *NJAC Case* [496].

50 to initiate an impeachment motion in the Rajya Sabha, judicial independence might plausibly be affected; however it could not be a reasonable claim to suggest that it affects judicial independence to such a degree that the basic structure will collapse.

This has the added benefit of setting an appropriate standard of proof to constitute a basic structure violation. Questions pertaining to standard of proof in this context have been an endemic and unresolved feature of basic structure jurisprudence. That the basic structure would have to be 'abrogated',[10] 'destroyed',[11] 'affected',[12] 'violated'[13] have all been used by judges in the context of testing the validity of a constitutional amendment. The possible discrepancies between these terms was brought out in the argument by the Union of India in the *NJAC Case*, arguing that a high threshold, that required the basic structure to be abrogated or destroyed should be adopted given the extraordinary nature of judicial power exercised while assessing a basic structure violation. It appears that the majority either dismissed the argument or rejected it implicitly. This is clear from Justice Khehar as well as Justice Goel's opinion both of which merely require the basic structure to be affected for a constitutional amendment to be bad.[14]

Adopting such a low standard of proof has two particular concerns. First, it is incommensurate to the extraordinary nature of judicial power exercised.[15] The power to strike down a constitutional amendment as a concept is alien to the common law. Even in constitutional democracies, judicial review ordinarily extends to striking down executive

[10] *See, e.g., M. Nagaraj v. Union of India* (2006) 8 SCC 212; *Ashoka Kumar Thakur v. Union of India* (2008) 6 SCC 11.

[11] *See, e.g., Waman Rao v. Union of India* (1981) 2 SCC 362; *Manoj Narula v. Union of India* (2014) 9 SCC 1.

[12] *See, e.g., Union of India v. Sankalchand Himatlal Sheth* (1977) 4 SCC 193 (*Sankalchand Sheth*); *Minerva Mills Ltd. v. Union of India* (1980) 3 SCC 625.

[13] *See, e.g., Charan Lal Sahu v. Neelam Sanjeeva Reddy* (1978) 2 SCC 500; *Kuldip Nayar v. Union of India* (2006) 7 SCC 1.

[14] *NJAC Case* [341], [258] (Justice Khehar); [1167] (Justice Goel).

[15] For a general discussion on basic structure review *see* Sudhir Krishnaswamy, *Democracy and Constitutionalism in India: A Study of the Basic Structure Doctrine* (Oxford University Press 2010); Satya Prateek, 'Today's Promise, Tomorrow's Constitution: 'Basic Structure', Constitutional Tranformations and the Future of Political Progress in India' (2008) 1(3) *NUJS Law Review* 417.

action, or at most parliamentary law.[16] If the Supreme Court is to exercise the power of judicial review to strike down a constitutional amendment, the ultimate expression of parliamentary sovereignty, a degree of caution is called for.[17] Striking down an amendment to the Constitution for merely affecting the basic structure is inadequately respectful of Parliament.

Second, it is incapable of balancing between two features that may form part of the basic structure, one of which may be furthered by the amendment, and the other derogated from. Unlike previous cases where basic structure violations have been found,[18] the NJAC provided a case where the government argued that the amendment was to promote checks and balances and a better separation of powers, both of which were part of the basic structure, in addition to judicial independence. The Court was called upon to adjudicate on this balance—however, adopting a low standard of proof, by which any amendment that merely affected the basic structure would be bad, is *per se* incapable of assessing such a balance.

On the contrary, Justice Chelameswar's two-step test is fit for this purpose. First, it incorporates two distinct standards of proof in its two limbs—the lower threshold (affects) is used to determine whether at all the constitutional amendment raises a relevant question pertaining to a basic feature and if it does, the number of basic features that are at play in every case. The higher threshold (destroys) determines whether the sum total of how the amendment affects the various basic features, leads to an unconstitutionality. Second, it is designed in order to assess the constitutionality of hard cases pertaining to the basic

---

[16] *See* Jeremy Waldron, 'The Core of the Case against Judicial Review' (2006) 115 (6) *The Yale Law Journal* 1346.

[17] In fact, the Supreme Court has been cautious when challenges to constitutional amendments have been brought before it. In the past, the Court has struck down constitutional amendments in six instances, that too only in part. These instances have been discussed in K.T. Thomas, 'Judicial Review and Parliamentary Power: Reorienting the Balance', pp. 73–83 in this volume.

[18] *Kesavananda Bharati* (n. 4); *Indira Nehru Gandhi v. Raj Narain*, 1975 Supp SCC 1; *Minerva Mills Ltd. v. Union of India* (1980) 3 SCC 625; *P. Sambamurthy v. State of Andhra Pradesh* (1987) 1 SCC 362; *L. Chandra Kumar v. Union of India* (1997) 3 SCC 261.

structure—when one feature which is part of the basic structure may be positively affected and the other negatively.

Applying the test to the 99th Amendment, Justice Chelameswar holds that the primacy of the opinion of the Chief Justice of India in appointments is not a basic feature; instead, a checks and balances scheme with non-investiture of power to appoint in the President is. Understood in this manner, the amendment by creating the NJAC and including the Law Minister and two eminent persons from civil society, does not affect this basic feature. If, on the contrary, it entirely excluded the executive branch, that might have created an unconstitutionality. Similarly, the inclusion of eminent persons furthers the same goal preventing 'unwholesome trade-offs'[19] between the judiciary and the executive. Thirdly, the requirement of a super-majority, i.e., 5 out of 6 affirmative votes[20] to confirm all appointments is also constitutionally sound since primacy of the judiciary according to Justice Chelameswar is not a basic feature in the first place.[21] Each of these inferences flows logically from his clear statement of the law.

The Government and the Court: A History of Necessary Tension

The relationship between the executive and the judiciary subsequent to the *Second Judges' Case* has been portrayed as founded on mutual distrust.[22] Much of this has its genesis in the law laid down in the *Second Judges' Case*—vesting the executive with the last word on appointments would be detrimental to judicial independence; on the contrary giving such power to the Chief Justice and a collegium of senior justices would better ensure such independence. This rather simplistic belief, belied by two decades of mixed experiences, was considered to be entrenched constitutional law by the majority judges in the *NJAC Case*. Justice Chelameswar however adopts a longer-term view of executive–judiciary

---

[19] *NJAC Case* [520].

[20] NJAC Act, proviso to s 5(2).

[21] *NJAC Case* [517].

[22] Nakul Dewan, 'Revisiting the Appointment of Judges: Will the Executive Initiate a Change?' (2005) 47(2) *Journal of the Indian Law Institute* 199, 210.

relations in India. He offers a contrarian perspective and questions the significance of past incidents on the declaration of constitutional law.

Insofar as the working of the appointments process post-collegium is concerned, Justice Chelameswar is blunt, saying, 'Instead of ministers, judges patronised.'[23] He points to two recorded instances in the cases of Justice Ashok Kumar and Justice P.D. Dinakaran who were confirmed and elevated to the Supreme Court respectively, despite widely held doubts about their conduct and suitability.

Further, when discussing the mass transfer of judges by the executive during the Emergency, he points out a salient fact: each of these transfers had been acquiesced to by the Chief Justice of India.[24] This implies that the solution to ensuring judicial independence in the *Second Judges' Case* and held to be part of the basic structure by his brethren in the majority in the *NJAC Case* would not have been able to stave off the threats to independence posed during the Emergency.

These two examples are offered in the backdrop of the general perception of the executive branch being opposed to judicial independence and judges best placed to secure it. Two key inferences emerge from this nuanced discussion: first, that it is dangerous to lay down constitutional law on the basis of incidents pertaining to executive–judiciary relations. Executive interference in judicial appointments was certainly a reality in the 1970s and 1980s, as noted by Justice Chelameswar. But the Chief Justice of India was, on occasion, complicit in such interference. Further, it was the executive itself, owing to considerable political pressure, which reversed its transfer orders issued during the Emergency. To lay down constitutional law on the basis of a particular interpretation of specific incidents would be hasty.

Second, the discussion demonstrates that the separation of powers scheme in India is not a simplistic exhortation of the insulation of the branches of government. The scheme envisaged by Dr Ambedkar, particularly pertaining to the role of distinct organs in appointment of judges, quoted and analysed at length by Justice Chelameswar, presupposes a role for both the executive and the judiciary in appointments.[25]

---

[23] *NJAC Case* [471].

[24] *NJAC Case* [457]. *See also Sankalchand Sheth* (n. 12), where such transfers had been challenged.

[25] *See NJAC Case* [508] where Justice Chelameshwar refers to the Federalist papers (No. 51), wherein he quotes James Madison to the effect that insisting

This is part of a larger separation of powers scheme, where separation is maintained by mutual checks and balances, that ensures that while one organ is invested in another, it does not have the incentive to takeover or subvert the other's functioning. It is consequently difficult in law to draw bright lines as to when executive interference in judicial appointments is such that judicial independence is breached. Needless to say, the mere presence of the Law Minister, or two eminent persons from civil society in the process, as envisaged by the NJAC, would not *per se* violate judicial independence.

This is precisely why Justice Chelameswar upholds the 99th Amendment as consistent with the separation of powers envisaged in the Constitution. The presence of one member of the executive cannot be contrary to such a scheme since the Constitution does not envisage a strict insulation of organs of government. In a similar vein, representatives of civil society, who are key stakeholders can also constitutionally be part of the appointments process. His refusal to strike down either of these provisions is a testament to a judgment that is based on law and legal reasoning rather than hypothetical possibility.

At the same time, there are two aspects of his judgment that require closer scrutiny. First, while upholding the requirement of two eminent persons on the NJAC, he believes that there should be greater safeguards as to how such persons are chosen. Consequently he proposes that such persons be confirmed by a vote of all Supreme Court judges.[26] Unfortunately, his judgment fails to demonstrate why the

---

on a strict separation of powers in the context of judicial appointments may be 'inexpedient' owing to the 'peculiar qualifications' that such candidates are required to have:

> In order to lay a due foundation for that separate and distinct exercise of the different powers of government, which to a certain extent is admitted on all hands to be essential to the preservation of liberty, it is evident that each department should have a will of its own, and consequently should be so constituted that the members of each should have as little agency as possible in the appointment of the members of the others. [...] In the constitution of the judiciary department in particular, it might be inexpedient to insist rigorously on the principle: first, because peculiar qualifications being essential in the members, the primary consideration ought to be to select that mode of choice which best secures these qualifications.

[26] *NJAC Case* [522].

existing selection mechanism, by a committee with the Prime Minister, Leader of Opposition in the Lok Sabha, and the Chief Justice of India is not constitutionally adequate to ensure appropriate selections to the NJAC. There are several references to why Chief Justices of India in the past have been pliable, but whether that can form a justified basis for reading in a confirmation process that the Constitution is silent on is questionable.

Secondly, in a conspicuous omission, Justice Chelameswar does not examine the validity of the NJAC Act. He says that he does not engage in this exercise because 'in view of the majority decision, [he] did not see any useful purpose'.[27] This is curious—judicial propriety demanded that a full examination of the enactments be carried out irrespective of the views of other judges on the issue. Such an examination became all the more relevant given that there was a sharp division within the majority as to whether an Act can be challenged on the ground of being violative of the basic structure. This is a surprising omission in an otherwise comprehensive and well-reasoned judgment.

The Legacy of a Dissent

Justice Chelameswar's opinion joins an illustrious list of dissenting judgments by judges of the Supreme Court of India which boldly spoke truth to power. Justice Saiyid Fazl Ali in *A.K. Gopalan v. State of Madras*,[28] Justice Hidayatullah in *Naresh Shridhar Mirajkar v. State of Maharashtra*[29] and Justice H.R. Khanna in *Additional District Magistrate, Jabalpur v. Shivakant Shukla*[30] all expressed powerful views on how the Constitution ought to be interpreted. What makes Justice Chelameswar's opinion in this case a particularly illustrious member of this list is his courage to call out his own fraternity for its failings. This is especially so when his brethren remained united in their conviction of their own suitability to appoint judges without adequate introspection and unconvincing legal reasoning. In this context Justice Chelameswar's view is remarkable both for its clear argumentation and bold introspection about the

---

[27] *NJAC Case* [534].
[28] AIR 1950 SC 27.
[29] AIR 1967 SC 1.
[30] (1976) 2 SCC 521.

shortcomings of judges themselves. It is for posterity to judge its legacy, particularly in explicating basic tenets of constitutional law and shaping the process of appointment of judges. In both these respects one can only hope that his wise words to the keepers of the judiciary in closing are heeded: 'Reform that you may preserve.'[31]

---

[31] *NJAC Case* [535].

The NJAC Case and Judicial Independence

Conceptual and Contextual Safeguards

14

GOPAL SUBRAMANIUM*

The debate around appointment of judges to the higher judiciary has raised profound questions that warrant a deeper understanding of our Constitution. This essay argues in favour of the autonomy of the judiciary in the appointment process that the Supreme Court boldly reaffirmed in the *NJAC Case*. Further, it discusses how sincere concern about existence of well-defined criteria and procedures in matters of appointments led to the Union of India proposing an executive veto, while being asked to prepare a simple Office Memorandum to describe interstitial steps in the appointment process.[1] This, as I argue, is not surprising. By providing a conceptual understanding of judicial independence and delving into some lesser known aspects of India's judicial history, I advance the view that executive interference in the appointments process to undermine the independence of the judiciary has been endemic. I look back further—to the early years of the Indian Republic and the seldom-discussed, but pivotal case, involving the transfer of Justice Sankalchand Sheth and 15 other judges. Using these, I demonstrate that the judgment in the *NJAC Case* is a much-needed affirmation of judicial independence and rule of law. It firmly keeps

* The author is grateful to Talha Abdul Rahman, Anusha Ramesh, and Utkarsh Saxena for their assistance with research for this essay.

[1] *See NJAC Case. See also, NJAC Case* orders dated 5 November 2015 and 16 December 2015 in W.P. (C) No. 13/ 2015.

the overweening executive at arm's length from the judiciary, which has and must continue to be the guardian of human rights in the country.

Living Constitution and Breathing Judiciary

The Indian Constitution was conceived as a living document that would have new life breathed into it continuously by the pulsating organs of the State, allowing it to grow and evolve with the times. When critics of the *NJAC Case* wave the Constitution and point towards the words of Article 124 and Article 217—the textual abode of the appointment process of the higher judiciary—they neglect other historical facts relating to contrarian acts emasculating the independence of the judiciary. The autonomy of the judiciary as an independent organ has proved its value not merely when we petition it for justice (*cri de coeur*) but when it has struck down invalid executive actions and arbitrary legislations and demanded a culture of accountability of the executive and the legislature. This necessarily had led to power hungry politicians to seek pliant members of a sympathetic higher judiciary and thus leave the judiciary morally disempowered, if not 'defrocked'.

As Professor Laurence Tribe lucidly described in his intriguing work, *The Invisible Constitution*,[2] the Constitution, like the night sky, is an 'inter-temporal collage'[3] that entails concerns and elements from profoundly differing eras of history. The shape and size of the Constitution is moulded, reshaped, and redefined every day. Alterations through the legislature or the judiciary directed at some specific part of the Constitution end up changing the entire document. The Constitution is never static: every amendment affects other parts of the Constitution in deep ways, rather than remaining stationary in fixed silos. In *R. C. Cooper v. Union of India*,[4] the Supreme Court used this dynamic idea of the Constitution to break down the walls of watertight compartments of different provisions under Part III of the Constitution—as understood in *A. K. Gopalan v. State of Madras*[5]—and concluded that provisions of

---

[2] Laurence H. Tribe, *The Invisible Constitution* (Oxford University Press 2008) (Tribe).

[3] Tribe (n. 2) Part III: Explorations beyond the Text.

[4] (1970) 1 SCC 248 (*Bank Nationalisation Case*).

[5] AIR 1950 SC 27.

the Constitution could be read with other parts of the Constitution for deciphering their true import. Therefore, to understand the judicial appointment process, one must read the evolving constitutional material—constitutional text, Constituent Assembly Debates, other constitutional doctrines, and the contemporary history of the working of the Constitution—in its entirety. Constitutionalism prevents the delamination of constitutional text into literal and the moral, textual, and the spirit. Thus, the desquamation of interested motives of powerful men is essential to appreciate how valuable an independent judiciary is for the Constitution and the people. It follows that solely a textual scrutiny of the words of Article 124 and Article 217 or of the literal understanding of the Article at the time of the ratification of the Constitution would provide an incomplete and outdated answer.

Dr B.R. Ambedkar in his final address to the Constituent Assembly noted the conscious decision of the Drafting Committee to keep the amendment clause 'facile' and less onerous than those found in its American or Australian counterparts, to permit evolution of the Constitution with changing times.[6] On the issue, he bluntly conceded: '... the principles embodied in the Constitution are the views of the present generation or if you think this to be an overstatement, I say they are the views of the members of the Constituent Assembly.'[7] In several judgments, the Supreme Court has confirmed the 'essential organic and evolutionary character of a Constitution and its flexibility as a living entity to provide for the demands and compulsions of the changing times and needs'.[8] As a result, the Court has rejected the doctrine of 'originalism', requiring a strict adherence to the literal and original intention and meaning of the Constitution at the time of its founding. The Indian Supreme Court, on the other hand, has often taken positions contrary to the express intentions of the Constituent Assembly. It has discountenanced excessive delegation, voided arbitrary legislation, and upheld the jurisdiction of the Court to speak on the interpretation of the basic structure of the Constitution beyond the pale of the amending power and substantive due process. Such progress

[6] *Constituent Assembly of India Debates*, vol. 11, no. 5 (Lok Sabha Secretariat) 25 November 1949, 976 (CAD vol. 11).

[7] CAD, vol. 11 (n. 6) 975.

[8] See *Kihoto Hollohan v. Zachilhu*, 1992 Supp (2) SCC 651; *Rameshwar Prasad v. Union of India*, (2005) 7 SCC 157.

was possible because of the autonomy of the institution, which could uphold its independence in a spirit of detachment.

To have oblique powers to interfere in judicial appointments and insist on comfortable candidates who may be politically 'suitable' and 'non-inconvenient' is a dispiteous blow to the Constitution. There is bound to be a conflict of interest if merit is subordinated to convenience and comfort. The power of the courts to judge, given their standing in public space, would naturally dispose politician kingmakers to seek a say in the appointment process. That motive cannot be couched as a just struggle to restore the textual supremacy of the Constitution. The once acknowledged supremacy becomes a hankering; the amendment to interfere with independence is a mere inroad to achieve the subjugation of the judiciary and is not borne out of conviction or a deep analysis of the history of the Constitution.

As noted earlier, Article 368 provided simple prerequisites for constitutional amendments to enable the legislature to change the Constitution in a manner it deemed fit without any conception of inherent limitations or entrenchment, an idea that was otherwise gaining popularity in constitutions around the world after the experiences of the Second World War, which witnessed a 'constitutional' rise of autocratic regimes through a distortion of the amendment process. The Supreme Court erected the canopy of the basic structure above the Constitution, as a shield from the amendment power of the legislature, through creative interpretations of overarching and underlying principles found *beneath* the text, not *in* the text, and equipped itself with the power to strike down even constitutional amendments, a historic, tectonic, and unprecedented step. A strict literal interpretation could not have allowed for the constitutional revolution triggered by the creation of the basic structure doctrine in *Kesavananda Bharati v. State of Kerala*.[9]

These were structural revolutions and adjustments made by the Supreme Court of India to revelations and insights gained from the working of the Constitution that the original framers did not and could not fathom. A Constitution that is rigid and does not account for possibilities that could not be envisioned at its birth cannot survive the onslaughts of time. In the context of the American Constitution, Justice Thurgood Marshall said:

---

[9] (1973) 4 SCC 225 (*Kesavananda Bharati*).

The men who gathered in Philadelphia in 1787 could not have envisioned these changes. They could not have imagined, nor would they have accepted, that the document they were drafting would one day be construed by a Supreme Court to which had been appointed a woman and the descendant of an African slave. 'We the People' no longer enslave, but the credit does not belong to the Framers. It belongs to those who refused to acquiesce in outdated notions of 'liberty', 'justice' and 'equality', and who strived to better them... We will see that the true miracle was not the birth of the Constitution, but its life, a life nurtured through two turbulent centuries of our own making, a life embodying much good fortune that was not.[10]

Members of the Constituent Assembly could not have prophesized the controversies that awaited the Constitution and the need for a basic structure doctrine, realized by the judiciary in light of creeping, shellacking executive attempts to shorten the reach of judicial review; or the necessity of a substantive due process doctrine in light of the precarious implementation of fundamental rights by the State. After all, the violation of human rights has an interesting sigillography.

As Upendra Baxi remarked presciently, the judgment in *Kesavananda Bharti* 'is in some sense, the Indian Constitution of the future'.[11] The Supreme Court used the basic structure doctrine to save our constitutional republic from egregious attacks, such as those in *Indira Gandhi v. Raj Narain*,[12] *Minerva Mills Ltd. v. Union of India*,[13] *L. Chandra Kumar v. Union of India*,[14] and *S. R. Bommai v. Union of India*[15] and ushered an era of transformative fundamental rights, public interest, and environment litigation, amongst others, with the aid of the substantive due process doctrine, instead of adhering to the literal text of the Constitution. Constitutional discourses do require stereogramic interpretations since

---

[10] Charles S. Zelden, *Thurgood Marshall: Race, Rights, and the Struggle for a More Perfect Union* (Routledge 2013) 196.

[11] Upendra Baxi, 'The Constitutional Quicksands of Kesavananda Bharati and the Twenty-Fifth Amendment' in Surendra Malik (ed.), *Fundamental Rights Case: The Critics Speak* (Eastern Book Company 1975) 130.

[12] (1975) Supp SCC 1

[13] (1980) 3 SCC 625 (*Minerva Mills*).

[14] (1995) 1 SCC 400.

[15] (1994) 3 SCC 1.

the intention of the founding fathers was to create a living Constitution, and not a studentized textbook.

The doctrine of complete autonomy of the judiciary is not a torentic. It is born out of the vicissitudes surrounding the appointment process. After all there have been experiences with the appointment process during which the executive reduced judges and their inner ambitions to a game of tresette. The true test of an institution is often its survival of identity and spirit against ugglesome challenges. *Maneka Gandhi v. Union of India*,[16] *Kesavananda Bharati*, the *Second Judges' Case* and *Power, Privileges, and Immunities of State Legislatures, Re*[17] were such examples of constitutional supremacy.

Independent, Free, and 'Untouchable' Judiciary

The Court should interpret the Constitution 'with an enlightened liberty' and administer the law with 'goodwill and sympathy for all', said Chief Justice Kania after taking his oath from President Dr Rajendra Prasad. To do this, it will 'be quite untouchable by the legislature or the executive authority in the performance of its duties'.[18]

Judicial independence is a universal aspiration that is achieved through differing constitutional structures. But what does it mean? 'What am I, a Potted Plant?' asked Judge Richard Posner of the Court of Appeals, of the Seventh Circuit, while expounding thoughts about his duties as a judge of the Court.[19] What may a judge think and consider during the discharge of his or her duties, after being ushered out of the courtroom at the end of business every day? This part attempts to unravel this question and chalk out the attributes of an independent judicial mind, and an examination of the thoughts of great judges from

[16] (1978) 1 SCC 248.

[17] AIR 1965 SC 745.

[18] Kania's observation was reiterated by Justice Y.K. Sabharwal in Y.K. Sabharwal, 'Address on the Occasion of Silver Jubilee Celebrations of the All-Assam Lawyers' Association' (Silver Jubilee Celebrations of the All-Assam Lawyers' Association, Guwahati, 28 January 2006) <http://www.supremecourtofindia.nic.in/speeches/speeches_2006/assam.pdf> accessed 26 October 2016.

[19] Richard A. Bosner, *Overcoming Law* (Harvard University Press 1995) 229–36.

the past provides some insights. The obvious place to start is with the four great judges whose portraits adorn the walls of the Supreme Court. The first, Chief Justice Kania, who led the way; Justice B.N. Mukherjea, an epitome of learning, dignity, and scholarship marked by an inspiring personal life; Justice T.L. Venkatarama Iyer, a capable learned judge who wrote with elegance and was one of the great masters of Carnatic music; and Justice H.R. Khanna whose dignity, conduct, and conscientiousness marked by high moral resonance left him a universe of admirers.

It is evident that judicial independence operates at the individual or internal level and an institutional or external level. At the individual level, it relates to the notion of conflict resolution by a 'neutral third', that is, someone who can be trusted to settle controversies after considering only the facts and their relation to relevant laws free from corrupting influences.[20] From a normative viewpoint, judges should be autonomous moral agents, who can be relied on to carry out their public duties independent of venal or ideological considerations.

A court which is afflicted by pre-judgment is likely to fail in dealing fully and fairly with the reasoning advanced against the winning party, not only in oral argument, but also in judgment.[21] It renders the fairness quotient of the process of adjudication doubtful. It is not the power, authority, and jurisdiction which speaks for an institution because that would have an element of *vi et armis*. Rather, the judge is a warrantor of rational and careful reasoning.

Judicial independence is also a question of optics and perception: the judiciary must not only be independent, but also appear to be dispensing justice without being influenced by any extraneous considerations. 'Doing justice' involves not only the courage of a judge to formulate an independent view, but the ability of a judge to pass orders expressing

[20] Martin M. Shapiro, *Courts: A Comparative and Political Analysis* (University of Chicago Press 1986) 17–27; *See also,* Christopher M Larkins, 'Judicial Independence and Democratization: A Theoretical and Conceptual Analysis' (1996) 44(4) *American Journal of Comparative Law* 605 605.

[21] Justice Dyson Heydon, 'Threats to Judicial Independence: The Enemy Within' (2013) 129 *Law Quarterly Review* 205–22. He writes at 210, 'Authorities are followed because they are authorities, not because their reasoning is admired.' However, the importance of reasoning lies in the fact that losing parties must have confidence that their arguments have been adequately considered and dealt with. It is therefore noted, English decisions were addressed to the losing party.

that view and giving effect to it. This ideal is indispensably rooted in the dispensation of 'equal justice for all', and in the preservation of rule of law, which runs through the fabric of our entire Constitution.[22]

At the external level, judicial independence implies dispensation of duties free from the influence of vested interests of other organs of the State, i.e., the legislature and executive. Judicial independence is essential to the preservation of rule of law at the institutional level, which is achieved through the separation of powers between the executive, legislature, and the judiciary. This is especially so in India since the Constitution has guaranteed several fundamental rights to citizens and empowered the Supreme Court and the High Courts, under Article 32 and Article 226 respectively, to protect these rights against acts of the State and those charged with performance of public duties.

The manner of appointment and selection of judges is an integral component of allowing the judiciary to function independently. With regard to appointment of judges, the framers of our Constitution were unanimously of the view that independence of the judiciary was paramount. Dr Ambedkar expressed the unanimous opinion of the Constituent Assembly that 'our judiciary must both be independent of the executive and must also be competent in itself'.[23] However, in order to ensure independence without creating any power imbalances (or *imperium in imperio*), no sympathy was shown towards a strict separation of powers. Instead, an attempt was made to steer a middle course by which the judiciary would have ample independence to act without fear or favour of the executive.

The constitutional debate around the NJAC needs to be grounded in this legal and constitutional context. The tendency of a judge to be

[22] In *Subhash Sharma v. Union of India*, 1991 Supp (1) SCC 574 [29], the Supreme Court observed that,

> An independent non-political judiciary is crucial to the sustenance of our chosen political system. The vitality of the democratic process, the ideals of social and economic egalitarianism, the imperatives of a socio-economic transformation envisioned by the Constitution as well as the Rule of Law and great values of liberty and equality are all dependent on the tone of the judiciary. The quality of the judiciary cannot remain unaffected, in turn, by the process of selection of judges.

[23] *Constituent Assembly of India Debates*, vol. 8, no. 3 (Lok Sabha Secretariat) 24 May 1949, 258.

influenced by his or her internal prejudices and aspirations is not primarily an institutional phenomenon, but a human one. As Benjamin
Cardozo elegantly surmised in his *Nature of Judicial Process*, 'The great
tides and currents which engulf the rest of men, do not turn aside in
their course, and pass the judges by.'[24] Every judge suffers from internal
prejudices that he or she is trained to quarantine during judicial deliberations. Hence, irrespective of the nature of the appointing body, the
internal independence of the judiciary depends on the attributes of the
individual appointed as a judge. This independence has nothing to do
with the institutional architecture of the appointment process and can
be termed *internal* independence.

The 'constitutional' problem with regard to the independence of the
judiciary arises in the area of *external* independence at an institutional
level. By design, the fate of the members of the executive and legislatures, whose actions are tested on the anvil of the Courts on a daily
basis, lies in the hands of the judges. The appointment of judges to
courts, as a result, has always been a subject of keen interest for members of other organs of the State. This is the crux of the issue with regard
to judicial independence: adoption of an institutional framework that
ensures that judges appointed to the higher judiciary, under whose
gaze, actions of the establishment are tested every day, are not compromised. The true constitutional concern regarding the independence of
the judiciary is not about the merit of the judges or their understanding
of the law, but the distance that they keep from those whose actions
they judge while discharging their official functions.

This distinction is important to be able to appreciate the context
and perspective that I am trying to set for this debate. Criticism of the
collegium system is based on the quality of the judges that have been
elevated ever since its introduction, which may be difficult to contest.
A 'bad' judge, i.e., a judge with a slow clearance rate or with a poor
understanding of the law or facts of cases or with a stubborn attitude
or impatient temperament, while a malaise for the system, is, however, not an illustration of a compromised judiciary, and certainly not
a constitutional violation. The constitutional concern centres on the
appointment of independent judges. A bright and intelligent judiciary,

---

[24] Benjamin Nathan Cardozo, *The Nature of the Judicial Process* (Yale
University Press 1946 rep) 168.

while highly desirable, is not the basic feature of the Constitution that the courts are steadfastly defending; but an independent one, that is institutionally equipped to protect its people from the excesses of the establishment.

Therefore, the true constitutional quest is not for a mechanism that appoints the smartest judges, but the freest. The bench that delivered judgment in the *NJAC Case* pronounced its constitutional view on independence of the judiciary, yet as an institution, the judiciary continues to strive towards internal reform for the selection of bright and qualified judges, for which it sought recommendations and views from the Government, members of the bar and other stakeholders.[25] Moreover, the conceptual idea of the independence of the judiciary is an evolving idea.

At this stage, it may be beneficial to retrace the precise details of the nature of attacks suffered by the judiciary from the executive and legislature, before the introduction of the collegium, and revisit the corridors of history to remind ourselves why we chose this path of appointment of judges, less travelled by other judiciaries.

Illuminating Text and Judicial Structure with History

The true test of the strength of an institution is often not in its day-to-day functioning, but its survival through existential threats that challenge its identity and spirit. The movement towards the collegium system of appointments was triggered by dark lessons of history that must be appreciated before devising any prophylactic mechanisms.

Contrary to popular opinion, rumblings of executive interest in judicial appointments began before the Emergency, which was perhaps the culmination of on-going skirmishes. In 1950, Granville Austin recounts, appointments to the Madras High Court became controversial because Chief Justice Kania resisted a move by the Chief Minister, P.S. Kumaraswami Raja and the Chief Justice of the High Court, P.V. Rajamannar to appoint an Indian Civil Service (ICS) officer as a judge.[26] Austin says:

---

[25] *See NJAC Case*, order dated 5 November 2015 in W.P. (C) 13/2015.

[26] Granville Austin, *Working a Democratic Constitution: A History of the Indian Experience* (Oxford University Press 1999) 126 (Austin).

This so irritated the Chief Minister that he protested in an intemperate letter, which Patel declined to place in the file. Instead, Patel drafted a letter for Kumaraswami, to send back to him, reiterating his and the Madras Chief Justice's support for the officer.[27]

Chief Justice B.P. Sinha wrote in his autobiography about instances where governors who 'had been known to toe the line of the Chief Ministers' had tried to block judicial appointments for personal reasons by making false allegations about the candidate's communal bias.[28]

Early controversies in the appointment process was one of the reasons that led to the constitution of the Law Commission led by Mr M.C. Setalvad in 1955, within five years of the adoption of the Constitution. In its questionnaire, the Commission received several replies about executive interference. This included a stinging reply from K.M. Munshi where he stated that Chief Ministers were becoming a source of patronage in the appointment process causing the High Court judiciary to deteriorate.[29] Chief Justice Patanjali Sastri replied that politicians were only seeking a 'complaisant judiciary'.[30] The 'almost universal chorus of comment' alleged that unsatisfactory selection had 'been by executive influence' reflecting 'political expediency or regional or communal sentiments'.[31]

On 17 October 1957, the *Statesman* reported about an interim note of the Law Commission that said that the 'weight of testimony' collected by the Commission led one to believe that numerous appointments had been cleared on factors 'of political expediency or regional or communal sentiment'.[32] The Home Minister at the time, Pandit Govind Ballabh Pant, reacted strongly to this letter and suggested that every appointment made was on the advice of the Chief Justice of India. Setalvad contested the claim: he argued that the information collected by the Law Commission of India came from oral testimonies

---

[27] Austin (n. 26) 126.

[28] B.P. Sinha, *Reminiscences and Reflections of a Chief Justice* (B.R. Publishing Corporation 1985) 93–8.

[29] Austin (n. 26) 129–30.

[30] Austin (n. 26) 130.

[31] Law Commission of India, *Reform of Judicial Administration: Vol. I* (14th Report, Ministry of Law and Justice, Government of India 1958) 69, 105.

[32] *See* Austin (n. 26) 131.

in confidence. He shared the following answer from an anonymous former Chief Justice of India with the Minister: 'In olden days,' this answer said, the Chief Justice had a 'preponderant voice' and the Governor could act in his individual discretion. Now, the Governor had to be guided by his ministers and the 'Chief Minister thinks it is his privilege to distribute patronage and that his recommendation should be the determining factor'. This demoralized some of the High Court judges who, before making their recommendations, had tried to ascertain the Chief Minister's views to spare themselves of any loss of prestige in case their nomination was unceremoniously turned down.[33] This note created an uproar after it was leaked to the press.

The wavering trust of the early years led to full-blown 'court packing' attempts in the early 1970s, as per Justice Jaganmohan Reddy.[34] This was epitomized by the executive-led supersession of judges, which has left a lasting suspicion of the executive's role in judicial appointments.

The first 'grievous blow'[35] came after *Kesavananda Bharti*. Few realize the extent of pressure and threats faced by the sitting judges during the deliberation of *Kesavananda Bharti*. Justice Reddy alludes to it in the judgment itself referring to the dire consequences that the court would have to face if the judgment went against the government and that 'we should free ourselves of considerations which tend to create pressures on the mind'.[36]

Three judges, who voted against the government in the case, Justice Shelat, Justice Hegde, and Justice Grover, were superseded with Justice A.N. Ray being appointed the Chief Justice of India on 25 April 1973, in defiance of the seniority convention and with a complete disregard for the objections of President V.V. Giri. Austin described this as a 'grievous blow at democratic constitutionalism, for, by attempting to make the Court obedient to her government, she was unbalancing the power equation among the three branches of government and distorting the seamless web'.[37] Chief Justice A.N. Ray, incidentally was the lone dissenter in

---

[33] Austin (n. 26) 132.

[34] P.J. Reddy, *We Have a Republic: Can We Keep It?* (Tirupati 1984) 100.

[35] H.R. Khanna, *Judiciary in India and Judicial Process* (Ajoy Law House 1985), as cited in Austin (n. 26) 278.

[36] *Kesavananda Bharati* (n. 9) [1103].

[37] Austin (n. 26) 278.

the *Bank Nationalisation Case*[38] and one of the two dissenters in the *Privy Purses Case*,[39] and had earlier ruled in favour of the government.

It ought to be quickly added that the views of Chief Justice Ray were 'doctrinaire' and he personally enjoyed an impeccable reputation. I was privileged to meet him in his reclusive life after retirement when I could assess more accurately his belief in neo-classical parliamentary supremacy and not to aid any political setup. He had a keen eye for appointing good judges and persuaded one of his great successors, Justice M.N. Venkatachaliah, to accept the office of a judge. His passion for the freedom of the press, and his independent posture in administration is also well-known. Although I disagree with the readiness with which Justice Ray became Chief Justice and with his dissent in *Kesavananda Bharati*, yet a historical account would be incomplete without reference to his personality. I also remember the dignity with which Chief Justice S.H. Kapadia paid him a tribute at the full court reference.

The second blow was in the form of the supersession of Justice H.R. Khanna as Chief Justice, though it may be fair to argue that the judgment that led to it, the infamous *Additional District Magistrate, Jabalpur v. Shivakant Shukla*[40] was an instance of a compromised judiciary itself. Upendra Baxi writes that during the Emergency there was a 'diffuse and subtle... feeling pressing upon the Court... that its actions were being watched by the regime and there were hints that judicial power might be curbed in the days to come'.[41] Those who wandered in the Court could see fear even amongst members of the bar. As a young aspirant, when I came to watch the proceedings in Court, I saw that a great lawyer like V.M. Tarkunde was shunned because of his strong and determined protest of the Emergency.

No judiciary could be independent under the glare of the executive, with the fate of the personal and professional careers of the judges in the hands of the establishment. About the judgment in *ADM Jabalpur*, Austin said:

---

[38] *Bank Nationalisation Case* (n. 4).

[39] *Madhav Rao Scindia v. Union of India* (1971) 1 SCC 85 (*Privy Purses Case*).

[40] (1976) 2 SCC 521 (*ADM Jabalpur*).

[41] Upendra Baxi, *The Indian Supreme Court and Politics* (Eastern Book Company 1980) 42–5, 70–6.

> The common view is that the four judges (in the majority, who had voted in favour of the government) either were protecting the institution from an ill-intentioned government or protecting their personal futures or both... In cynics' eyes, three of the bench saw a relationship between their rulings and their prospects on the Court. Justices Beg, Chandrachud, and Bhagwati aware that in the normal practice of seniority they would become Chief Justice one day, held for the government to assure that this took place according to this view.[42]

However, history will record that Chief Justice M.H. Beg concurred with some of the most outstanding appointments by the Janata Government and that Justice Chandrachud and Justice Bhagwati strengthened the Court and the institution by brilliant jurisprudential contributions. The judiciary very quickly recognized its credibility in higher moral consistency. This was, in no small part, the legacy of Justice Khanna, the brave dissenting judge. The greatest tribute paid to him by placing his portrait on the wall of the Supreme Court is a reminder to all that the greatest Supreme Court judges are ones who did not budge. One of the great judges, U.R. Lalit, an outstanding lawyer, who would never toe the line, was not confirmed. But as great men, he never showed the mildest rancour and became a leading light of the Supreme Court bar.

The executive continued to interfere with judges who disagreed with it through the Emergency. Sixteen judges were transferred from their 'home' High Courts to others without their consent, and in several instances, over their objections. The executive rationalized these heinous acts by using straw man justifications like national integration, while continuing to move judges who disagreed with it like pawns. The chilling experience of the 1970s should be a complete answer to those who question complete autonomy in the judicial appointment mechanism. Years of judicial performance are irrelevant if in the most challenging times, when the liberties and freedoms of the citizens are closest to being extinguished, the judiciary is unable to stand up to its oath. A republic is as strong as its weakest organ in the most difficult of times.

---

[42] Austin (n. 25) 343.

Sankalchand Sheth and the Quest for Judicial Independence

The Supreme Court in 1977, in *Union of India v. Sankalchand Himatlal Sheth*,[43] a case often ignored by scholars, laid the foundation of our evolving jurisprudence on the appointment of judges before any of the traditional *'Judges' Cases'*, and nearly a decade before the *First Judges' Case*. Sankalchand Himatlal Sheth was a judge of the High Court of Gujarat. He was a Gandhian, spartan by nature, extremely learned and methodical. One of the sixteen transferred judges referred to above, he was sought to be transferred as a judge of the Andhra Pradesh High Court.

Being a man of great dignity, he complied with the order of transfer and took charge of his office as a judge of the Andhra Pradesh High Court. Yet before doing so, he filed Writ Petition No. 911/76 on the file of the Gujarat High Court challenging the constitutional validity of the transfer notification. He urged four grounds in support. The first was that the order was passed without his consent; second, it was in breach of an assurance given by the Government of India in 1963 that no transfer would take place except by consent, a statement on the strength of which Justice Sheth had accepted judgeship; third, since no considerations of public interest justifying the transfer were made out, the order was void; and fourth, the order was not preceded by an effective consultation with the Chief Justice of India. Sheth impleaded Justice Ray as a respondent to the petition, while the Union of India was described as the first respondent. It must be stated in fairness to Justice Ray, who was the then Chief Justice of India, that he neither filed an affidavit nor participated in the proceedings.

The writ petition was heard by a bench comprising Justice J.D. Mehta, Justice A.D. Desai, and Justice D.A. Desai. As far as the first ground was concerned, Justices J.D. Mehta and D.A. Desai held that the consent of Justice Sheth was not necessary and hence the order transferring him as a judge to the Andhra Pradesh High Court was not void for lack of consent. Justice A.D. Desai dissented and held that a judge of the High Court cannot be transferred without his consent. The third and the fourth grounds were taken together and there was a unanimous verdict by the full bench that there was no effective consultation with the

---

[43] (1977) 4 SCC 193 (*Sankalchand Sheth*).

Chief Justice of India. Justices Mehta and D.A. Desai voided the order of transfer on the ground that there was no compliance with principles of natural justice and further, that there was no material to substantiate an effective consultation with the Chief Justice of India. Significantly, Justice D.A. Desai noted that sixteen judges were transferred with a single stroke. Since the Union of India had failed to disclose the nature and content of the consultation, Justice Desai held that the consultation was not meaningful and, therefore, the order was void. Justice A.D. Desai proceeded to hold that the order was passed for a 'collateral purpose'.[44] The High Court granted a certificate of fitness to the Union of India to file an appeal to the Supreme Court.

In the Gujarat High Court, the Central Government had raised what must be termed as an unstatable objection that, on the ground of bias, the three particular judges hearing the matter ought not to continue the hearing. The objection was overruled. But, however, while discussing the independence of the judiciary, one must not overlook the aberrations of conduct by the executive as recorded in legal history. Justice Chandrachud pointed out in the judgment delivered by the Supreme Court in *Sankalchand Sheth* that '... the Learned Attorney General has spared us from having to consider the untenable contention by stating that he does not want to canvass it....'[45]

It must be said in fairness to Attorney General S.P. Gupte that he was one of the foremost Attorneys General who maintained the high traditions of the office and did not feel bound by 'instructions' from the executive government. He was an Attorney General who maintained the same character and independence as M.C. Setalvad and C.K. Daphtary. These three Attorneys General in my opinion have set a benchmark which, even today, is viewed as the best possible standard of independence that must be displayed by those who hold that high constitutional office and are leaders of the bar. Gupte made a statement when the hearing of the matter commenced. The statement was recorded by the Supreme Court in an order dated 26 August 1977:

> On the facts and circumstances on record the present government does not consider that there is any justification for transferring Justice Sheth

---

[44] *Sankalchand Himatlal Sheth v. Union of India*, (1976) 17 GLR 1017.

[45] *Sankalchand Sheth* (n. 43) [6].

from Gujarat High Court and propose to transfer him back to that High Court.

On this statement being made by the Learned Attorney General, Mr. Seervai, Counsel for Respondent No.1 [Justice S.H. Sheth], withdraws the petition with leave of the Court.[46]

It is submitted that the standard of consideration by an executive government respecting the independence of the judiciary, the posture of the Attorney General in Court, the dignity and manner in which the case was dealt with are indicative of what could be described as a fair and appropriate attitude of executive government towards the independence of the judiciary.

To return to the judgment, the first contention raised by Seervai was that a judge of a High Court could not be transferred without his consent. The Attorney General did not dispute that '... the greatest care ought to be taken to preserve the independence of the judiciary which the Constitution so copiously protects, nor does he join issue on the question of hardship which a transfer ordinarily entails...'[47] However, he submitted that consent was not a condition precedent for transfer. Justice Chandrachud referred to Justice George Sutherland's (who was an Associate Justice of the United States Supreme Court) dissenting opinion in *Home Building and Loan Association v. Blaisdell*[48] that, '... if the provisions of the Constitution be not upheld when they pinch as well as when they comfort, they may as well be abandoned...'.[49] After referring to various rules of interpretation, Justice Chandrachud held that

> ... where if the provision is clear and explicit, it cannot be reduced to a nullity by reading into it a meaning which it does not carry and, therefore, Courts are very reluctant to substitute words in a statute or to add words to it and it has been said that they will only do so where there is a repugnancy to good sense...[50]

Justice Chandrachud acknowledged that

> It is beyond question that independence of the judiciary is one of the foremost concerns of our Constitution. The Constituent Assembly

---

[46] As recorded by the Supreme Court in *Sankalchand Sheth* (n. 43) [44].
[47] *Sankalchand Sheth* (n. 43) [8].
[48] (1934) 78 L Ed 413.
[49] *Sankalchand Sheth* (n. 43) [10].
[50] *Sankalchand Sheth* (n. 43) [11].

showed great solicitude for the attainment of that ideal devoting more hours of debate to the subject than to any other aspect of judicial provisions: if the beacon of the judiciary was to remain bright, the courts must be above reproach, free from coercion and political influence…[51]

Justice Chandrachud recalled Jawaharlal Nehru:

> It was important that the High Court Judges should not only be first rate but should of the highest integrity, people who can stand up against the executive government and whoever come in their way. Dr. Ambedkar, while winding up the debate on the judicial provisions, said that the question as regards the independence of the judiciary was 'of the greatest importance' and that there could be no difference of opinion that the judiciary had to be 'independent of the executive'.[52]

I am quoting the above passage and the reasoning in *Sankalchand Sheth* because this case was a classic example of direct interference by the government in taking punitive actions against judges who were possibly suspected to be non-compliant. It is submitted that if autonomy of the judiciary has to be truly perceived, there must be an appreciation of the space between independence and fearful consequences being inflicted by the executive. In my view, the judiciary which is acknowledged to act as the bastion of the freedom of the people and which is expected to be protected from the influence of the executive, can only do so when the executive is kept at arm's length regarding appointments and transfers. It is submitted that the government cannot exercise unseen and malignant pressures upon the judiciary to influence its thought. The freedom from such pressures can only be guaranteed by the safeguard of a vigilant democratic society.

However, who speaks for that vigilant society? It can be done only by those who have power and authority to exclaim that such autonomy is capable of impugnation by the executive and the legislature. It is the duty of the judiciary to preserve itself. If it were to do otherwise, it shall be accused of not merely a dereliction of constitutional duty, but would be charged with possessing an impuissant character unable to act as 'sentinel on the qui vive'.[53]

---

[51] *Sankalchand Sheth* (n. 43) [12].

[52] *Sankalchand Sheth* (n. 43) [12].

[53] As noted in the immortal words of the Chief Justice Patanjali Sastri in *State of Madras v. V. G. Row*, 1952 SCR 597 [13].

In this context, the suggestion that checks and balances operate at every level and with regard to every function discharged by an institution is erroneous—no organ checks the other in every task that it performs. Therefore, the reading by some critics of the judgment in the *NJAC Case* that an in-house appointment process implies an erosion of all checks and balances on the judiciary as a whole is incorrect. While the appointment process, which is one cog of the judicial wheel, is beyond any executive or legislative influence (for good reason), the Constitution provides a plethora of other means that check and balance the judiciary. Parliament may by simple law (and not a constitutional amendment) change the number of judges of the Union Judiciary (under Article 124(1)), the age of the judge of a Supreme Court (under Article 124(2A)), salaries (under Article 125(1)) and privileges and allowances (under Article 125(2)) of the Supreme Court, the appellate jurisdiction of the Supreme Court with regard to civil matters (Article 133(3)), appellate jurisdiction with regard to criminal matters (Article 134), and even the review jurisdiction of the Supreme Court (Article 137), though a strong case may be made against some of these provisions being altered in such a manner.[54]

Parliament is also equipped with powers of impeachment of judges of the Supreme Court (under Article 124(4)) and may by law regulate the procedure for the investigation and proof of the misbehaviour or incapacity of a judge under Article 124(4) (Article 124(5)). There is considerable wisdom in this scheme of appointment and removal of judges. The executive is kept out of the fray during the stages of induction of judges, since, as history has shown, they derive considerable interest and benefit from their appointment *ex ante*. Moreover, it is significantly easier to tamper and interfere with the appointment mechanism since discretions and subjectivity, which are inevitable in selection processes, abound. However, the executive and the legislature play a crucial role *ex post* in the impeachment process. Since the impeachment process has higher demands and prerequisites, the executive and legislature will hesitate from resorting to it, unless absolutely necessary.

---

[54] *See* Gopal Subramanium, 'A new beginning by the Supreme Court', *The Hindu* (Delhi, 17 October 2015) <http://www.thehindu.com/opinion/op-ed/gopal-subramanium-writes-on-supreme-court-bench-order-on-njac/article7770998.ece> accessed 26 October 2016.

It is this delicate balance, that Justice Chandrachud attempted to capture. He wrote that if concurrence was to be read as a condition precedent, then, 'we will be confusing our own policy views with the command of the Constitution....'.[55] Yet Justice Chandrachud voiced:

...but we hope and trust that in his fight against an overbearing executive, the Judge will not be waging a lone or unequal battle. The ink on recent history is still not dry and its pages contain a tribute to the gentlemen standing in black robes who, though small in number, championed public causes with a courage which dumbfounded even that world in which Martin Luther King and Lord Coke had lived and died...[56]

This observation made by Justice Chandrachud in *Sankalchand Sheth* is a tribute to his own perception of Indian history and the manner in which the members of the legal profession rose to the occasion to sustain human rights and speak up for an independent judiciary. Hence, Justice Chandrachud held that the consultation with the Chief Justice of India was mandatory and had to be full and effective to be valid.

Justice Bhagwati described in his opening words why the question raised by *Sankalchand Sheth* was important:

This is an unusual case where a Judge of a High Court has been compelled to seek justice in a court of law against an unwarranted executive action. It raises questions of great constitutional significance affecting the entire High Court judiciary?[57]

Justice Bhagwati correctly analysed the constitutional provisions to hold that:

Two propositions clearly emerge on a consideration of these provisions read in the context of the constitutional scheme. The first is that the appointment contemplated under these provisions is appointment of a person as a Judge of a particular High Court and not as a Judge simpliciter. There is no All-India Cadre of High Court Judges. Secondly, a Judge of the High Court is not a Government servant, but he is the holder of a constitutional office. He is as much part of the State as the executive Government.... In fact a High Court Judge has no employer: he occupies

---

[55] *Sankalchand Sheth* (n. 43) [16].
[56] *Sankalchand Sheth* (n. 43) [16].
[57] *Sankalchand Sheth* (n. 43) [45].

a high constitutional office which is coordinate with the executive and the legislature.[58]

It is submitted that the above lines contained in the judgment of Justice Bhagwati have not received the careful attention which it warranted at the hands of scholars or even in subsequent judgments of the Supreme Court. It is respectfully submitted that if the Constitution guaranteed coordinated stature and respect for a judge of the High Court, it necessarily follows that in matters of appointment the said stature cannot be abrogated. Reference to Articles of the Constitution in a logographic manner will not in any way address the primary issue—does the constitutional amendment or executive action which is attempted to be undertaken pursuant to the said amendment, thwart the autonomy of the judiciary? If it does, there can only be one answer that the amendment is void and violates the basic structure of the Constitution.

In a sense, all subsequent landmark cases pertaining to judicial appointments were seeking to answer this question alone. The *Second Judges' Case* held that if such institutional autonomy were to be protected, judicial primacy in the appointments process would be crucial. The *Third Judges' Case* provided the details of how judicial primacy was to be maintained. The *NJAC Case*, confronting a challenge to judicial primacy, on the basis of a holistic assessment of the exact composition of the National Judicial Appointments Commission (NJAC), and the procedures for selection of its members, affirmatively held that any dilution of primacy, as envisaged in the *Second Judges' Case* would thwart the autonomy of the judiciary. We now turn to a detailed analysis of the judgment in the *NJAC Case*.

The NJAC Case

The effect of the *Second Judges' Case* in vesting power of appointment of judges in a collegium was sought to be undone by the 99th Amendment. The judgment in the *NJAC Case*, notwithstanding certain valid observations made by Justice Chelameswar in the dissenting judgment, is a sign of splendid independence of the judiciary in declaring the constitutional amendment as void. The structure of the majority

---

[58] *Sankalchand Sheth* (n. 43) [49].

reasoning of Justice Khehar that independence of the judiciary was violated by the constitutional amendment is admirable.

Yet, the subsequent proceedings by which the government was asked to prepare a Memorandum of Procedure was somewhat disappointing. It may be noted that an office memorandum or a memorandum of procedure is purely an administrative circular to inform officers in different ministries about the timelines which must be observed in implementation of the processes pertaining to appointment. This is because every appointment must take place in a timely manner and that there should be no backlog of vacancies. While the office memorandum may guarantee consultation, the opportunity to rework the office memorandum given by the consequence proceeding has placed the Court in a somewhat unenviable position. It is respectfully submitted that the office memorandum was no more than an administrative document and not a replacement of the charter of autonomy for the judiciary, affirmatively upheld in the *Second Judges'* and *NJAC Cases*.

The Constitution (One Hundred and Twenty-first Amendment) Amendment Bill, 2014 received Presidential assent on 31 December 2014 when it became the 99th Amendment. Along with the 99th Amendment, the NJAC Act was also enacted. The 99th Amendment attempted to overcome the law laid down in the *Second Judges' Case* by amending Article 124 of the Constitution. Article 124A came to be inserted, which provided for the establishment of a six-member NJAC comprising

1. the Chief Justice of India,
2. two senior-most judges of the Supreme Court,
3. the Union Minister for Law and Justice (Law Minister); and
4. two eminent persons nominated jointly by the Prime Minister, Chief Justice of India, and the leader of the Opposition in the Lok Sabha.

Thus, the judicial component, which prior to the 99th Amendment had primacy, was reduced to half its strength in the NJAC. The Chief Justice of India would have equal voting rights as other members, and even though designated as the Chairman of the NJAC, the Chief Justice was not vested with a casting vote in the event of a tie. If the Chief Justice and two other senior judges on the NJAC supported the appointment/transfer of an individual, the same could be negatived by any of the other two members, including two eminent persons. Through Article 124C the details of the selection process were delegated to Parliamentary legislation, in pursuance of which the legislature framed the NJAC Act.

In the judgment in the *NJAC Case*, the 99th Amendment and the NJAC Act were struck down by a majority of 4:1 headed by Justice Khehar, for being *ultra vires* the basic structure of the Constitution. The Court also held that the earlier collegium method of appointments had revived.

It is evident from the submissions of the Union of India recorded in the *NJAC Case* that they were completely inconsistent with our constitutional scheme. While contending that the *Second Judges' Case* ought to be overruled, it was also contended on behalf of the Union of India that the *Second Judges' Case* did not have any relevance because the basic structure of the Constitution would not be emasculated by the 99th Amendment. The basis of this contention, it was asserted, was that judicial appointments did not affect independence of the judiciary. Rightly rejecting the contentions, the majority judgment in the *NJAC Case* held that independence of the judiciary forms an integral part of the basic structure of the Constitution and is inextricably linked with the constitutional process of appointment of judges.

In the sole dissenting opinion, Justice Chelameswar accepted that independence of the judiciary forms part of the basic structure of the Constitution and the process of judicial appointments is one of the elements essential to establish an independent judiciary. After an analysis of various judgments commencing from *Kesavananda Bharti*, Justice Chelameswar opined that the abrogation of a particular basic feature could be said to destroy the basic structure of the Constitution depending upon the nature of the basic feature sought to be amended and the context of the amendment. He observed that the basic feature of the Constitution was not primacy of the opinion of the Chief Justice or collegium, but lay in the non-investiture of absolute power in the executive to choose and appoint judges, a feature which was not abrogated by the 99th Amendment. There was, however, no difference in opinion in Justice Chelameswar's judgment on the content of the law laid down in the *Second Judges' Case* and *Third Judges' Case* regarding independence of judiciary being an immutable feature of the Constitution.

Justice Lokur in his concurring opinion referred to the Constituent Assembly Debates and held that there was nothing therein to indicate that the Constituent Assembly had an objection to an integrated participatory role of the judiciary and executive as laid down in the *Second Judges'* and *Third Judges' Cases*. Pertinently, it was held by Justice Lokur that the Constitution being an organic and living document ought to be meaningfully, and positively interpreted. Consequently, 'consultation' with the Chief Justice of India has to be understood in that light and 'not as a "consulted and opinion rejected" situation'.[59] Justice Lokur and Justice Joseph also referring to various international conventions and documents including the Bangalore Principles of Judicial Conduct, 2002 which lay down six essential values for a judge[60] (which are accepted both in civil law and common law countries) held that such values would be totally unworkable if a person appointed as a judge, at the time of appointment, lacked basic competence and independence. It was rightly suggested that appointment of a person as a judge at the instance of a party appearing before it may impact the impartiality principle.

Another pertinent aspect dealt with in the *NJAC Case* was that consequent upon the participation of the Law Minister, a judge approved for appointment with the Minister's support may not be able to resist or repulse a plea of conflict of interest, raised by a litigant, in a matter when the executive has an adversarial role. Relying on *Madras Bar Association v. Union of India*,[61] where it was held that it was not possible to accept that a party to a litigation can participate in the selection process whereby members of the adjudicatory body are selected, the majority in the *NJAC Case* held that such a system of appointment would have an inevitable effect of undermining the independence of the judiciary. After taking note of Dr Ambedkar's observation in the Constituent Assembly Debates that the chances of influencing the conduct of a member of the judiciary by the government was very remote since the judiciary was very rarely engaged in deciding issues between the citizen and the government, the Court asserted that times had dramatically changed since the observations were made by Dr Ambedkar, and that the government, in recent times was unashamedly the biggest

---

[59] *NJAC Case* [694].

[60] United Nations Office on Drugs and Crime, 'The Bangalore Principles of Judicial Conduct' (The Hague 2002) <http://www.unodc.org/pdf/crime/corruption/judicial_group/Bangalore_principles.pdf> accessed 26 October 2016.

[61] (2014) 10 SCC 1.

litigant in the country.[62] In this view, it was held that a greater need was felt to insulate the judiciary and the judicial appointment process if independence of the judiciary were to be maintained.

To the credit of the five-judge bench in the *NJAC Case*, having stood up for the basic structure of the Constitution, they demonstrated acceptance of the criticism towards the collegium system and willingness to remedy possible errors in the future. In a new beginning for the Supreme Court, in the final order dated 3 November 2015, suggestions were invited to further transparency, define eligibility and qualifying criteria, establishment of a secretariat and a mechanism to deal with complaints or adverse reports.

I believe that the Supreme Court would be benefited by a very careful and serious dialogue with the bar to determine what possible changes can be brought about for ensuring that even after the 99th Amendment is struck down, the true aspirations of the Court reflected in its earlier judgments could be realized. Indeed, one must not forget that the life-blood of an independent judiciary has been the contribution made by many judges who have given their lives quietly and stoically in service of the cause of justice. The portraits of Justices Harilal J. Kania, Bijan Kumar Mukherjea, T.L. Venkatarama Ayyar, and H.R. Khanna in the Supreme Court are meant to signify the four separate facets of judicial excellence which they embodied, and which must guide the Supreme Court. It must be said to the great credit of the Supreme Court that the judgment in the *NJAC Case* exhibits these facets.

Conclusion

It cannot be forgotten that the quality of judicial appointments has serious implications upon the expectations of citizens in their dealings with the State. There exists the peril of altering the ecology of the human relationship between the citizen and the State.[63] As Justice M.N. Venkatachaliah said in an inaugural address as Chief Justice of India:

> No legal system, however lofty, high sounding and emotive in its professions, will mean anything by itself. The political traditions and the innate sense of honour, dignity, friendship and of liberty and justice are

---

[62] *NJAC Case* [471].
[63] Subramanium (n. 54).

the ultimate assurances of a just society. Even a nation pays, as anyone else, for what it takes out of life. It is not law alone but the psychology of a people for Law that matters. Did not Judge Learned Hand say, 'I often wonder whether we do not rest our hopes too much upon constitutions, upon laws and upon courts. These are false hopes. Liberty lies in the hearts of men and women; when it dies there, no constitution, no law, no court can save it ... while it lies there it needs no constitution, no law, no court to save it...'[64]

The strength of enforceability of a constitutional amendment must only be tested with reference to the Constitution. The amending power of Parliament is not absolute and Parliament by no means possesses the power to amend the basic structure of the Constitution.[65] To the extent that the majority judgment in the *NJAC Case* rejected the argument of majoritarianism as a means of testing the validity of the 99th Amendment, and defended the independence of the judiciary, a great service has been rendered in preserving the rule of law true to the spirit of our Constitution.

While it may be true that India has a rare distinction of being a democracy where judges appoint themselves, having regard to the general deficit of constitutional morality, and the present social and political environment, it is presently incompatible with the foundational living document to arrogate this power to the elected representatives thriving on either a fractured or an absolutist mandate.

The point is not whether judges while appointing new judges lack democratic pedigree. In some sense, it can be argued that precisely to save democracy and the rule of law, there must be judicial primacy and a consequent lack of democratic pedigree in the matter of selection of judges. Anything else might lead to a clear conflict of interest as the government by virtue of being the largest litigant in Court is an interested party in judicial selections. It is respectfully submitted that the Supreme Court of India has stood up against any attempt to make an inroad to its independence and the *NJAC Case* is a manifestation of that.

---

[64] M.N. Venkatachaliah, 'Introspection of Administration of Justice and Legal Profession' (Inaugural Address to the Supreme Court of India, New Delhi, 26 June 1993).

[65] *Indira Nehru Gandhi v. Raj Narain* (1975) Supp SCC 1.

At the same time, securing judicial independence is as much a question of law, as it is one of tradition. It is a combination of scores of judges with outstanding personal and impeccable character, a Court whose head has always been viewed as a leader, and the public perception in the hearts and minds of citizens that Courts will always be there to stay and stand up against executive encroachments and legislative aggression. Any compromise with the autonomy or independence of the judiciary would be a death knell for the rule of law.

There is also no scope for trial and error in ensuring the rule of law. Hoping that there would always be an outstanding Minister who would respect judiciary for judiciary's sake or the Constitution for Constitution's sake or eminent persons who would uphold the dignity of the institution is too risky a proposition. Judicial independence cannot be the subject of an experiment. While it is not inconceivable that such Ministers and politicians may exist, in a world of power and pelf, it is safer to act with caution, to preclude any possible manipulation in such a serious event. It is only if this is done that the Supreme Court can fulfil its tryst with destiny assigned to it under the Constitution.

III

COMPARATIVE PERSPECTIVES

Comparative Law in the NJAC Judgment

15 *A Missed Opportunity*

SUHRITH PARTHASARATHY

In October 2015, a five-judge bench of the Supreme Court delivered a portentous verdict of far-reaching significance for the state of judicial independence in India. In pronouncing as null and void the 99th Amendment, the Court not only quashed the NJAC but it also ensured the survival of the much-maligned collegium.

Given the weighty questions at stake, the judgments rendered by each of the four judges that comprised the majority—Justice Khehar, Justice Lokur, Justice Joseph and Justice Goel—ran into reams of pages. But, unfortunately, the opinions turned out to be an exercise in pleonasm. What's more, even where a thread of reasoning can be spotted in them, the explanations supplied brim with several inconsistencies and flaws. None of the judgments provide any rational, coherent argument elucidating how the 99th Amendment infracts the basic structure of the Indian Constitution;[1] none of them engages sufficiently with the Court's own precedent; each of them eschews what the Constitution's bare text tells us; and, significantly, together the judgments virtually incinerate the principle of separation of powers that sits at the bedrock of Indian democracy.

Also salient in each of the majority's opinions, and exemplifying the quality of these judgments, is an absence of even a reasonable comparative analysis. This elision is especially bemusing given that several examples were cited at the bar from other countries which look

---

[1] *See generally, Kesavananda Bharati v. State of Kerala* (1973) 4 SCC 225.

beyond the judiciary's own views—often to civil society too—in their quests to choose the best women and men as judges for their courts. The perfunctory manner in which the majority judgments engage with comparative laws is especially damning; it presents to us a picture of a Supreme Court that considers itself as not merely authoritative but also as a quasi-sovereign for whom its own superiority appears to be far too dear to be compromised.

History of Comparative Analysis and the Indian Example

Some scholars trace the use of comparative constitutional studies to as far back as Aristotle's *Politics*,[2] which involved an analysis of the laws of various Greek states in theorizing a perfect constitution. Tom Ginsburg and Rosalind Dixon, in fact, point to the tradition of using comparative analysis even in ancient India and imperial China, where assessments of statecraft—which we would today consider as matters of constitutional law—often engaged with tactics used by other territories. In the West, at the beginning of the modern era, many legal philosophers incorporated a comparative analysis to buttress arguments for the existence of a natural law.[3] This included Baron de Montesquieu, who is often regarded as the father of comparative law.[4] In his masterpiece, *The Spirit of Laws*, Montesquieu famously used foreign laws as a specific source of legislation. 'As the civil laws depend on the political institutions, because they are made for the same society,' he wrote in Chapter XIII of Book XXIX, 'whenever there is a design of adopting the civil law of another nation, it would be proper to examine beforehand whether they have both the same institutions and the same political law.'[5] Therefore the practice

---

[2] Tom Ginsburg and Rosalind Dixon (eds), *Comparative Constitutional Law* (Edward Elgar Publishing 2012) 1 (Ginsburg and Dixon). *See* David S. Clark, 'History of Comparative Law and Society' in David S. Clark (ed.), *Comparative Law and Society* (Edward Elgar Publishing 2014).

[3] Ginsburg and Dixon (n. 2).

[4] Konrad Zweigert-Hein Kotz, *An Introduction to Comparative Law* (3rd edn, OUP 1998) 50.

[5] Montesquieu, *The Spirit of Laws* (Batoche Books 2001) 612, 613 <http://socserv2.socsci.mcmaster.ca/econ/ugcm/3ll3/montesquieu/spiritoflaws.pdf> accessed 18 September 2016.

of adopting comparative analysis is certainly far from new—it has, as Ginsburg and Dixon describe it a 'long and distinguished lineage'.[6]

Today, in a world that is more internationalized than ever before, comparative constitutional law has treaded newer territories, in a bid to not necessarily arrive at homogeneity, but at least with a view to enriching national-level discussions on matters of uniform significance. Or, as Anne Marie Slaughter has put it, 'informed divergence' is just as likely an outcome.[7] A failure, though, to conduct a reasonable comparative analysis where material exists on matters of serious political and public significance could prove deeply detrimental to a proper development of the law; such insulation from global practice is usually far from beneficial.

India's approach to judicial review, although unusual, is certainly neither unique nor incomparable. There are many other countries that, like India, treat constitutional amendments as amenable to a court's appraisal. The highest courts of Germany, Turkey, South Africa, Israel, Colombia, and Brazil have each devised theories of judicial review that allow judges to rule on the substantive validity of acts that amend the respective country's constitution.[8] In recent times, there has been a considerable movement across the Commonwealth that has seen many states revise—or at least debate and deliberate over revisions to—their laws governing judicial appointments.[9] These revisions have invariably involved the establishment of an independent commission that would elicit views from a spectrum of authorities and civilians, much like the

---

[6] Ginsburg and Dixon (n. 2).

[7] *See* Anne-Marie Slaughter, 'A Brave New Judicial World' in Michael Ignatieff (ed.), *American Exceptionalism and Human Rights* (Princeton University Press 2005) 297–8.

[8] Notably, though, unlike in India, this power to test constitutional amendments in these countries flows from the text of their respective constitutions. *See* Manoj Mate, 'State Constitutions and the Basic Structure Doctrine' (2014) 45 (2) *Columbia Human Rights Law Review* 441, 450. *See also* Kemal Gözler, *Judicial Review of Constitutional Amendments: A Comparative Study* (Ekin Press 2008) 52–3.

[9] *See* Jan van Zyl Smit, 'Judicial Appointments in the Commonwealth: Is India Bucking the Trend?' (*UK Constitutional Law Blog*, 7 March 2016) <https://ukconstitutionallaw.org/2016/03/07/jan-van-zyl-smit-judicial-appointments-in-the-commonwealth-is-india-bucking-the-trend/> accessed 28 September 2016 (Zyl Smit).

NJAC that was established by the Indian Parliament. The majority's judgments, therefore, effectively abjuring any comparative analysis with other countries and their constitutions, and in rejecting outright their respective rationales for the formation of an independent commission, are deeply disappointing, and are, in many ways, symptomatic of the self-created cocoon that the Indian Supreme Court finds itself in.

Justice Khehar's Opinion and the Flaws of its Comparative Analysis

Consider, at first, Justice Khehar's opinion, in which much of the arguments advanced in favour of the 99th Amendment have been reproduced. The judge states, quite explicitly, that various counsel had placed reliance on the manner of appointment of judges in the United States of America (USA), Australia, New Zealand, Canada, and Japan to contend that in all these countries judges appointed to the higher judiciary were discharging their responsibilities independently, and that 'it was presumptuous to think that Judges appointed by Judges alone, can discharge their duties independently'.[10] Justice Khehar also points to the Attorney General's reliance on the system of judicial appointments in 15 different countries—in nine of these countries, as the Attorney General averred, a judicial appointments commission selected the higher judiciary's judges; in four countries appointments were made directly by the executive; in one European country judges were nominated by the Minister of Justice and confirmed by a Parliamentary committee; and in the USA, judges to the Supreme Court were nominated by the President and confirmed by the Senate.

The Union's intention in highlighting the process of appointment in these 15 countries was clear. It had sought to establish that in none of these states was executive involvement in the process of appointing judges considered an affront to judicial independence; on the contrary, executive involvement, and, in some cases, executive prerogative, was, in fact, seen as being necessary to ensure a proper separation of powers. However, in his leading opinion, Justice Khehar offers no rational explanation for why the NJAC—which was to comprise the Chief Justice of India, his two senior-most colleagues, the Law Minister and

---

[10] *NJAC Case* [276].

two 'eminent persons' to be appointed jointly by the Chief Justice of India, the Prime Minister and the Leader of the Opposition—ought to be treated any differently from similar commissions established by other countries. Instead, what we get is an almost-cursory dismissal of such comparative analysis, a submission, which according to Justice Khehar, did not 'require an elaborate debate'.[11]

The judge then goes on to cite paragraph 194 from a concurring opinion rendered by Justice Ratnavel Pandian in the *Second Judges' Case*:

> The outcry of some of the critics is when the power of appointment of Judges in all democratic countries, far and wide, rests only with the executive, there is no substance in insisting that the primacy should be given to the opinion of the CJI in selection and appointment of candidates for judgeship. This proposition that we must copy and adopt the foreign method is a dry legal logic, which has to be rejected even on the short ground that the Constitution of India itself requires mandatory consultation with the CJI by the President before making the appointments to the superior judiciary.[12]

This observation by Justice Pandian was both baseless and erroneous even at the time when it was made. It is therefore all the more bizarre that Justice Khehar would rely on his remark to counter the Union Government's arguments, especially when the Attorney General had specifically cited instances of countries where executive prerogative in matters of appointments was considered as conforming to the need for an independent judiciary. The idea that Justice Pandian's observation somehow negates the comparative analysis made by the proponents of the NJAC simply defeats all conceptions of common logic and reason.

Having thus brusquely dismissed the government's reliance on practices adopted in other countries by simply quoting the above paragraph from the *Second Judges' Case*, Justice Khehar proceeds to cite a study conducted by Nuno Garoupa and Tom Ginsburg of the University of Chicago's Law School. This study, according to Justice Khehar, shows that countries around the world are proceeding towards a model of appointment that insulates judges from partisan politics, and that makes selections to the judiciary 'based purely on merit'.[13] From this,

[11] *NJAC Case* [321].
[12] *NJAC Case* [321].
[13] *NJAC Case* [329].

Justice Khehar concludes, rather astonishingly, that the inclusion of the Law Minister in the NJAC, and the involvement of the Prime Minister and the Leader of Opposition in selecting the eminent persons of the NJAC is somehow a 'retrograde step'.[14]

However, there is nothing in Garoupa and Ginsburg's study to show that the NJAC would be a movement away from the popular consensus of other democratic nations; if anything, a close look at their study shows us that the use of commissions involving a broad spectrum of members is often a useful tool in furthering judicial independence; in many countries, the participation of a wide range of selectors, including members of civil society, has been seen as vital to the checks and balances required of a democracy.[15] The trend towards insulating judicial selection from partisan politics in the USA, write Garoupa and Ginsburg, 'is reflected in the growing scholarly consensus in favour of "merit selection"', and in other countries, 'it is reflected in the adoption of judicial councils, an international "best practice" designed to help ensure judicial independence and external accountability'.[16] The idea of having a judicial commission that would serve to make selections based on merit is therefore seen by Garoupa and Ginsburg as a worldwide trend. But while the question of whether these commissions help further judicial independence might well require separate analysis, any nuance in Garoupa and Ginsburg's study has been withered away by the Court's near-mechanical dismissal of the government's arguments that the NJAC is in keeping with comparative constitutional practices.

Justice Lokur's Perfunctory Dismissal of Comparative Analysis

Justice Lokur's separate, concurring opinion is characteristic of this fractured approach to comparative constitutionalism. His judgment follows no set pattern in terms of addressing arguments advanced on the basis

[14] *NJAC Case* [329].

[15] *See* Zyl Smit (n. 9).

[16] Nuno Garoupa and Tom Ginsburg, 'Guarding the Guardians: Judicial Councils and Judicial Independence' (2008) John M. Olin Program in Law and Economics Working Paper No. 444, 2–3 <http://chicagounbound.uchicago.edu/cgi/viewcontent.cgi?article=1221&context=law_and_economics> accessed 26 September 2016.

of comparative legal provisions. Citations of foreign cases are haphazardly made, and the only real reliance on any practice that transcends India is on the Beijing Statement of Principles of the Independence of the Judiciary in the LAWASIA Region.[17] Analysing these along with the Bangalore Principles of Judicial Conduct, 2002,[18] Justice Lokur concludes that 'the process for appointment and the actual appointment of a judge to a High Court or the Supreme Court is a predominant part of the independence of the judiciary and, therefore, an integral part of the basic structure of the Constitution'.[19] This is a truly stupefying inference and involves a significant logical leap. The purpose of comparative law is to relate to practices in other countries, to see how other countries and their courts interpret their own laws and constitutions, and to see whether our own practices conform to larger international standards. The Beijing Statement and the Bangalore Principles are scarcely capable of telling us what the basic structure of our Constitution is made of; but where they can be useful is in an analysis of how other signatories construe their provisions and whether these countries consider executive involvement in the appointment process as antithetical to the maintenance of an independent judiciary. But Justice Lokur conducts no such analysis. Instead he merely affirms, based on pure supposition, that judges must appoint their own brethren, as such a norm is necessary for the preservation of judicial independence.

Finally, having virtually concluded that the 99th Amendment infracts the Constitution's basic structure, Justice Lokur proceeds to avert a submission made on the basis of the United Kingdom's (UK) Constitutional Reform Act, 2005, through which a Judicial Appointments Commission was created to select judges to the courts and tribunals in England and Wales, along with *ad hoc* selection commissions for appointments to the Supreme Court. Here, rather peculiarly, Justice Lokur cites a speech made by the former Lord Chancellor Jack Straw who alluded to the difficulty in exercising an executive veto in the face of selections made by a commission comprising, among others,

---

[17] *NJAC Case* [755].

[18] Justice Lokur observes that these Principles lay down six integral values of a judge, viz., Independence, Impartiality, Integrity, Propriety, Equality, Competence, and Diligence. *NJAC Case* [756].

[19] *NJAC Case* [756].

judges. If anything, Straw's statements suggest that the view expressed by the judiciary within the confines of a commission would often be conclusive. In the NJAC too, the three judges—the Chief Justice and his two senior-most colleagues—enjoyed a majority. Although the two eminent persons on the commission can together veto a nomination suggested by its judicial wing, no person can be selected without the concurrence of any less than two of the judges. A comparative analysis with the UK's position, therefore, suggests that there is little chance of a judicial appointments commission impeding the independence of the judiciary; and what's more, the according of an executive veto in the UK only suggests that such powers are considered to be in conformity with any necessity to ensure an independent judiciary. From this, Justice Lokur somehow blithely concludes as follows: 'So much for the appointment process in the UK and the "judges appointing judges" criticism in India.'[20] Stranger still is Justice Lokur's citation of literature from Australia and South Africa, both of which allude towards the need for new systems of appointments which partake principles of transparency and accountability to conclude simply that, 'The considerations in different countries are, to put it simply, different. We need to have our own indigenous system suited to our environment and our own requirements.'[21] At their best these statements may be described as curious; at their worst, they represent a facile dismissal of comparative constitutional analysis, a factor that is, even if not at the core of the judgment's deficiencies, certainly indicative of a missing rigour.

What the Others Said

While Justice Joseph offers no independent opinion on the merits of the controversy, choosing instead to add but a few paragraphs in agreement with the other judges in the majority, Justice Goel does refer to the comparative arguments made by the Union of India. But he concludes that the Indian Constitution 'has its own background and personality', and therefore that these arguments carry little weight. He goes on to add:

---

[20] *NJAC Case* [875].

[21] *NJAC Case* [917]–[918], where Justice Lokur deals with literature from Australia and South Africa.

Models of other countries could not be blindly followed so as to damage the identity and personality of the Indian Constitution. The Judicial Commissions referred to by learned Attorney General do not show the trend of reducing the pre-existing role of judiciary. In fact, the trend is for reducing the pre-existing role of the Executive. In the impugned amendment it is the reverse....[22]

What Justice Goel does not recognize is that the reason behind his assertion—that there is no prevailing international trend towards reducing the role of the judiciary in matters of appointments—is because nowhere other than in India is the collegium system of appointment led by the judiciary prevalent. The rationale for the trend is not to reduce one organ's role vis-à-vis the other, but rather to effectuate a better balance between stakeholders in the appointments process. Seen in this light, international trends, if anything, point to a clear consensus that the involvement of the executive in matters of appointments is not in and of itself injurious to the maintenance of an independent judiciary. In fact, it is often necessary to provide a proper check and balance on the powers of judges.

Quite contrary to what the majority holds, Justice Chelameswar does recognize the importance of the comparative experience. He points out that Articles 124 and 217 of the Constitution were, in fact, themselves products of comparative analysis.[23] He notes that it was after studying the various models used by other democracies at the time that the Constituent Assembly decided to adopt, in Dr Ambedkar's words, 'a middle course'.[24] While he does not conduct a detailed analysis of the reliance placed by the Attorney General on judicial appointments in other jurisdictions, he steers clear of shunning comparative experience altogether.

Conclusion

The Supreme Court of India has historically adopted a rather chaotic approach to comparative law.[25] It has grappled with the extent to which

[22] *NJAC Case* [1103].

[23] *NJAC Case* [1146].

[24] *NJAC Case*[1146]–[1147].

[25] *See* Arun K. Thiruvengadam, 'Foreswearing "Foreign Moods, Fads of Fashions"?—Contextualising the Refusal of Koushal to Engage With Foreign Law' (2013) 6(4) *NUJS Law Review* 595 (Thiruvengadam).

it must cite—and rely—particularly on judgments of foreign courts.[26] As Arun Thiruvengadam has pointed out, in spite of a lack of consistency, the Supreme Court has used material from foreign sources for a wide stream of purposes.[27] The Court has, *among other things*, cited, often with approval, foreign cases to develop tests for violation of the equal protection clause of Article 14,[28] to find in Article 21 a right to privacy,[29] to rule against prior restraints of speech,[30] to read a due process

[26] Thiruvengadam (n. 25).

[27] Thiruvengadam (n. 25).

[28] *State of West Bengal v. Anwar Ali Sarkar*, AIR1952 SC 75.

[29] *Gobind v. State of Madhya Pradesh* (1975) 2 SCC 148. Here, Justice K.K. Mathew cited both *Griswold v. Connecticut*, 381 US 479 and *Roe v. Wade*, 410 US 113, to conclude that the U.S. Supreme Court has said that although the Constitution of the U.S.A. does not explicitly mention any right of privacy, it recognizes that a right of personal privacy, or a guarantee of certain areas or zones of privacy, does exist under the Constitution, and 'that the roots of that right may be found in the First Amendment, in the Fourth and Fifth Amendments, in the penumbras of the Bill of Rights, in the Ninth Amendment, and in the concept of liberty guaranteed by the first section of the Fourteenth Amendment' and that the 'right to privacy is not absolute'. [18] Furthermore, he stated that

> There can be no doubt that the makers of our Constitution wanted to ensure conditions favourable to the pursuit of happiness. They certainly realised as Brandeis, J. said in his dissent in Olmstead v. United States 277 U.S. 438, the significance of man's spiritual nature, of his feelings and of his intellect and that only a part of the pain, pleasure, satisfaction of life can be found in material things and therefore they must be deemed to have conferred upon the individual as against the government a sphere where he should be let alone. [20]

[30] *R. Rajagopal v. State of Tamil Nadu* (1994) 6 SCC 632. Justice B.P. Jeevan Reddy wrote,

> As observed in New York Times v. United States [1971] 40 U.S. 713, popularly known as the Pentagon papers case, 'any system of prior restraints of (freedom of) expression comes to this Court bearing a heavy presumption against its constitutional validity' and that in such cases, the government 'carries a heavy burden of showing justification for the imposition of such a restraint'. We must accordingly hold that no such prior restraint or prohibition of publication can be imposed by the respondents upon the proposed publication of the alleged autobiography of 'Auto Shankar' by the petitioners. [22]

requirement in Article 21,[31] and to explicate a fundamental, inalienable right to legal aid.[32] These citations, however, are invariably made when it appears to suit the court's ordained conclusion. When rejecting a foreign opinion, or when abjuring a constitutional practice adopted by a foreign country, the court is routinely dismissive of comparative law as a tool of decision-making. It rarely sees comparative constitutional analysis as furthering 'a process of collective judicial deliberation on a set of common problems', as Anne Marie Slaughter once said of such reflections.[33] What's foreign is foreign for a reason, the Supreme Court often seems to suggest. In the *NJAC Case*, the Court expectedly did not buck this trend.

As various studies cited before the Supreme Court show us, the practice of nations around the world is to treat independence of judiciary as integral to the maintenance of democracy. But it does not follow, as a corollary, that primacy to judges in matters of appointments is necessary to achieve this independence. It is a matter of regret that the majority's judgments in the *NJAC Case* eschew these international traditions, instead choosing to tread a course that is *sui generis* not because of any peculiar Indian requirements, but purely out of a belief that it is only judges who are capable of selecting their successors and their brethren. The logic in this argument, and its anti-democratic temper, are scarcely justifiable, whether on application of comparative principles or on application, purely, of Indian constitutional law. Therefore, in quashing the 99th Amendment, and doing so in a manner that shows little devotion to the best practices of both Indian and foreign constitutionalism, the Supreme Court has abnegated a most wonderful opportunity.

---

[31] *Maneka Gandhi v. Union of India* (1978) 1 SCC 248.

[32] *Madhav Hayawadanrao Hoskot v. State of Maharashtra*, (1978) 3 SCC 544. 'Gideon's trumpet,' wrote Justice VR Krishna Iyer, 'has been heard from across the Atlantic,' [15] and that it is clear from Justice Brennan's words that the philosophy of free legal aid is 'an inalienable element of fair procedure.' [16]

[33] Anne-Marie Slaughter, 'A Typology of Transjudicial Communication' (1994) 29 *University of Richmond Law Review* 99.

Judicialization of Judicial Appointments?

16

A Response from the United Kingdom

CHINTAN CHANDRACHUD

The United Kingdom's uncodified Constitution offers dilemmas that are exciting for theorists but confounding for the general public, in equal measure. The nature of the Constitution leaves ample ground for contestation about whether changes are best described as refinements of practice, or amendments to the Constitution itself. If ever any phase in British constitutional history were to qualify as one characterized by frequent constitutional amendments, Prime Minister Tony Blair's New Labour government would surely be towards the top of the list.[1] The amendments introduced by the New Labour government included changing the composition of the House of Lords (the Upper House of Parliament), devolving law-making authority and some executive powers from Westminster Parliament to Scotland and Wales, enacting the Human Rights Act 1998 (a domestic statute intended to give effect to the European Convention on Human Rights) and passing freedom of information legislation. The Constitutional Reform Act 2005 (CRA)—which modified the office of Lord Chancellor, established a new Supreme Court, and reformed the judicial appointments process—was amongst the most significant changes introduced by New Labour.

Perhaps unsurprisingly, the CRA played an important role in a constitutional case in a different part of the Commonwealth. In the *NJAC*

---

[1] These changes were so significant that some scholars argued that Britain had a 'new' constitution by the end of 2007. *See* Vernon Bogdanor, *The New British Constitution* (Hart 2006).

Case, the Indian Supreme Court cited the CRA (as well as developments in Australia and New Zealand) in support of the proposition that the 99th Amendment violated the basic structure of the Constitution. Justice Khehar argued that recent trends in the Commonwealth pointed towards the 'judicialisation' of the judicial appointments processes.[2] This increased role of the higher judiciary in appointments processes corresponded with the diminishment of the role of the executive. Changes would, by and large, be in the direction of reducing executive participation from existing default positions.

This essay considers whether the Supreme Court was correct in suggesting that the CRA demonstrates the trend towards judicialization of appointments processes. It concludes that the Court's analysis was reductionist at best and plainly incorrect at worst. The Court either misread a trend towards balanced appointments processes as one favouring judge-centric appointments processes, or correctly identified a trend of 'judicialisation' whilst ignoring other, equally significant trends.

The Appointments Process before the CRA

In order to deconstruct what prompted the changes brought about by the CRA, it is instructive to briefly consider the appointments process as it existed before the CRA was enacted. The Lord Chancellor, an office that goes back to at least the eleventh century,[3] played a decisive role. As head of the judiciary and a member of the cabinet, the Lord Chancellor's office exemplified Britain's modest compliance with separation of powers principles. In addition to appointments, the Lord Chancellor had several other functions concerning the judiciary: determining salary and pensions, investigating complaints, imposing disciplinary measures, and running the courts' service. The Lord Chancellor could also sit in on cases not involving the government, although this entitlement

---

[2] *NJAC Case* [329]—'[I]n the process of evolution of societies across the globe, the trend is to free the judiciary from executive and political control, and to incorporate a system of selection and appointment of Judges, based purely on merit.'

[3] Roger Smith, 'Constitutional Reform, the Lord Chancellor, and Human Rights: The Battle of Form and Substance' (2005) 32 *Journal of Law and Society* 187, 189.

was exercised very rarely in the years leading up to the CRA.[4] Of course, seldom did these overlapping functions give rise to allegations of impropriety in specific cases. Nevertheless, this 'dazzling amalgamation of titles and duties'[5] across the three branches of government gave rise to perceptions of partiality and prejudice. While one scholar described the Lord Chancellor's role as 'unsustainable' on the basis of separation of powers theory, a former Lord Chancellor conceived of the office itself as contravening essential characteristics of the Constitution.[6]

That the procedure for appointments was mired in secrecy further undermined its legitimacy in the years before the CRA. To start with, the Lord Chancellor collected information on potential candidates through what came to be known as 'secret soundings' with judges and members of the bar.[7] The widespread impression was that these soundings encouraged self-replication, since judges and members of the bar would be most likely to recommend to the bench those with similar social and professional backgrounds. Since the Lord Chancellor could not be expected to individually evaluate all candidates, the screening process involved confidential contact with unnamed informants.[8] The fact that vacancies were not advertised, the criteria for appointment were not formally articulated, and diversity was not acknowledged as an overriding principle of the appointments process, meant that it

---

[4] Lord Windlesham, 'The Constitutional Reform Act 2005: Ministers, Judges and Constitutional Change: Part 1' (2005) *Public Law* 806, 807.

[5] Lord Falconer, 'The Role of the Lord Chancellor after the 2005 Reforms' (Bentham Association Presidential Address, London, 11 March 2015) <https://www.laws.ucl.ac.uk/wp-content/uploads/2015/03/The-Role-of-The-Lord-Chancellor-After-the-2005-Reforms-Lord-Falconer-of-Thoroton-PC-QC.pdf> (accessed 24 August 2016).

[6] Diana Woodhouse, *The Office of the Lord Chancellor* (Hart 2001) 18–19.

[7] Sophie Turenne, 'Judicial Independence in England and Wales' in Anja Seibert-Fohr (ed.), *Judicial Independence in Transition* (Springer 2012) 157—'Before the CRA, the opinions of judges and senior lawyers were sought on the applicants. This was known to its critics as secret soundings, with the result that the appointment depended on the visibility of the individual to the judges through social and work networks.'

[8] Mary Clark, 'Advice and Consent versus Silence and Dissent? The Contrasting Roles of the Legislature in US and UK Judicial Appointments' (2011) *Louisiana Law Review* 451, 482.

was widely suspected that appointments to the bench could be used as instruments of political patronage.

Concerns had also been raised about the fact that an overwhelming majority of judges came from a remarkably narrow social background. The imagery of a judge as a public school educated elite white male from Oxford or Cambridge remained powerful. Representation of women and ethnic minorities on the bench was shamefully low, even compared to other professions at the time. Some reports suggested that whereas 59 per cent of all law graduates were women, they constituted only 28 per cent of district judges, 11 per cent of circuit judges, and 7 per cent of High Court judges.[9] In 2001, less than 2 per cent of judges across England and Wales belonged to ethnic minorities.[10] Diversity of professional background was also lacking, since the pool of candidates under consideration was restricted to barristers.

The Design and Functioning of the CRA

Although disagreements between the Lord Chancellor (Lord Irvine) and the Home Secretary (David Blunkett) formed the immediate impetus for the CRA,[11] the CRA was more broadly aimed at addressing the concerns raised by the incumbent appointments process. As Beatson explains, the CRA strengthened the separation of powers in at least three ways: first, by divesting the Lord Chancellor of his role as head of the judiciary; second, by establishing a permanent judicial appointments commission which restricted the role of members of the political executive in the appointments process; and third, by transferring the functions of the Appellate Committee of the House of Lords to a new

[9] Commission on Women and the Criminal Justice System, *Women Working in the Criminal Justice System* (Interim Report, Fawcett Society, March 2004).

[10] Courts and Tribunals Judiciary, *Annual Diversity Statistics 2001* (23 March 2010) <https://www.judiciary.gov.uk/publications/annual-ethnicity-statistics-2001/> (accessed 24 August 2016).

[11] Lord Mance, 'Constitutional Reforms, the Supreme Court, and the Law Lords' (2006) *Civil Justice Quarterly* 155, 157. The long-standing feud between Lord Irvine and David Blunkett was based on a multitude of issues, including conflicting policy approaches towards immigration and asylum, as well as an attempt to shift ministerial responsibility for the courts from the Lord Chancellor to the Home Office.

Supreme Court established in a building in the south-west corner of Parliament Square in London.[12] The CRA also codified many aspects of a 'concordat' addressing the allocation of authority between the Lord Chancellor and the Lord Chief Justice.

For England and Wales, a Judicial Appointments Commission (JAC), an independent body which is not an agent of the Crown and does not form part of the executive, was entrusted with the appointments process for judges of all higher courts except for the Supreme Court. The JAC is a permanent, fifteen-member Commission. It consists of five judicial members, two professional legal members (one solicitor and one barrister), six lay members who have never practiced law or held judicial office, one member from a tribunal or other similar offices, and one lay justice.[13]

The JAC has the responsibility for advertising vacancies and assessing candidates for appointment. Only candidates recommended by the JAC may be appointed. Appointments are made solely on the basis of merit, although this requirement was clarified in 2013 to indicate that when candidates are of equal merit, the JAC is free to appoint the candidate that improves diversity on the bench.[14] With the introduction of the JAC, the Lord Chancellor's powers were heavily circumscribed. The Lord Chancellor has the power to accept, reject, or seek reconsideration of the candidate recommended by the JAC, up to three times for each vacancy.

Appointments to the Supreme Court are made by an *ad hoc* commission which is convened each time a vacancy arises. The commission consists of the President of the Supreme Court, a senior judge nominated by the President of the Supreme Court, and one member each from the judicial appointments commissions for England and Wales, Northern Ireland and Scotland.[15] As is the case with the JAC, the Lord Chancellor may accept, reject, or seek reconsideration of the candidate.[16] Since the commission presents a single name, rather than a list

---

[12] Jack Beatson, 'Reforming an Unwritten Constitution' (2010) *Law Quarterly Review* 48, 54.

[13] CRA, schedule 12, part 1.

[14] *See* Crime and Courts Act 2013, schedule 13, part 2 (amending s 63 of the CRA).

[15] CRA, schedule 8, part 1.

[16] CRA, s 29.

of names, the Lord Chancellor's discretion is significantly restricted.[17] The CRA requires at least one of the members of the commission to be a lay person. Further, when the appointment of the President of the Supreme Court is under consideration, the outgoing President cannot be a member of the commission, and the commission must be chaired by one of the lay members.[18]

Having considered the design of the judicial appointments process, it is worth examining whether the Indian Supreme Court was accurate in its analysis that the CRA evinces the increasing judicialization of the judicial appointments processes. Quite remarkably, the CRA contains a specific guarantee of judicial independence. Section 3 provides that '[t]he Lord Chancellor, other Ministers of the Crown and all with responsibility for matters relating to the judiciary or otherwise to the administration of justice must uphold the continued independence of the judiciary'. This section entails two specific duties. The first is a duty on Ministers of the Crown not to seek to influence particular judicial decisions through specific access to the judiciary. The second duty requires the Lord Chancellor to have regard to the need to defend the continued independence of the judiciary, the need for the judiciary to have proper support necessary to enable them to exercise their functions, and the need for public interest in matters relating to the judiciary or otherwise to the administration of justice to be properly represented in decisions affecting those matters.

In many ways, the CRA increased judicial influence over the appointments process. Seven of the fifteen commissioners of the JAC and at least two out of the five members of the selection commissions for the Supreme Court are judges. At the lower levels, judges make formal appointments—the Lord Chief Justice, for the lower courts and the President of the Tribunals, for the tribunals. When the JAC makes appointments, the Lord Chief Justice is consulted before each cycle. Judges prepare case studies and qualifying tests and write references.[19] A judge also sits on the interviewing panel. Interestingly, despite the

---

[17] *See* Robert Hazell, 'The Continuing Dynamism of Constitutional Reform' (2007) 60 *Parliamentary Affairs* 3, 18.

[18] CRA, schedule 8, part 1.

[19] Graham Gee, Robert Hazell, Kate Malleson, *The Politics of Judicial Independence in UK's Changing Constitution* (CUP 2015) 180.

increase in judicial influence occasioned by the CRA, large sections of the judges strongly criticized the proposals at the outset. The criticism, however, seemed to be directed predominantly towards the fact that with the change in responsibilities of the Lord Chancellor, judicial interests would no longer be adequately represented before the political branches. At a public event in 2003, Lord Woolf (then the Lord Chief Justice) was reported to have queried about who would 'take on the Lord Chancellor's role of speaking up for the judiciary in Government and Parliament,'[20] should the Lord Chancellor's duties be circumscribed as planned.

However, to conceive of the changes brought about by the CRA purely through the prism of judicial independence misses important parts of the picture. The Lord Chancellor-led appointments process before the CRA was widely criticized for its secret soundings and 'tap on the shoulder' system,[21] in which proposed candidates would be approached directly without advertisements of posts or open competition. This was seen as undermining public confidence in the appointments process in particular and in the courts in general. One of the major objectives of the new regime was to reaffirm public confidence through a range of transparency promoting measures, such as advertisements of posts. Selection methods of the JAC now involve a number of activities, including interviews, written tests and role play. As one scholar observes, 'Much judicial business which was previously conducted behind closed doors in the old Lord Chancellor's Department is now out in the open.'[22]

Of course, it was also acknowledged that a fully transparent appointments process would have a chilling effect on applications—the argument being that potential applicants would be concerned by the reputational ramifications of being unsuccessful. The balance between increasing public confidence and encouraging applications was achieved by providing that the applications to the JAC would remain

[20] Joshua Rozenberg, 'Lord Woolf Discards the Sheep's Clothing', *The Telegraph* (London, 10 July 2003).

[21] Penny Derbyshire, *Sitting in Judgment: The Working Lives of Judges* (Hart 2011) 56; Mark Elliott and Robert Thomas, *Public Law* (2nd edn, OUP 2014) 248.

[22] Robert Hazell, 'Judicial Independence and Accountability in the UK Have Both Emerged Stronger as a Result of the Constitutional Reform Act 2005' (2015) *Public Law* 198, 203.

confidential. Further, candidates concerned with maladministration in handling their application would be entitled to make complaints to an Ombudsman, who would have the power to uphold the complaint and make recommendations for redress.

The CRA also sought to address the lack of diversity in the judiciary and alter the 'white-male-public school-Oxbridge' image described earlier. Amongst the concerns of having a judiciary-controlled or judiciary-dominated appointments process is that it promotes self-replication based on background and social characteristics. It is hardly difficult to imagine why incumbent judges would consider those with similar backgrounds as most suitable successors. This is precisely the reason for which the JAC and the Supreme Court selection commissions include lay persons. In addition to the objective of minimizing self-replication, lay persons also offer different perspectives to the evaluation of candidates. The JAC includes more robust lay person participation than the Supreme Court selection commissions. Nevertheless, since an overwhelming majority of Supreme Court judges are appointed from amongst existing members of the bench, it is likely that, *ceteris paribus*, most Supreme Court judges would have been assessed by lay persons at some stage of their career. Overall, the appointments process established by the CRA ensured that responsibility for appointments is fragmented, rather than vested singularly in the office of the Lord Chancellor.

The discussion thus far has focused predominantly on the institutional design established by the CRA, rather than on the way in which the CRA has impacted upon the appointments process in practice. Serious questions continue to linger about whether the CRA has genuinely increased diversity on the bench. While the representation of women as well as people from black or minority ethnic backgrounds has improved considerably in the lower courts and tribunals, progress in the higher judiciary has been far slower. Baroness Hale was the only female judge of the House of Lords when the CRA was being considered. She remains the only female judge in the Supreme Court's seven-year history. Only seven of the thirty-eight judges of the Court of Appeal are women.[23] This has prompted many scholars to argue in favour of a quota system

---

[23] Geoffrey Bindman QC and Karon Monaghan QC, *Judicial Diversity: Accelerating Change* (Report submitted to Sadiq Khan, Shadow Secretary of State for Justice, November 2014) [5.7] (Bindman QC and Monaghan QC).

based on gender and ethnicity for appointments to the judiciary.[24] A large proportion of judges were barristers. As the only current member of the Supreme Court not to have been a practicing barrister, Baroness Hale once again constitutes the exception to the norm.

In a similar vein, it is often argued that the CRA judicialized the appointments to a far greater extent than that intended by its designers. Although the chair of the JAC is a lay person, the judicial members exercise decisive control in the appointments process. The JAC is accused of playing into the very self-replication concerns that it was intended to avoid. Although the Lord Chancellor theoretically has three options on the table (accept, reject, or reconsider), on only four occasions has he done something other than accepted a recommendation.[25] In two of these cases, the Lord Chancellor preferred to turn down the candidacy on the basis that it was 'it was better to have fewer judges' than to appoint the proposed candidates and in the others, he was 'stretched to find the number of candidates' that he was being asked to select.[26]

Of course, Justice Khehar's judgment in the *NJAC Case* was concerned solely with the design of the CRA, and did not investigate whether there was a disjunction between the promise of the CRA and its performance in practice. The Indian Supreme Court was operating in the domain of intentions, since the petitioners in the case challenged the validity of the 99th Amendment before it could take effect. Thus, even if we were to accept the claim that the CRA has effectively judicialized the appointments process, that is different from the Court's claim that the CRA was *self-consciously designed* to do so.

To be fair, not all of the opinions in the *NJAC Case* examined the CRA as a matter of constitutional design. Justice Lokur, for example, considered how judicial appointments operated *in practice* since the

---

[24] Kate Malleson, 'Diversity in the Judiciary: The Case for Positive Action' (2009) 36 *Journal of Law and Society* 376. *See also* Bindman QC and Monaghan QC (n. 23).

[25] Select Committee on the Constitution, *Judicial Appointments* (House of Lords 2012, 272) [2] <http://www.publications.parliament.uk/pa/ld201012/ldselect/ldconst/272/272.pdf> accessed 29 August 2016 (House of Lords Select Committee).

[26] House of Lords, *Transcript of Evidence Taken before the Select Committee on the Constitution* (7 December 2011) (Lord Toulson) 10–11.

CRA entered into force. His opinion concluded (quite fairly) that the appointments process was dominated by the judiciary, prompting him to comment that the 'judges appointing judges' syndrome is hardly distinctive to India.[27] Nevertheless, the opinion did not consider whether the system operated in the manner it was designed to function, or whether the transfer of power to the judiciary was an unintended consequence of the reforms. If increasing judicialization is attributable to the second reason rather than the first, it is difficult to see how the CRA validates the collegium system in any way.

The disproportionate influence of the judiciary in the appointments process has, in fact, prompted the House of Lords Select Committee to suggest changes to redraw the balance of decision-making power.[28] For instance, the Committee acknowledged the problems associated with the judge-heavy *ad hoc* Supreme Court selection commissions, and recommended increasing the lay presence from one to two members (one of them as the chair). It also reiterated that the composition of the JAC must consist of a balance of lay and judicial members. Thus, the direction of travel in recent years has been with a view to moderating judicial involvement in the appointments process in favour of the involvement of lay members, in order to achieve the balance originally envisaged by the CRA.

Conclusion

Experience from the UK tells us that the Indian Supreme Court's reliance on comparative law in support of the claim that the Commonwealth is moving in the direction of 'judicialising' processes for judicial appointments is either plainly wrong or highly reductionist. One way of construing the narrative is that the focus in the UK was not on enhancing the role of the judiciary at the expense of the executive, but instead on fragmenting the appointments process amongst a range of actors, including the government, judges, and civil society. In other words, the 'most favourable position' on the 'spectrum of possibilities'[29] would not

[27] *NJAC Case* [478].

[28] House of Lords Select Committee (n. 25).

[29] Jan van Zyl Smit, 'Judicial Appointments in the Commonwealth: Is India Bucking the Trend?' (*UK Constitutional Law Blog*, 7 March 2016) <https://

give judges exclusive control over the appointments process, but would balance control amongst different actors. On this analysis, the Court's approach was plainly mistaken. In fact, this narrative would consider the 99th Amendment—an attempt to balance control over appointments amongst stakeholders—as consistent with, rather than antithetical to, the changes in appointments processes in the Commonwealth.

However, even if we were to accept the Court's narrative that the CRA evinces increasing judicialization of appointments processes, its approach was highly reductionist. The CRA espoused objectives aside from increasing the influence of the judiciary (or insulating appointments from executive control), including procuring civil society participation, promoting transparency, and diversifying the composition of the judiciary at all levels. For the Indian Supreme Court to selectively recognize one trend without identifying the others is deeply problematic.

---

ukconstitutionallaw.org/2016/03/07/jan-van-zyl-smit-judicial-appointments-in-the-commonwealth-is-india-bucking-the-trend/> accessed 28 September 2016.

17 South Africa—Analysing a Commission Model

CHRIS McCONNACHIE

Judicial primacy in the selection of judges is a foreign concept in South Africa. Like many other countries, South Africa has developed a version of the commission model for judicial selections. Under this model, judges are picked by bodies made up of members from different branches of the state and other institutions. This is in contrast with unitary models, which leave this decision to a single branch of the state, such as the judiciary or the executive.[1]

South Africa's Judicial Service Commission (JSC) plays a central role in the selection of judges.[2] The JSC was the product of the negotiations that resulted in South Africa's transition to democracy in 1994. Its design reflects a complex mix of hard-fought compromise, international borrowing, and lessons from the country's difficult history. As a result, the JSC is very specific to South Africa's context, although it still offers some helpful comparative insights.

---

[1] For deeper analysis of the available models, *see* Nuno Garoupa and Tom Ginsburg, 'Guarding the Guardians: Judicial Councils and Judicial Independence' (2009) 57 *The American Journal of Comparative Law* 103, 105–19 (Garoupa and Ginsburg); Sujit Choudhry and Katherine Glenn Bass, *Constitutional Courts after the Arab Spring: Appointment Mechanisms and Relative Judicial Independence* (IDEA 2014) ch 4.

[2] This essay will not address the appointment of magistrates, who are selected by a separate Magistrates' Commission.

The JSC's performance over the last two decades has been the subject of much debate.[3] It has achieved many successes, including bringing greater transparency to the selection process and improving the diversity of the judiciary. There have also been concerns. The large contingent of politicians on the JSC has been a source of constant anxiety, as many have feared undue political influence over appointments. Yet for all these fears (and several scandals), the South African judiciary remains independent and credible.

In this essay I critically analyse the JSC as an example of the commission model. A full assessment of its performance over the last two decades would require a book in itself. I will instead highlight some general trends which offer insights for judicial selection in India and elsewhere.

I argue that the JSC's record shows the complex relationship between selection processes and judicial independence. The combined effect of the judgments in the three *Judges' Cases* in India seems to suggest that judicial primacy in selections is an essential requirement for independence. The South African experience shows that this is not necessarily true. Whether selection processes enhance or undermine judicial independence depends on a range of variables; the identity of those doing the selection is just one factor.

This analysis of the JSC will be divided into three parts. In the first part, I provide some background to the creation of the JSC. The second part analyses the JSC's role in the judicial selection process and its composition. The third part assesses three broad themes in the JSC's work: first, its impact on the independence of the judiciary; second, its contribution to transparency in the selection process; and, third, its role in transforming the judiciary after apartheid.

Background

South Africa's transition to democracy in 1994 brought about many changes, not least to the role and selection of judges.

---

[3] For general appraisals of the JSC, *see*, e.g., Kate Malleson, 'Assessing the Performance of the Judicial Service Commission' (1999) 116 *South African Law Journal* 36; Penelope Andrews, 'The South African Judicial Appointments Process' (2006) 44 *Osgoode Hall Law Journal* 565; Morné Olivier and Cora Hoexter, 'The Judicial Service Commission' in Cora Hoexter and Morné Olivier (eds), *The Judiciary in South Africa* (Juta 2014) (Olivier and Hoexter).

Before 1994, South Africa operated under a system of white minority rule with Westminster-style parliamentary sovereignty. Under this system, judicial appointments were entirely controlled by the executive. The Minister of Justice selected judges, with the State President rubber-stamping his decisions. There was some informal consultation with the judiciary and the legal profession, but the Minister was not bound by their advice. These selection processes were also opaque and there was no public involvement of any kind.[4]

The system of apartheid had a significant effect on judicial appointments. After taking power in 1948, the National Party set about implementing its apartheid policies. Judicial appointments during this time were heavily weighted in favour of those sympathetic to the regime. Pockets of independence remained, but most judges were executive-minded and broadly supportive of the apartheid system.[5]

South Africa's transition to democracy in 1994 was made possible by a multi-party negotiation process in the early 1990s. Representatives of all major political groups came together to negotiate South Africa's new Constitution.

The negotiating parties agreed that South Africa would embrace constitutional supremacy, with a fully justiciable Bill of Rights. Given that the judiciary would be handed greater power, the role and appointment of the judiciary came under close scrutiny.

Unitary models of judicial appointment were unpalatable. On the one hand, the apartheid-era showed the danger of giving the executive complete control over judicial selection. On the other hand, judicial primacy in selections would have been disastrous. In 1994, the 166

---

[4] *See further* Hugh Corder, 'Appointment, Discipline and Removal of Judges in South Africa' in HP Lee (ed.), *Judiciaries in Comparative Perspective* (Cambridge University Press 2011) 96, 98; Morné Olivier, 'The Selection and Appointment of Judges' in Cora Hoexter and Morné Olivier (eds), *The Judiciary in South Africa* (Juta 2014) 116, 117–20.

[5] The extent to which the judiciary retained its independence under apartheid is a matter of some debate. For deeper analysis, *see* Hugh Corder, *Judges at Work: The Role and Attitudes of the South African Appellate Judiciary, 1910–50* (Juta 1984); Christopher Forsyth, *In Danger for their Talents: A Study of the Appellate Division of the Supreme Court of South Africa from 1950–80* (Juta 1985); Christopher Forsyth, 'The Judiciary under Apartheid' in Cora Hoexter and Morné Olivier (eds), *The Judiciary in South Africa* (Juta 2014).

judges in South Africa included just three black men and two white women.[6] The prospect of an overwhelmingly white, male, conservative judiciary perpetuating itself through judicial appointments made this option untenable.

Ultimately, the negotiating parties agreed on a hybrid system of judicial selection, which included the creation of the JSC. The JSC would have the final say over some judicial appointments while the President would decide others, as is explained below. In choosing this model, the parties were heavily influenced by the growing use of judicial commissions in other countries.[7] However, the final design and composition of the JSC owed much to the political bargains struck between the negotiating parties.

The JSC was established under the interim Constitution, which came into force in April 1994.[8] Its composition and functions were refined in the 1996 Constitution.[9] In what follows, I will describe the JSC as it exists under the 1996 Constitution.

Overview of the JSC and the Selection Process

Functions

The JSC has three broad functions. First, it plays a leading role in the selection of judges. Second, it plays a role in the discipline and removal of judges. Third, it is also empowered to advise the government on judicial affairs. I will concentrate on the JSC's role in judicial selection, as it has been far more active in this area.

The Selection Process

As mentioned earlier, the 1996 Constitution creates a hybrid process for the selection and appointment of judges. Section 174 of the Constitution allocates the President and the JSC different roles in the

---

[6] Catherine Albertyn, 'Judicial Diversity' in Cora Hoexter and Morné Olivier (eds), *The Judiciary in South Africa* (Juta 2014) 245, 246 (Albertyn).

[7] *See also* Hugh Corder, 'The Appointment of Judges: Some Comparative Ideas' (1992) *Stellenbosch Law Review* 207; Olivier and Hoexter (n. 3) 155–6.

[8] Constitution of the Republic of South Africa (Act 200 of 1993).

[9] Constitution of the Republic of South Africa, 1996 (1996 Constitution).

selection process, depending on what type of judicial vacancy needs to be filled.

South Africa's superior court system has three tiers. At the apex is the Constitutional Court, which is the highest court in all matters. The Supreme Court of Appeal is the second highest court and exercises appellate jurisdiction. The High Court has divisions in all nine provinces.[10] It sits as a court of first instance and also exercises appellate jurisdiction over its own decisions and decisions of the lower courts.

The President has the final say in the appointment of the Chief Justice and Deputy Chief Justice of the Constitutional Court. The President exercises this power 'after consulting' with the JSC and the leaders of opposition parties. The President also appoints the President and Deputy President of the Supreme Court of Appeal, after consulting the JSC.[11] In contrast with India, the phrase 'after consulting' is interpreted as giving the decision-maker the final say, after taking advice from others.

In respect of all other judges of the Constitutional Court, the JSC must prepare a list of candidates for the President, which must include three names more than the number of vacancies. If there is one vacancy, four names should be put forward. The President then selects a candidate from the list. The President may request the JSC to supplement the list if none of the candidates are deemed suitable.[12]

The JSC makes the final decision in the selection of all judges of the Supreme Court of Appeal and the High Court.[13] The President must make these appointments 'on the advice' of the JSC, which leaves the President with no discretion.

Public interviews and public comment form an integral part of the JSC's selection process.[14] Once a judicial vacancy has been

---

[10] There are also a range of courts with similar status to the High Court, including the Labour Court and the Land Claims Court.

[11] 1996 Constitution (n. 9) s 174(3).

[12] 1996 Constitution (n. 9) s 174(4).

[13] 1996 Constitution (n. 9) s 174(6).

[14] This process is detailed in the 2003 JSC Procedures, published as GNR 423 in *Government Gazette* No 24596 of 27 March 2003. For analysis of these steps in the process, *see* Democratic Rights and Governance Unit, *Judicial Selection in South Africa* (DGRU 2013) <http://www.dgru.uct.ac.za/usr/dgru/downloads/Judicial%20SelectionOct2010.pdf> accessed 15 April 2016 (JSC Procedures).

declared, the JSC issues an invitation for nominations. Any person may nominate a candidate in writing, provided the candidate accepts the nomination. Nominations are then screened and shortlisted candidates are invited to interview with the JSC. In preparation for these interviews, the nominations are made available for public comment. The respective bar councils and civil society groups play an important role in this process, as they regularly submit extensive comments on the candidates.[15] Interviews are then held in open forums, attended by the media and members of the public. Interviews have been broadcast on television and the radio and are now also available via live streaming services.[16] The JSC's deliberations happen behind closed doors, but the JSC is required to give reasons for its decisions on demand.

Composition

The JSC's composition is one of its most controversial features. Section 178(1) of the 1996 Constitution provides that the JSC consists of 23 regular members, which increases to 25 members when the JSC considers matters relating to a particular division of the High Court. In those cases, the Premier (the head of the provincial executive) and the Judge President of that division join the JSC's ranks.

Of the 23 regular members of the JSC, only three are judges. The Chief Justice chairs the JSC, joined by the President of the Supreme Court of Appeal and a Judge President of one of the divisions of the High Court. A further four members are required to be lawyers, including two attorneys and two advocates (the South African equivalents of solicitors and barristers). One member must be a legal academic.

Eleven of the 23 members are politicians. They include the Minister of Justice, six members of the National Assembly, and four members of the National Council of Provinces (the two houses of Parliament). Of the six members of the National Assembly, at least three must be

---

[15] The bar councils generally elect not to make their comments available to the public, but civil society groups often publicise their comments, particularly where they raise matters of public interest.

[16] *See* Judges Matter <http://www.judgesmatter.co.za/> accessed 15 April 2016 (Judges Matter).

members of opposition parties. The final four members are selected by the President after consulting with opposition parties. In practice, these members tend to be drawn from the legal profession, although this is not a requirement.

The JSC is also supported by a full-time secretariat that is responsible for the administration, finances, and logistics.

The JSC's size and its large political membership set it apart from judicial commissions in other countries. India's proposed NJAC was conservative by comparison, with judges making up three of its six members. The NJAC was more in line with the international trend, as most commissions are smaller bodies with a greater proportion of judges relative to politicians.

The JSC's Record

I now turn to analyse the JSC's record over the last two decades, considering three broad themes: judicial independence, transparency, and transformation.

Judicial Independence

The JSC's influence on judicial independence is complex and contested. The JSC's composition creates the possibility for party-political manipulation of the selection process. However, this danger has been largely prevented by the range of interests represented on the JSC, the power-dynamics between members, and the checking role of the media and civil society.

Since the JSC's creation, there have been constant fears that the judicial selection process would be captured by party-political interests. The ruling African National Congress (ANC) has at least eight politicians on the JSC. When the President's four appointees are included, the ANC determines at least 12 of the 23 regular members. The ANC's dominance over political life and its policy of 'deploying' ANC members to senior positions in the civil service have added to these anxieties.

Some of the JSC's decisions have appeared to confirm these fears. Over the past two decades, there has been criticism of the JSC for not selecting several candidates who had a record of opposing the government. The JSC has also been slow to act in instituting disciplinary proceedings against judges who are perceived to be favoured by the government.[17]

Partisan politics have also been displayed at the JSC's public interviews, as these interviews have often become sparring grounds for politicians. This was again evident in the April 2016 round of interviews, which took place in the shadow of the Constitutional Court's judgment in *EFF v. Speaker of the National Assembly* (the *Nkandla* judgment).[18] In that judgment, the Court held that President Jacob Zuma had a duty to repay public money spent on upgrades to his private residence at Nkandla. In the JSC interviews, ANC-aligned members asked questions that showed thinly veiled distaste for the judgment. Members of the opposition parties shot back with their own questions, designed to show the full extent of the President's misconduct.[19] To add to the political drama, these interviews took place the day before Parliament debated whether to impeach the President for his unconstitutional conduct.

Despite these concerns and difficulties, there has been no ANC-led capture of the selection process. It is not possible to identify a definite pattern of appointments that favour the government, despite some questionable decisions.

The selection process has also not diluted the judiciary's actual or perceived independence. The judiciary retains a reputation for independence and this continues to be displayed in its judgments. Following a series of high-profile decisions against the ANC government, including the recent *Nkandla* judgment, this reputation is perhaps stronger than at any time in South Africa's history.

What explains the JSC's ability to avoid political capture of the selection process? A full answer is beyond the scope of this piece, but some tentative suggestions can be offered.

---

[17] For further analysis of these controversies, *see* Olivier and Hoexter (n. 3) 172–98.

[18] *Economic Freedom Fighters v. Speaker of the National Assembly and Others; Democratic Alliance v. Speaker of the National Assembly and Others* [2016] ZACC 11 (31 March 2016).

[19] Niren Tolsi, 'Aspirant Judges Find That JZ Saga Weighs on the JSC', *Mail & Guardian Online* (8 April 2016) <http://mg.co.za/article/2016-04-07-jz-saga-weighs-on-the-jsc> accessed 15 April 2016.

First, the composition of the JSC allows for a balance of perspectives. The inclusion of opposition party members, judges, and members of the legal profession certainly dilutes the influence of the ruling party.

Second, the Chief Justice's role as chairperson of the JSC also has an influence. In the early years, some JSC members expressed concern that members were too deferential to the Chief Justice's views in deliberations.[20] Whether this remains the case is unclear. What is certain is that the Chief Justice exerts a measure of control over interviews, keeping questioning in line, and generally bringing an air of dignity to proceedings.

Third, the media and civil society have also played an important role. The media reports extensively on interviews, analysing the performance of candidates, and trends in questioning. The legal profession and civil society have also helped to hold the JSC accountable, primarily through their written comments on candidates and by monitoring JSC proceedings. The recently formed civil society coalition, Judges Matter, will play an increasingly important role in monitoring the JSC and making its work more accessible to the public.[21]

Debates about the composition of the JSC and its influence on judicial independence will continue to rage. This level of public debate and scrutiny is made possible by the relatively transparent way in which the JSC conducts the selection process. The JSC's contribution to transparency is perhaps one of its greatest achievements.

Transparency

The JSC's practice of holding public interviews started in 1994. This practice has since been formalized in the JSC's rules of procedure.[22] The process of calling for public comment on nominees has also helped to make the process more transparent. The legal profession and NGOs submit detailed comments and analysis of candidates. The quality

---

[20] Malleson (n. 3) 38.

[21] Judges Matter (n. 16). Judges Matter is a coalition led by the University of Cape Town's Democratic Governance and Rights Unit. The coalition publishes extensive commentary on candidates and JSC proceedings on its website as well as providing a live streaming service.

[22] JSC Procedures (n. 14).

of this input can be variable, but there appears to be a growing level of scrutiny of nominees. The JSC has extended this transparency to the appointment of the Chief Justice. The President makes the final decision on the appointment of the Chief Justice and no provision is made for the JSC to hold a public interview for the President's nominee. Nevertheless, the JSC insisted on holding an interview before the President appointed Chief Justice Mogoeng in 2011. The two-day interview was aired on live television, with all aspects of the candidate's professional and personal life scrutinized in detail. This resulted in unprecedented levels of public interest in the judicial selection process. One of the fears in India is that open interviews and public comments would provide a platform for character assassination of candidates. The JSC interviews have a reputation for being bruising, with occasional inappropriate questions or comments. Anecdotal evidence suggests that some candidates have not applied for appointment out of fear of public humiliation. However, there has never been any suggestion that the comments and questioning are malicious. On balance, the benefits of transparency have far outweighed the occasional indelicate treatment of candidates.

While public interviews and comment allow for greater openness, there has been less transparency in other aspects of the JSC's work. The JSC's process of short-listing nominees for interview remains largely opaque. The public is also barred from the JSC's deliberations after interviews. For some time, the JSC insisted that it was not obliged to give reasons for its decisions, as its decisions are taken by secret ballot. However, in *Judicial Service Commission v. Cape Bar Council*, the Supreme Court of Appeal affirmed that the JSC, as an organ of state, has a duty to give reasons for all of its decisions following a proper request.[23] The JSC's reasons tend to be terse, but a culture of reason-giving is likely to develop over time.

Transparency is, of course, not the preserve of a commission model. There is no reason in principle why unitary models of judicial selection cannot emulate these features of public hearings and public comment. While a commission model does not necessarily breed transparency, the South African experience shows that transparency plays an important role in guarding against political capture.

---

[23] *Judicial Services Commission v. Cape Bar Council*, 2013 (1) SA 170 (SCA).

Transformation

The literature tends to characterize the choice between different models of judicial selection as being a choice between different degrees of independence and political accountability.[24] In South Africa, a third element should be added to this choice: the need to transform the judiciary. As mentioned earlier, if judicial selection had been left to judges, the judiciary would likely have remained dominated by white men.

The JSC has made transformation one of its central aims. This in line with the Constitution, which requires decision-makers to consider the need for racial and gender diversity in selecting judges.[25] The diverse membership of the JSC has played a role in advancing this goal as it has avoided the danger of a legal elite selecting judges in their own image.

Transformation remains a contested and complex goal in South Africa.[26] Understood purely in demographic terms, there has been substantial transformation in the judiciary. From an overwhelmingly white judiciary in 1994, black judges are now in the majority, with all three tiers of the superior court system headed by black judges.

Gender transformation has been far slower, with women making up just over 30 per cent of the judges.[27] While the pace of gender transformation leaves much to be desired, there are promising signs. In the December 2015 round of appointments, eight of the 12 vacancies were filled by women. Earlier in 2015, all four candidates to fill a vacancy on the Constitutional Court were women. The President appointed Justice Nonkosi Mhlantla to the Constitutional Court, bringing the number of women on the Court to three out of the eleven judges. In the previous two decades, the Court had never had more than two women on the bench at any given time.

Despite progress, transformation is still a fraught topic. The JSC has not been able to articulate precisely what it means by transformation and how transformation goals are to be balanced against other selection criteria. It is perhaps too much to expect a multi-member body to

---

[24] *See* Garoupa and Ginsburg (n. 1) 105–6.

[25] 1996 Constitution (n. 9) s 174(1).

[26] *See also* Andrews (n. 3); Murray Wesson and Max Du Plessis, 'Fifteen Years On: Central Issues Relating to the Transformation of the South African Judiciary' (2008) 24 *South African Journal on Human Rights* 188.

[27] Albertyn (n. 6) 246.

offer a single definition of this broad aim. However, the uncertainty about this aim has led some to speculate that transformation is often used as a sub-text for partisan politics. No doubt, this subject will continue to fuel public debate.

Conclusion: Lessons from the South African Experience

The JSC is a product of South Africa's particular history and context. It would be naïve to think that the JSC model could or should be duplicated in other countries. However, if the South African experience can offer one lesson, it is this: the impact of judicial selection processes on the independence of the judiciary cannot be reduced to categorical statements.

The JSC has shown that the involvement of politicians and members of the executive in judicial selection does not necessarily erode judicial independence. A commission's performance and impact are dependent on many variables, including the different internal and external checks and balances. Over the last twenty years, the JSC's selection processes have largely supported judicial independence. In a different context, with different political forces and a weaker civil society, the selection process could have been captured by partisan political interests. That danger is not a reason to jettison the JSC or to criticize the commission model. Instead, it is a reason for greater public scrutiny and efforts to hold these bodies accountable. No selection model is perfect. Whether judicial selections produce the right outcomes will depend on a measure of faith, good leadership, and a healthy dose of public scrutiny.

Appointments to the Supreme Court of Canada

18

Procedures and Controversies

PETER McCORMICK

In recent times, the procedure for appointments to the Supreme Court of India, as well as the High Courts in its states has occupied centre stage in public discourse, with the Indian Supreme Court having delivered a constitutionally significant judgment in the *NJAC Case* in October 2015. Recently, if briefly, Canada's Supreme Court appointment procedures were also a major focus of the national news. In 2014, the Court decided over a single solo dissent that the recent appointment of a new justice, Justice Marc Nadon, to the Supreme Court was invalid because he lacked the full set of relevant qualifications.[1] This was as unprecedented as the public battle of words that ensued between the Prime Minister and the Chief Justice. The immediate public drama aside, the case is lastingly important less for what it said about the appointment process than for how it clarified the constitutional status of the Supreme Court itself.[2] Unfortunately, the immediate consequence of the contretemps was the abandonment of recent experiments in favour

---

[1] *Reference Re Supreme Court Act ss. 5 and 6*, 2014 SCC 21 (Supreme Court of Canada).

[2] A lack of textual clarity in the Constitution Act 1982 made it unclear which of the various amending formulae applies to which aspects of the Supreme Court—or (on the most technical reading) whether anything about the Supreme Court was 'in' the Constitution in the first place. The Court has now made it clear that only the most routine procedural aspects of the institution can be modified without formal constitutional amendment.

of a reversion to a more closed and secretive judicial appointment procedure. This essay will explore the history and the practice of Supreme Court appointment procedures in Canada that provide the context for this remarkable episode.

Canada's Supreme Court: Status and Powers

As in most other common law countries, the Supreme Court of Canada is the single apex court of the Canadian judicial system. It has ultimate legal authority with respect to constitutional matters while also serving as a final court of appeal for civil, criminal, and public law cases. The balance between the various types of appeals has varied over time; civil appeals dominated the caseload for many decades, with a growing criminal caseload since the 1950s and a more recent burgeoning of public law and constitutional cases. A major factor in this recent evolution of the caseload was the constitutional entrenchment of the Canadian Charter of Rights and Freedoms in 1982 (Charter), although there has always been a steady flow of constitutional cases involving federalism issues as well. Constitutional cases of various sorts are a major part of the Supreme Court caseload, making up about 40 per cent of all cases, and this proportion was even higher (over 50 per cent) in the early 1990s.[3]

In recent decades, the Supreme Court's constitutional role has been a major element of Canadian politics, more so because the Court has been willing to apply the entrenched Charter very vigorously, and because it has championed a conception of federalism that has sometimes conflicted with the national government's approach. The Supreme Court of Canada was once famously described, seriously and entirely credibly, as 'the quiet court in an unquiet country';[4] the same claim today would lack all credibility. The Court is so publicly visible and active that, much to the Court's displeasure, it was recently presented

---

[3] For a closer consideration of the evolving caseload of the Supreme Court, *see* Peter McCormick, *Supreme at Last: The Evolution of the Supreme Court of Canada* (James Lorimer & Company Ltd 2000).

[4] Ronald I. Cheffins, 'The Supreme Court of Canada: The Quiet Court in an Unquiet Country' (1966) 4(2) *Osgoode Hall Law Journal* 259.

with a 'Policy Maker of the Year' award from a national think-tank for its constant interventions in the public policy process.[5]

Although Canada is a federal country, its judicial system can be diagrammed as a unitary hierarchical pyramid. Below the Supreme Court are the provincial superior courts of appeal, and below them are the provincial superior trial courts. Although both are provincial courts established by provincial statutes, the judges who serve on them are appointed and paid by the federal government. In recent decades, almost all Supreme Court justices have been elevated from the provincial courts of appeal, while most appeal court judges in turn previously served on the provincial superior trial courts. The lowest tier of the court system is the 'purely provincial' courts, also established by provincial statute, whose judges are appointed and paid by the provincial government. Both the (provincially appointed) provincial courts and the (federally appointed) provincial superior courts deal with matters involving either provincial or federal law[6]—they are different levels within a single judicial pyramid, rather than American-style parallel pyramids—and there is in theory no legal matter that could not be appealed all the way to the Supreme Court.[7] A relatively small federal court system (including both trial and appellate levels) is appended to this single pyramid, with a limited jurisdiction dominated by federal administrative law and immigration matters; its decisions can also be appealed to the Supreme Court.

Establishing the Supreme Court and Appointing Its Judges

The Supreme Court of Canada was not directly established by the country's initiating constitutional document, the British North America Act

[5] *See* Benjamin Perrin, *The Supreme Court of Canada: Policy-Maker of the Year* (Macdonald-Laurier Institute November 2014) <http://www.macdonaldlaurier.ca/files/pdf/MLI_SupremeCourt_NewFinal_web_r2.pdf> accessed 5 March 2016.

[6] Criminal law is federal legislative jurisdiction, but many criminal charges are dealt with by provincial court judges; civil law is provincial jurisdiction, but civil law suits dealing with large amounts of money are handled by the higher—federally appointed—trial courts.

[7] This making Canada unlike the United States, where most matters of state law, and even of state constitutional law, cannot be appealed to the United States Supreme Court.

1867 (since renamed the Constitution Act 1867).[8] However, there is a permissive provision (Section 101) which empowers the Parliament of Canada to establish a 'General Court of Appeal for Canada',[9] and this is what it did when it passed the Supreme Court Act[10] in 1875. This genesis and the dominance of the national government at this early stage of Canadian federalism explain why the appointment procedure described in the Supreme Court Act is so brief and unilateral,[11] involving the national government alone with no role for provincial governments in staffing a court that is, among other things, the referee of Canadian federalism. Only the francophone majority (and civil law) province of Quebec is statutorily guaranteed a presence on the Court,[12] although there is a long-standing convention that the other seats are assigned to specific regions—in addition to the three judges from Quebec, there are normally three judges from Ontario, one from the four Atlantic provinces,[13] and two from the four Western provinces.[14]

The fact that the Supreme Court was the creature of a regular federal statute rather than formal constitutional entrenchment has meant that the federal government could unilaterally make any desired changes to the institution through routine statutory amendments. In 1927 and 1949 it increased the size of the court from the initial six justices to seven and then nine; and in 1975 (and again in 1999) it reduced the category of 'appeals by right' in favour of a leave process that has given the Supreme Court extensive (but not yet complete) control

---

[8] It is similarly curious that the Supreme Court Act was not one of the statutes listed in the Constitution Act 1982 as forming part of the Constitution of Canada.

[9] Constitution Act, 1867, s 101 (Canada).

[10] The current version is Supreme Court Act, 1875, RSC 1985, c S-26 ('Supreme Court Act') (Canada); although the Act has been amended a number of times, (for example, expanding it from six to seven and then nine judges) it has not been changed in any fundamental way.

[11] Supreme Court Act, s 4.2—'The judges shall be appointed by the Governor in Council by letters patent under the Great Seal.'

[12] Supreme Court Act, s 6.

[13] These four provinces are Nova Scotia, New Brunswick, Prince Edward Island, and Newfoundland and Labrador.

[14] These four provinces are British Columbia, Alberta, Saskatchewan, and Manitoba.

over its own docket.[15] The most important change in the status of the Supreme Court was accomplished in 1949, when the federal statute was amended to abolish appeals beyond the Supreme Court to the Judicial Committee of the Privy Council after a reference case had been taken to the Judicial Committee itself to confirm that Parliament had this legislative capacity.[16]

However, there have never been any statutory changes to the appointment procedure, which continues to be legally defined by Section 4.2 of the 1875 statute. In practice, of course, 'Governor in Council' means the federal cabinet, more so because there is no suggestion that the Governor-General has ever hesitated over a recommendation; and 'federal cabinet' has in practice always meant the Prime Minister himself (with varying degrees of involvement by federal Ministers of Justice), on the basis of whatever criteria and whatever investigation process he thought appropriate at the time. Some limits are included in the Supreme Court Act—an appointee must be 'a judge of a provincial superior court of a province, or a barrister or advocate of at least ten years standing of the bar of a province'.[17] The wording is slightly different in Section 6.1 for the appointment of judges from the francophone-majority province of Quebec, and this is what gave rise to the unusual case mentioned earlier.[18]

Although there have been no statutory (let alone constitutional) changes to the appointment procedure for Supreme Court justices since

---

[15] The 1999 changes have reduced the proportion of appeals by right to about 5 per cent of the total caseload, mostly criminal cases in which there was a dissent on a matter of law in the provincial court of appeal; most appeals by right are dealt with summarily with oral decisions 'from the bench' immediately after oral argument.

[16] *Attorney-General for Ontario v. Attorney-General for Canada (Privy Council Appeals Reference)* [1947] AC 127 (Judicial Committee of the Privy Council).

[17] Supreme Court Act, s 5.

[18] Looking at the wording of the current statute is misleading because it continues to include (in s 6.1) the words of a parliamentary amendment to the Supreme Court Act that was declared by the Supreme Court in 2014 to be unconstitutional. This situation is not unusual, because neither the federal nor the provincial governments have any established practice of dealing with such judicial rebukes by removing sections or phrases that have been found unconstitutional.

the Court was established in 1875, significant changes in actual practice emerged in the 1970s. This was a remarkable decade for the Canadian judicial system, with major changes (new courts established, long-standing courts transformed or amalgamated, new institutions created and new procedures laid down to handle complaints against judges) put in place by the national government and all ten provincial governments. With respect to the Supreme Court, the Prime Minister and the Minister of Justice established a new system of broad consultation for all federal judicial appointments which involved gathering of personal and professional information to create a standing 'bank' of names for consideration, regular interaction with the various Chief Justices and law school deans and provincial justice ministers to solicit names of possible candidates, and a close connection with the Canadian Bar Association's national committee on the judiciary.[19]

The result of this new process has been a major transformation of the 'normal' credentials of federally appointed judges generally and of the Supreme Court in particular. Most significantly, the previous importance of political party connections and experience (D.C. Abbot in 1954 was appointed straight out of the federal cabinet, I.C. Rand and J.W. Estey in 1943 and 1944 from provincial cabinets) has been replaced by an emphasis on experience in public service, most notably service on Law Reform Commissions.

There was an important new emphasis on judicial experience. Before 1970, about half of the appointees to the Supreme Court lacked prior judicial experience, and the others often had only brief trial court experience. Since 1970, all but a handful of the appointees have had significant appeal court experience. Academic backgrounds have also become more important, with a string of former deans and professors from law schools to have been appointed to the Supreme Court. The first products of this new process for appointments have been described as 'the most learned and scholarly set of judges ever to join the Supreme Court'.[20] Finally, there was a new emphasis on a more visibly representative Court, replacing the long-standing monopoly of middle-aged (or

[19] Edward Ratushny, 'Judicial Appointments: The Lang Legacy' in Allen M. Linden (ed.), *The Canadian Judiciary* (Osgoode Hall Law School 1976) 31–46.

[20] James G. Snell and Frederick Vaughan, *The Supreme Court of Canada: History of the Institution* (University of Toronto Press 1985) 236.

older) white males of French or British descent. Bora Laskin became the first Jewish justice in 1970 (there have been three others since); Bertha Wilson the first woman to serve on the Court in 1982 (there have been eight others since); John Sopinka the first Ukrainian-Canadian in 1988; and Frank Iacobucci the first Italian-Canadian in 1991.

Modern Experiments in Appointment Reform

More substantive changes have also emerged in the appointments process. In the late 1980s, Prime Minister Brian Mulroney was briefly willing to consider a system whereby the Prime Minister would appoint justices from shortlists submitted by provincial premiers, but this notion died with the failure of the Meech Lake Accord[21] without there having been a Supreme Court vacancy that would have necessitated working out the details. A decade later, a new Prime Minister, Paul Martin, spoke of a 'democratic deficit' in the way Supreme Court justices were appointed, and touched off a dozen years of short-lived innovations, the changes coming so steadily that no two successive appointments were handled in quite the same way.

The first such innovation occurred in 2004, for a pair of new appointments (Rosalie Abella and Louise Charron). When the names were announced, the Minister of Justice appeared before the House of Commons Standing Committee on Justice to answer questions about the search process and the qualifications of the individuals concerned. The nominees themselves did not appear before the Committee, and the hearings closed without a vote of any kind. Commentators found the process more curious than transformative; one referred to it as the equivalent of sending your mother to your job interview.[22]

The next Supreme Court vacancy, two years later, involved a more robust process. An advisory committee was established which included politicians from each recognized party in the House of Commons, a

---

[21] A package of proposed constitutional changes negotiated between the Prime Minister and the provincial premiers in 1987, so named for the locale of the meeting where the negotiations took place.

[22] See Editorial, 'A Feeble New System for Screening Judges' The Globe & Mail (Toronto, 25 August 2004) <http://www.theglobeandmail.com/opinion/a-feeble-new-system-for-screening-judges/article1332965/> accessed 5 March 2016.

nominee of the provincial law societies, a nominee of the provincial Ministers of Justice, and two lay members; this group received a 'long shortlist' from the federal Department of Justice and reduced it to a 'short shortlist' of three names, from which the Prime Minister made a selection.[23] The nominee then appeared before a 12-member *ad hoc* House of Commons committee chaired by the Minister of Justice. The dean of one of the country's major law schools presided over the proceedings, which were nationally televised. The idea of a formal protocol that would have restricted the scope of the questions was considered but abandoned. The process lasted three and a half hours; as before, it closed without a vote of any kind, and the nominee was formally appointed to the Court a week later.[24]

The use of the same procedure for the next Supreme Court vacancy was interrupted by inter-party wrangling because of which the seat sat empty for an unprecedented length of time. The Prime Minister simply announced the name of a nominee, and although there was an indicated intention of having that person appear before an *ad hoc* Commons committee, this plan was abandoned when the Commons was dissolved for an early election.[25] The process was therefore changed again, with the Minister of Justice submitting a 'long shortlist' to a special committee of five House of Commons backbenchers, three from the governing party, whose confidential deliberations reduced the list

[23] The procedure was followed even though the government that set it up was defeated in a general election partway through the process, such that a new Prime Minister from a different party was in office to receive the recommendations; this created an interesting and genuinely multi-partisan dimension to the process. *See* Peter McCormick, 'The Serendipitous Solution to the Problem of Supreme Court Appointments' (2006) 44(36) *Osgoode Hall Law Journal* 539, 542.

[24] For accounts of the process by the law school dean who presided, *see* Peter Hogg, 'Appointment of Justice Marshall Rothstein to the Supreme Court of Canada' (2006) 44(3) *Osgoode Hall Law Journal* 527.

[25] *See* Peter Hogg, 'Appointment of Thomas A. Cromwell to the Supreme Court of Canada' (2009) Supreme Court Working Paper 2009-5, Institute of Intergovernmental Relations, School of Policy Studies, Queen's University <http://www.queensu.ca/iigr/sites/webpublish.queensu.ca.iigrwww/files/files/pub/archive/DemocraticDilemma/ReformingTheSCC/SCCpapers/HoggFINAL.pdf> accessed 5 March 2016.

to three names from which the Prime Minister made the final choice. But this was the procedure that on next use culminated in 'l'affaire Nadon', the appointment of a justice who was determined by the Court itself not to be qualified for appointment, so it in turn went by the board in the scramble to deal with the unexpected embarrassment and the continuing vacancy.

The next three appointments—including the 'replacement' of Nadon—were handled in *ad hoc* and much more secretive ways. The appointment procedure has been susceptible to constant changes because none of them ever took statutory (let alone constitutional) form, but were simply self-constraining announcements by the Prime Minister. The curious consequence, then, is that despite more than a decade of experiments with more nuanced procedures for the appointments to the Supreme Court, Canada has reverted to closed and unilateral secrecy. The public contretemps between the Prime Minister and Chief Justice dramatically highlighted the challenge of institutional interactions between Court and government in this new age of judicial power,[26] but at the apparent cost of completely undoing what little progress had been made on the appointment process.

Challenges That Lie Ahead

Another election in 2015 has resulted in another change of government, and again there is talk of institutional reform—but the Supreme Court does not seem to be on the list. The first item on the new government's reform agenda is electoral reform to replace the current single-member plurality-vote electoral system; the next is the issue of Senate reform, or at least of an interim appointment procedure pending more substantial reform, that body having been rocked by a recent string of embarrassing scandals. To date, there has been no suggestion of revisiting the judicial appointment process, nor was this matter featured in the 'mandate letters' that Canadian Prime Ministers now send to their newly appointed ministers after an election.

There has been a rapid turnover in the membership of the nine-judge Court, with 13 appointments having been made since 1 January 2000,

---

[26] Brent Cotter, 'The Prime Minister v the Chief Justice of Canada: The Attorney General's Failure of Responsibility' (2015) 18(1) *Legal Ethics* 73.

and this is continuing with a somewhat surprising retirement (Thomas Cromwell) in March 2016. A more significant vacancy, occasioned by mandatory retirement at the age of 75 will occur in the fall of 2018; this will involve Chief Justice Beverley McLachlin, the longest serving Chief Justice in the history of the institution. Consequently, there will be a double vacancy, first of one of the nine seats and second of the Chief Justice's centre seat. The formal provisions for the appointment of a Chief Justice are even more casual—the statute says only that '[t]he Court shall consist of a chief justice to be called the Chief Justice of Canada, and eight puisne judges'[27] without any indication of how the designation of the Chief Justice comes about. In practice, this has always been treated as a separate appointment in its own right, with Chief Justices serving until retirement rather than for specific time-limited terms followed by either possible reappointment or a return to the ranks.[28] The appointment of a new Chief Justice is almost always from within the ranks of the puisne judges at the time the vacancy occurs.[29]

Just as the Prime Minister has always had the ultimate say in appointments to the Supreme Court, so it is with the designation of the Chief Justice. Historically, there has been a general practice of recognizing seniority; Charles Fitzpatrick in 1906, Francis Anglin in 1924, and John Laskin in 1973 are the only three counter-examples.[30] Some have suggested an expectation of more recent vintage of a rotation between Quebec and non-Quebec judges.[31] This process has almost never been problematic; the only real example of controversy was the appointment as Chief Justice of the very junior Laskin over five more senior members of the Court in 1973, which was criticized publicly

---

[27] Supreme Court Act, s 4.1.

[28] Specific limited terms with a return to the ranks are now the regular practice for Chief Judges of the provincial courts established under s 92 of the Constitution. *See* Peter McCormick, *Judicial Independence and Judicial Governance in the Provincial Courts* (Canadian Association of Provincial Court Judges 2004) Part III.

[29] There is only a single exception, that being the 1906 appointment of Charles Fitzpatrick (the Federal Attorney General) to the Chief Justiceship.

[30] *See* Peter McCormick, 'Choosing the Chief: Duality, Seniority and Beyond' (2013) 47(1) *Journal of Canadian Studies* 5.

[31] Peter W. Hogg, *Constitutional Law of Canada* (Thomson Reuters Canada Ltd 2012) sec. 8.3.

and within the profession as undermining the Court's judicial independence.[32] Nothing, however, came of the complaints, and the system has remained unchanged, untouched by even the transient experiments in the appointment process described above.[33]

It is perhaps curious that the judicial appointment process has not been more of an issue, because its unilateral nature exposes the Court to political attack on grounds of being 'Ottawa's Court' rather than a genuinely neutral referee of federalism. As Peter Russell has pointed out, Canada is 'the only constitutional democracy in the world in which the leader of the government has an unfettered discretion to decide who will sit on the country's highest court'.[34] It must not be forgotten that in a country like Canada, where the Court is responsible both for protecting entrenched constitutional rights from governments and for maintaining the appropriate balance between the legislative pretensions of federal and provincial legislatures, this is highly problematic, even if it has (not yet, not quite) led to a major crisis.

[32] *See* Philip Girard, *Bora Laskin: Bringing Law to Life* (Osgoode Society/University of Toronto Press 2005) 407–27.

[33] This is, of course, partly because the modern Chief Justiceship does not change hands very often—the replacement of McLachlin in (presumably) 2018 will be only the second in a quarter century.

[34] Peter Russell, 'A Parliamentary Approach to Reforming the Process of Filling Vacancies on the Supreme Court of Canada' (Brief presented to the Standing Committee on Justice, Human Rights, Public Safety and Emergency Preparedness, 23 March 2004) 1.

Judicial Appointments in Pakistan

19 *The Seminal Case of the 18th Amendment*
SAMEER KHOSA

Extensive changes were made to the Constitution of the Islamic Republic of Pakistan, 1973 (Constitution), through the Constitution (Eighteenth Amendment) Act, 2010 (18th Amendment), which received Presidential assent on 19 April 2010. Among other things, the process for appointment of judges to the Superior Courts[1] was amended to include prior inputs from a much wider array of functionaries and individuals. Almost immediately after its passage, the Amendment was challenged before the Supreme Court in its original jurisdiction.[2] The Court was asked to strike down a constitutional amendment—something it had never done before.

The Supreme Court of Pakistan decided these constitutional challenges in *District Bar Association, Rawalpindi and others v. Federation of Pakistan and others.*[3] By a majority of 14 to 3, the Supreme Court dismissed the petitions and upheld the 18th Amendment.[4] However,

---

[1] The term 'Superior Courts' is used to denote collectively the various High Courts, the Supreme Court of Pakistan and the Federal Shariat Court.

[2] Constitution of the Islamic Republic of Pakistan (Constitution), art. 184(3). Under this provision, the Supreme Court has original jurisdiction to hear matters of public importance that relate to the enforcement of the Fundamental Rights conferred by Chapter 1 of Part II of the Constitution.

[3] PLD 2015 SC 401 (*District Bar Association*).

[4] In fact, in relation to the portion of the 18th Amendment relating to the appointment of judges, the majority was 16 to 1, as discussed later.

in essence, the judicial appointments process that has been upheld is different from the one originally envisioned by the 18th Amendment. This essay discusses the appointments process as it existed prior to the 18th Amendment, and the changes it brought about, along with the jurisprudence of the Superior Courts around the appointments process. The essay culminates with an examination of the judgment in *District Bar Association* and the appointments process which now exists.

Procedure Prior to the 18th Amendment

Before the 18th Amendment, Article 177 of the Constitution dealt with the appointment of the Chief Justice of Pakistan (CJP) and the judges of the Supreme Court. In relation to the CJP it provided simply that he 'shall be appointed' by the President. Judges of the Supreme Court were to be appointed by the President in consultation with the CJP. Under Article 193, the Chief Justice of a High Court was to be appointed by the President in consultation with the CJP and the Governor of the Province concerned. A judge of a High Court was to be appointed by the President in consultation with the CJP, the Chief Justice of the concerned High Court, and the Governor of the concerned Province.

These provisions had to be clarified in various judgments of the Superior Courts since problems arose in their practical implementation. The appointments procedure was therefore extensively clarified in a series of important cases commencing with the case of *Al-Jehad Trust v. Federation of Pakistan.*[5] Essentially, the Supreme Court held that there was a nexus between judicial appointments and judicial independence and interpreted the constitutional provisions in a manner that elevated the position of judicial functionaries in the appointments process and reduced the role of the executive functionaries.

---

[5] PLD 1996 SC 324 (*Al-Jehad Trust*). For a detailed account of the circumstances leading up to and following this case, as well as a summary of the basic judicial determinations held by the Supreme Court in this series of cases, *see* Hamid Khan, *Constitutional and Political History of Pakistan* (Oxford University Press 2005) 782–92.

The 18th and 19th Amendments

The 18th Amendment inserted Article 175A in the Constitution, which amended the method of appointment of judges to the Superior Courts. Under Article 175A, a Judicial Commission of Pakistan (JCP) was established for the purpose of such appointments.

For appointment of judges to the Supreme Court, the JCP was to consist of the CJP as its Chairperson, two senior-most judges of the Supreme Court, a former Chief Justice/Judge of the Supreme Court to be nominated by the CJP, in consultation with the two senior-most judges, for a period of two years, the Federal Minister for Law and Justice, the Attorney-General for Pakistan, and a senior advocate of the Supreme Court to be nominated by the Pakistan Bar Council for a period of two years.[6] Thus, the JCP was to consist of seven members, out of which three would have been serving judges.

For appointments to the High Courts of the various provinces, the membership of the JCP was expanded to include the Chief Justice and the senior-most judge of the concerned High Court, along with the provincial Minister for Law, and a senior advocate to be nominated by the Provincial Bar Council.[7] The expanded membership would be eleven out of which five will be serving judges. Similarly, for appointments to the Islamabad High Court (which is in Federal territory) and the Federal Shariat Court, the JCP was to include the Chief Justice and the senior-most judge of these courts respectively.[8]

The 18th Amendment also clarified that the President 'shall appoint' the senior-most judge of the Supreme Court as the CJP.[9] For appointment of the Chief Justice of the High Courts and Federal Shariat Court, the senior-most judge of that court who would otherwise have been a member of the JCP would be replaced by a former Chief Justice/Judge of that court to be nominated by the CJP in consultation with the two senior-most judges of the Supreme Court.[10]

---

[6] Constitution, art. 175A(2).

[7] Constitution, art. 175A(5).

[8] Constitution, arts. 175A(6), (7).

[9] Constitution, art. 175A(3).

[10] Constitution, art. 175A(5), first proviso. Similarly, if the Chief Justice of the relevant court is not available for any reason, he would be replaced in the JCP in the same manner.

Apart from the JCP, the 18th Amendment also constituted an eight-member Parliamentary Committee with representation from the National Assembly and the Senate (four members from each House) and two members each from the Treasury and Opposition benches in each House (to be nominated by their respective leaders).[11] The process laid down under the new Article 175A was that for each vacancy, the JCP (having the power to regulate its own procedure) would nominate one name and forward it to the Parliamentary Committee for consideration. The Committee would then have 14 days to confirm the nomination through a majority of its membership, failing which the nomination would be deemed approved. However, the Parliamentary Committee could reject a nominee acting only through a three-fourths majority, in which case the JCP would have to provide a fresh nomination.

In *Al-Jehad Trust*, the Supreme Court had insulated the judicial appointments process from excessive political interference. It had since been felt that the judiciary almost exclusively controlled the judicial appointments process and there was little accountability for the decisions made. The 18th Amendment was clearly aimed at changing this balance. It was no surprise, therefore, that when the challenges to the 18th Amendment were brought before the Supreme Court, one of the main issues argued by the petitioners was that the possibility of serving judges being outvoted on the JCP, and the nomination of the JCP being subject to confirmation by the Parliamentary Committee opened the way for outside interference in, and politicization of, the appointments process thereby affecting judicial independence. Even then, the 18th Amendment did have some safeguards built in. For example, while the serving judges could potentially be outvoted, the other members of the JCP were also genuinely linked with the legal profession representing valid stakeholders, and some members (such as the retired judge) were to be nominated by the serving judges and could bring genuine judicial insight by virtue of their experience. Furthermore, the nomination of the JCP could only be overturned within fourteen days, and after garnering a supermajority (three-fourths) in the Parliamentary Committee.

Nonetheless, an activist Supreme Court headed by Chief Justice Iftikhar Muhammad Chaudhry constituted a full bench of seventeen

---

[11] Pakistan has a bicameral legislature consisting of a National Assembly and a Senate.

judges to hear these challenges in *Nadeem Ahmed, Advocate v. Federation of Pakistan.*[12] The case was argued over several months and given the stakes—the Court was deciding whether it could overturn a constitutional amendment unanimously passed by the first freely elected Parliament in a decade in a matter that conveniently involved its own appointments procedure—there was a serious risk of an ensuing institutional and political crisis if the Amendment was overturned.

Perhaps this is why, while the Supreme Court had reserved the matter for judgment, when it did finally announce its decision on 21 October 2010, instead of giving a final judgment, the Court passed an interim order stating certain 'concerns/reservations' that had arisen during the course of arguments regarding the new procedure for appointments, and referred the matter back to the Parliament for reconsideration in light of these reservations and certain 'suggestions.'[13]

Interestingly, after referring the matter to Parliament, instead of disposing them of, the Supreme Court adjourned the pending petitions thus sending a clear message—even though the matter had been referred to Parliament, the issue was kept pending (and alive) with the obvious indication that if the 'concerns' were not addressed the Court could take up the matter again. The Supreme Court also held that pending reconsideration by Parliament the provisions of the 18th Amendment would be given effect. In this regard, if the Parliamentary Committee disagreed with any nomination made by the JCP, it would record specific reasons, which would be justiciable before the Supreme Court.[14] Hence, final say was also retained by the Court during the interim period. The Court was clearly engaging in institutional dialogue here through its quite unique interim order, and extending an opportunity to Parliament to head off a confrontation.

As a result, and in light of the interim order, Parliament passed the Constitution (Nineteenth Amendment) Act, 2010 (19th Amendment) further amending the new procedure that had been introduced by the 18th Amendment. The composition of the JCP was expanded to include four (instead of two) senior-most judges of the Supreme Court, to increase the weight of judicial opinion. Further, it was provided that

---

[12] PLD 2010 SC 1165 (*Nadeem Ahmed*).

[13] *Nadeem Ahmed* (n. 12) [8]–[10], [13].

[14] *Nadeem Ahmed* (n. 12) [15].

in case the Parliamentary Committee decided not to confirm a nominee of the JCP it would record its reasons for doing so and its decision, along with the reasons, would be sent to the JCP. However, it did not state that those reasons would be justiciable. Also, the deliberations of the Parliamentary Committee would be in camera, a record of which would be preserved.

The net effect of the two constitutional amendments is that the process of appointment of judges now involves a judicial commission, which has representation from the current judiciary, legal experts (in the form of lawyers, former judges, and the Attorney-General), and the executive (through the Minister for Law). Further, through the Parliamentary Committee the elected representatives of the public also have representation in the process. However, if the serving judges have agreed on a nomination they cannot be outvoted on the JCP, and the Parliamentary Committee can only disagree by a three-fourths majority within 14 days after giving reasons and keeping a detailed record of its proceedings.

As it so happened, after the legislative watering down of the 18th Amendment in the form of the 19th Amendment, the Court would further consider some cases that would strengthen the judiciary's role in the appointments process and minimize that of the Parliamentary Committee.

The Supreme Court's Examination of the Role of the Parliamentary Committee

While the extent of the role, equality of vote given to non-judicial members of the JCP, and possibility of the judges being outvoted were all issues raised in the petitions challenging the 18th Amendment, it was the introduction of the Parliamentary Committee that was most controversial. It was contended that the members of the Parliamentary Committee were ill-equipped and unqualified to judge legal acumen and calibre, and giving the last word in the matter of appointments to politicians would inevitably lead to undermining the independence of the judiciary.

While the 19th Amendment stated that the Parliamentary Committee had to provide reasons for rejecting any nomination of the JCP, it did not state that those reasons would be justiciable. Consequently, immediately upon passing of the 19th Amendment, this matter was raised in the Supreme Court.

The JCP had recommended the tenure of certain Additional Judges of the Lahore and Sindh High Courts to be extended for a further period. However, the Parliamentary Committee rejected the JCP's decision. The decision of the Parliamentary Committee was challenged in *Munir Hussain Bhatti, Advocate and Others v. Federation of Pakistan*.[15] A four-member bench of the Supreme Court held that even though the 19th Amendment did not state as much, a proper construction of Article 175A would lead to the conclusion that the decisions of the Parliamentary Committee were in fact justiciable by the Supreme Court. The Supreme Court also held that the Parliamentary Committee was not to be understood as a body that sat in review of the nominations made by the JCP. It was the JCP, comprising legal experts, that was best suited to judge the legal acumen, and competence of a candidate. If the JCP had decided to nominate an individual after consideration of the material before it, it was not open to the Parliamentary Committee to take a different view of the same material. The Parliamentary Committee, instead could look into the antecedents of a candidate, or consider material that was not before the JCP.

This was an immediate assertion of authority by the Supreme Court. In essence, by interpreting the role of the Parliamentary Committee in a way that corresponded almost exactly with the previous role of the executive prior to the 18th and 19th Amendments the Court through interpretation was taking the amended procedure, as far as possible, back to what it was prior to the amendments. In fact, it explicitly stated that the 18th and 19th Amendments were to be read consistently with the law established by the Supreme Court on judicial appointments prior to the two amendments.[16] Interestingly, as part of this interpretation, the Supreme Court held that the Parliamentary Committee (despite its explicit nomenclature) is better understood only as a 'Committee of Parliamentarians', actually performing an executive function and is an independent constitutional body not answerable to the Parliament.[17]

15 PLD 2011 SC 407 (*Munir Hussain Bhatti*).
16 *Munir Hussain Bhatti* (n. 15) [45].
17 *Munir Hussain Bhatti* (n. 15) [32].

Munir Hussain Bhatti had two important outcomes. First, the Supreme Court functionally restricted the nature and type of considerations that the Parliamentary Committee could have in its deliberations in a way that corresponded almost exactly with what the executive's role was prior to the 18th Amendment. This was notwithstanding the fact that the purpose of the amendments had clearly been to change that role. Further, by making the reasons of the Parliamentary Committee even in that limited sphere justiciable, it restored the last word in the matter to the serving judges on the JCP. A petition filed by the Federation for review of this decision was also rejected in *Federation of Pakistan v. Munir Hussain Bhatti.*[18]

The Judicial Commission of Pakistan

In stark contrast to their approach towards the Parliamentary Committee, the courts were quick to insulate the decisions of the JCP from any review. This became evident when controversy arose with regard to nominations made by the JCP to certain vacant positions in the Islamabad High Court. It had been a long-standing convention that where judges are appointed through the same notification, the senior in age is considered the senior judge as between them. However, the JCP that made these nominations included a judge who was not the senior-most judge of the Islamabad High Court as per that convention. Further, the senior-most judge was also not nominated for appointment as the next Chief Justice of the Islamabad High Court.

The issue was whether the JCP's decisions were invalid and vitiated the whole process since it was improperly constituted. The Parliamentary Committee also did not reject the nominations. However, the President issued a reference under the advisory jurisdiction of the Supreme Court. In *Reference No. 1 of 2012*[19] and *Nadeem Ahmed, Advocate v. Federation of Pakistan,*[20] the Supreme Court heard these challenges together and

---

[18] PLD 2011 SC 752.

[19] PLD 2013 SC 279 (*Presidential Reference*).

[20] 2013 SCMR 1062—This is a separate case of the same title and is not to be confused with the interim order passed in the challenge to the 18th Amendment mentioned earlier in *Nadeem Ahmed* (n. 12).

held that the proceedings of the JCP were not vitiated because it had reached its decisions by clear majorities and therefore the proceedings were not materially affected even if it was considered that one judge who sat in the proceedings did not belong there. It further held that after nomination by the JCP and the Parliamentary Committee, the role of the President in issuing the notification of appointment was simply ministerial.

Of interest is how the Court dealt with the issue regarding passing over the senior-most judge for appointment as the next Chief Justice. In *Munir Hussain Bhatti* the Supreme Court utilized the fundamental principles established by case law governing the appointment of judges prior to the 18th and 19th Amendments to diminish the role of the Parliamentary Committee.[21] At the same time, the Court conveniently shunned principles developed and recognized by case law while assessing the role of the JCP. For instance, *Al-Jehad Trust* recognized that the senior-most judge had a legitimate expectancy to be appointed as the Chief Justice. Evidently, this expectation was based not only on convention but had also received judicial sanction. Arguably, the JCP had acted in contravention of not just a convention, but also the law as declared in leading judgments of the Supreme Court which formed part of the fundamental principles governing the appointment of judges. The Supreme Court stated:

> 66. Although minutes of meeting of Judicial Commission have been placed on record by referring authority. We are not taking note of it nor making any comments for the reason that satisfaction of the Chief Justice of Pakistan prior to 19th Constitutional Amendment and of Judicial Commission now is 'subjective' as held in the cases of Al-Jehad Trust, Ghulam Hyder Lakho and Munir Ahmed Bhatti and not open to judicial review.
>
> 67. In this view of the matter, when this Court, time and again, by authoritative decisions held that the 'satisfaction' in the appointment of Judges of the superior Courts including the Chief Justice of the High Court is 'subjective' and not open to Judicial Review, the question of nomination by the Commission and confirmation by the Committee of a Judge who is not the most senior Judge of that Court as Chief Justice of High Court, cannot be answered in advisory jurisdiction and may be

---

[21] *Munir Hussain Bhatti* (n. 15) [45]–[48].

adjudicated upon in other jurisdiction. Although the practice of appointment of a Judge other than the most senior Judge is against the convention and may not be in the interest of the judiciary, however, the
appointment of a Judge not most senior as Chief Justice of the High
Court cannot be termed as violative of the Constitution.[22]

Far from subjecting them to scrutiny for departing from a legitimate
expectation, the Supreme Court refused to even bring on record the
minutes of the meeting of the JCP by saying that the satisfaction of the
JCP need only be subjective, in line with previous case law. Yet, it was
the same case law that also established that overlooking the senior-
most judge of the High Court required concrete and valid reasons.
Furthermore, even though it was hearing a petition and a presidential
reference together, it conveniently declined to exercise any review in its
advisory jurisdiction while stating that it 'may be adjudicated upon in
other jurisdiction'.[23]

Even though the Supreme Court had explicitly stated that the question of appointment of a judge, who was not the senior most judge, as
the Chief Justice may be answered in 'other jurisdiction', courts have
since been quick to foreclose any possibility of review. In *Sindh High
Court Bar Association, Sukkur v. Federation of Pakistan*[24] a three-member
bench of the Sindh High Court while summarizing the state of the case
law observed that the decisions of the JCP are not justiciable[25] (without
referring to authority for this point). The Supreme Court upheld this
judgment on merits without disturbing the said observation, possibly
because it was not material to the outcome.[26] Further, in *High Court Bar
Association, Hyderabad v. Federation of Pakistan*,[27] where the decisions
of the JCP were sought to be challenged, the Sindh High Court held
again that the decisions of the JCP are not justiciable 'by any forum'.[28]

---

[22] *Presidential Reference* (n. 19) [66]–[67].

[23] *Presidential Reference* (n. 19) [67].

[24] PLD 2012 Sindh 531 (*Sindh High Court Bar Association*).

[25] *Sindh High Court Bar Association* (n. 24) [10].

[26] *Federation of Pakistan through Secretary Ministry of Law, Parliamentary Affairs
and Justice v. Sindh High Court Bar Association, Sukkur through President,* [PLD
2012 SC 1067].

[27] 2016 CLC 25 (*High Court Bar Association*).

[28] *High Court Bar Association* (n. 27) [16(iv)].

Therefore, as far as decisions of the JCP are concerned, they can be subjective and free of review by any forum.

The Judgment in *District Bar Association*

In 2015, Parliament passed the Constitution (Twenty-First) Amendment Act, 2015 (21st Amendment) which purported to provide constitutional protection to trial by military courts of terrorism suspects. This amendment was challenged in the Supreme Court. It was then that the Supreme Court fixed a date for a consolidated hearing of challenges to the 21st as well as the 18th amendments to decide the question of whether a constitutional amendment could be judicially reviewed by the Court.

In *District Bar Association*, by a majority of 14 to 3, the petitions challenging the 18th Amendment were dismissed by the Supreme Court. It may be noted that the 18th Amendment carried out extensive changes in the Constitution, and of the three judges who struck down portions of that amendment, only one—Justice Dost Muhammad Khan—struck down Article 175A relating to the judicial appointments process. Of the 16 who dismissed challenges to the 18th Amendment, four—Justice Nasir ul Mulk, Justice Iqbal Hameedur Rahman, Justice Mian Saqib Nisar, and Justice Asif Saeed Khosa—did so on the ground that the Supreme Court lacked the jurisdiction to strike down a constitutional amendment.[29]

A plurality opinion authored by His Lordship Justice Sheikh Azmat Saeed joined by seven of his colleagues—Justices Anwar Zaheer Jamali, Sarmad Jalal Osmany, Amir Hani Muslim, Gulzar Ahmed, Mushir Alam, Umar Ata Bandial, and Maqbool Baqar—held that the Supreme Court is vested with the jurisdiction to examine the *vires* of a constitutional amendment 'so as to determine whether any of the Salient Features of the Constitution has been repealed, abrogated or substantively altered'.[30] However, on the question of the 18th Amendment in relation to the appointment of judges, they held that it did not offend the Salient Features of the Constitution 'in view of the provisions of the 19th Constitutional Amendment and the dictum laid down by this Court in

---

[29] Justices Nisar and Khosa, in their separate opinions do state positive opinions in relation to the 18th Amendment on merits but essentially hold that there is no jurisdiction to strike down a constitutional amendment.

[30] *District Bar Association* (n. 3) [180(d)].

the case, reported as *Munir Hussain Bhatti, Advocate and others v. Federation of Pakistan and another* (PLD 2011 SC 308 and PLD 2011 SC 407)'.[31]

This plurality opinion also stated that the litmus test was that the power to initiate, and primacy/decisiveness with regard to the final outcome 'must vest in the Chief Justices and the Members of the Judiciary' and that Article 175A as subsequently amended and interpreted passed the test 'with some difficulty'. It goes on to explicitly add a caveat that if Article 175A 'was to be amended or reinterpreted, compromising either of two limbs of the test mentioned above' it could be struck down.[32]

Similarly, in a separate opinion authored by His Lordship Justice Jawwad S. Khawaja, he held that the Supreme Court could strike down a constitutional amendment if it violated the commands of the people as contained in the Preamble of the Constitution. In relation to Article 175A he held that

> although the eighteenth amendment as it was originally passed, may have conflicted with the independence of the judiciary and may, therefore, have been liable to be struck down, the nineteenth amendment passed by Parliament brought about substantial changes ... and as a consequence, the amended Article 175A as interpreted in the two cases of *Munir Hussain Bhatti* are not open to judicial review on the ground that the Parliamentary Committee undermines the independence of the judiciary.[33]

Therefore, while the net result of the challenge was that the 18th Amendment survived, it is clear that out of the 16 judges who upheld the judicial appointments process at least 9 (a majority of the Court) upheld Article 175A only in view of the fact that as amended by the 19th Amendment, and interpreted in *Munir Hussain Bhatti*, it was not liable to be struck down. The plurality led by Justice Saeed explicitly added the caveat that if Article 175A was reinterpreted it may be liable to be struck down. His Lordship Justice Qazi Faez Isa, in his separate opinion, while striking down other parts of the 18th Amendment also upheld Article 175A stating that 'none of the petitioners could seriously point out that Article 175A, *as it presently stands*, in any manner violates the independence of the judiciary...'.[34]

[31] *District Bar Association* (n. 3) [180(e)] (emphasis original).
[32] *District Bar Association* (n. 3) [104].
[33] *District Bar Association* (n. 3) [96] (emphasis original).
[34] *District Bar Association* (n. 3) [37] (emphasis mine).

The result is that the process for appointment of judges to the Superior Courts originally introduced through the 18th Amendment, through a combination of institutional dialogue and judicial interpretation, has been watered down to restore primacy of the judges giving them the first and the final word in the matter, and immunizing their decisions from scrutiny while reducing the scope of inquiry, and ability to influence, of the non-judges, especially the Parliamentary Committee. It is this watered down process that has ultimately been upheld.

Conclusion

India also attempted to transition to the commission model for appointment of judges to its higher judiciary (the Supreme Court of India and the High Courts) by establishing the NJAC, comprising members of the judiciary, executive, and representatives of the public. In a manner similar to what unfolded in Pakistan, the amendment which introduced the NJAC to the Indian Constitution (the 99th Amendment) was challenged before the Supreme Court of India. The Parliamentary law which had to supplement essential details on the constitution of this commission, the NJAC Act, was also challenged. The Indian Supreme Court, by a majority of 4:1, struck down the 99th Amendment as well as the NJAC Act as unconstitutional and violative of the independence of the judiciary.

This was in contrast to the approach taken by the Supreme Court of Pakistan, which upheld a watered down version of the 18th Amendment. The decision of the Supreme Court of Pakistan to uphold the 18th Amendment did receive widespread praise for being an exercise in judicial restraint. However, both the decision itself (in which thirteen judges held—in some form or another—that the Court had jurisdiction to strike down a constitutional amendment) and the jurisprudence relating to the 18th and 19th Amendments prior to the final decision can hardly be categorized as an exercise in judicial restraint. The Court clearly upheld a judicial appointments process that was significantly different from the one originally enacted through the 18th Amendment and it played a key role in creating those differences.

Judicial Appointments in Sri Lanka

20 *A Politicized Trajectory*
REHAN ABEYRATNE*

In its judgment in the *NJAC Case*, the Supreme Court of India asserted its supremacy on appointments to the higher judiciary. The Court held that the NJAC was unconstitutional and that, under the 'basic structure' doctrine, judges must retain the final say on appointments. This case culminates the judiciary's takeover of the appointments process that began more than twenty years ago with what is known as the *Second Judges' Case* in India.

Sri Lanka has followed a very different trajectory. Unlike India, which retains its post-Independence Constitution, Sri Lanka has cycled through three constitutions since it achieved independence from the British in 1948. Each Constitution has been successively less protective of institutional judicial independence than the last. As a result, the judicial appointments process has become increasingly politicized. Such politicization assumed extreme proportions under President Mahinda Rajapaksa. His regime amended the Constitution to give the executive sole authority to appoint and remove judges belonging to the higher judiciary in Sri Lanka. This led to the controversial impeachment of Chief Justice Shirani Bandaranayake in 2013.

The politicization of judicial appointments in Sri Lanka was part of the broader erosion of the rule of law and separation of powers that has

* The author would like to thank Didon Misri for excellent research assistance.

occurred since the 1970s. Due to rising ethnic tensions and the civil war, Sri Lanka has been in an almost permanent state of emergency since 1971. In 1978, it adopted its most recent Constitution, which instituted a powerful—and largely unchecked—executive presidency. However, the victory of President Maithripala Sirisena and his allies in the 2015 elections provides cause for optimism going forward. Recent constitutional amendments and pledges to repeal emergency laws signal that judicial appointments will be depoliticized and rule of law will be reinstated.

This essay will proceed in four parts. Part I describes the judicial appointments mechanism under Sri Lanka's post-independence (Soulbury) Constitution, which protected the judiciary from undue political interference. Part II examines the two 'republican' constitutions of 1972 and 1978 and the decline in structural judicial independence. Part III analyses recent developments, including President Rajapaksa's extreme politicization of the appointments process and the impeachment of the Chief Justice. I conclude with a discussion of recent reforms that, while not sufficient, are a positive step towards an institutionally independent judiciary and a depoliticized judicial appointments system.

Appointments in the Soulbury Constitution

Sri Lanka's first post-independence constitution (1948–72) is widely referred to as the Soulbury Constitution. It drew substantially from a British Government Commission, headed by Lord Soulbury, sent to Sri Lanka in 1944–5 to propose constitutional reforms. While India assembled a diverse Constituent Assembly to draft an independent Constitution, Sri Lanka (then Ceylon) drafted and adopted the Soulbury Constitution in a more top–down fashion. This difference is largely due to the fact that Sri Lanka did not achieve full independence in 1948; it remained a British dominion until 1972, with the British monarch as its head of state. Thus, the principal drafters of the Soulbury Constitution were Sri Lanka's First Prime Minister, D.S. Senanayake and his inner circle, which included eminent constitutional scholar Sir Ivor Jennings.[1]

---

[1] Radhika Coomaraswamy, *Ideology and the Constitution: Essays on Constitutional Jurisprudence* (International Centre for Ethnic Studies 1997) 19.

The Soulbury Constitution essentially transplanted the Westminster parliamentary system to Sri Lanka.[2] Executive power was vested in a Crown-appointed Governor-General, who had the authority to appoint and remove Supreme Court judges, which he exercised on the advice of the Prime Minister.[3] In this sense, the Soulbury Constitution somewhat resembled the pre-collegium system of appointments in India, where the President appointed Supreme Court justices on the advice of his cabinet, the Chief Justice of India, and various other justices.[4]

In another sense, the appointments process in Sri Lanka resembled India's present collegium system. The Soulbury Constitution instituted a Judicial Services Commission (JSC) chaired by the Chief Justice, which included two other Supreme Court justices appointed by the Governor-General.[5] The JSC was empowered to appoint, transfer, dismiss and discipline judges, except for those sitting on the Supreme Court.

Thus, the Soulbury Constitution limited undue political interference on judicial appointments. However, it granted the judiciary very limited powers of judicial review. While Part III of the Indian Constitution sets forth a comprehensive set of fundamental rights that can be judicially enforced through Articles 32 and 226, the Soulbury Constitution contained but a single rights-protective provision. This provision, Section 29(2), prevented Parliament from passing legislation that would interfere with the free exercise of religion or discriminate against any community on the basis of religion.

Yet even this minimal check on parliamentary supremacy had limitations. For instance, Section 29(2) prevented the judiciary from reviewing any law concerning citizenship. The judiciary, for its part, did not challenge these limitations. Soon after independence, Parliament enacted the Citizenship Act of 1948 that disenfranchised the 'Indian Tamil' community on the basis that their Indian ancestry precluded them from obtaining Sri Lankan citizenship.[6] In *Mudanayake v.*

---

[2] The Ceylon (Constitution) Order-in-Council, Statutory Rules and Orders [1946] (Soulbury Constitution).

[3] Soulbury Constitution (n. 2) s 52(1), 52(2); LJM Cooray, *Constitutional Government in Sri Lanka: 1797–1977* (Stamford Lake 1984) 205.

[4] Constitution of India, arts 124(2), 217(1).

[5] Soulbury Constitution (n. 2) s 53–56.

[6] *See* Deepika Udagama, 'The Sri Lankan Legal Complex and the Liberal Project: Only Thus Far and No More' in Terence C. Halliday, Lucien Karpik, and

Sivagnanasunderam,[7] the Supreme Court ruled that the Citizenship Act was constitutional on the grounds that it regulated citizenship and was therefore exempt from the protections in Article 29. The Privy Council—Sri Lanka's highest appellate court until 1972—upheld this judgment in *Kodakan Pillai v. Mudanayake*.[8]

A few years later in *The Attorney General v. Kodeswaran*,[9] a Tamil civil servant challenged the constitutionality of the Official Language Act of 1956 that instituted Sinhala as the sole official government language. The plaintiff was an officer of the General Clerical Service, who had recently been promoted to the Executive Clerical Class. Members of this Class were required to pass a Sinhala language proficiency test. The plaintiff refused to take the test, which resulted in a pay suspension. He filed a suit claiming this policy, and the Official Language Act, violated the anti-discrimination provisions in Section 29(2). The case eventually reached the Supreme Court, which disposed of the case on alternate grounds. It held that a civil servant had no right to sue the Crown on a contract dispute, and declined to comment on the constitutionality of the impugned Act. On appeal, the Privy Council also declined to rule on the constitutionality of the Official Language Act and remanded the case back to the Supreme Court for a judgment on merits.[10] The Supreme Court never produced such a judgment.

These judgments demonstrated the Sri Lankan judiciary's reluctance to exercise meaningful judicial review under the Soulbury Constitution. As we shall see, Sri Lanka's subsequent constitutions would further limit the judicial role and also politicize the judicial appointments process.

Appointments in the Republican Constitutions

In 1972, Sri Lanka shed its British dominion status and became an independent republic. This led to the adoption of a new, republican

---

Malcolm M. Feeley (eds), *Fates of Liberalism in the British Post-Colony: The Politics of the Legal Complex* (Cambridge University Press 2012) 227–8 (Udagama).

[7] [1952] 53 NLR 25.

[8] [1953] 54 NLR 433.

[9] [1967] 70 NLR 121.

[10] *Kodeswaran v. The Attorney General* [1969] 72 NLR 337.

Constitution that replaced the Soulbury Constitution. The 1972 Constitution vested judicial appointment authority for the Supreme Court and Court of Appeal in the President.[11] This was not particularly worrisome at the time because this Constitution followed the Westminster tradition in making the President responsible to a Cabinet of Ministers drawn from the National Assembly—a unicameral legislature.[12] Since the President was bound by the advice of his ministers, the actual judicial appointments authority—and executive authority generally—was vested in the Cabinet.

However, this Constitution would be substantially amended in 1978 to effectively create a new Constitution and alter this balance of power. The 1978 Constitution was adopted following Prime Minister J.R. Jayewardene's landslide election victory in 1977 in which his United National Party (UNP) won approximately eighty per cent of National State Assembly seats. Jayewardene favoured a more powerful executive presidency, along the lines of the French 'Gaullist' model.[13]

The 1978 Constitution gave the President authority to appoint judges to the higher judiciary.[14] In theory, this was in line with the Soulbury and 1972 Constitutions, which vested this authority with the Governor-General and President, respectively. In practice, however, the 1978 Constitution marked an important shift in the judicial appointments authority. While past executives acted on the advice of their ministers, the 'Gaullist' President of the 1978 Constitution presided over a separate and powerful executive branch. The new Sri Lankan President would be the Head of State, Head of Government, and the Commander-in-Chief of the Armed Forces.[15] He would be directly elected to office and preside over a Cabinet of Ministers.[16] Following the French model, the Prime Minister and the Cabinet of Ministers are drawn from the majority party in the legislature (renamed the 'Parliament' in 1978).

---

[11] *Constitution of the Republic of Sri Lanka* (1972), art 122(1) (1972 Constitution)

[12] 1972 Constitution (n. 11) arts 91–2.

[13] A.J. Wilson, *The Gaullist System in Asia* (Macmillan 1980) 42–4.

[14] *Constitution of the Democratic Socialist Republic of Sri Lanka* (1978), art 107 (1978 Constitution).

[15] 1978 Constitution (n. 14) art 30.

[16] 1978 Constitution (n. 14) Chs VII–VIII.

However, Sri Lankan Presidents enjoy far greater powers than their French counterparts.[17] For instance, the President has complete discretion in nominating the Prime Minister and Cabinet of Ministers, who serve at the President's pleasure.[18] The President may also assign herself any portfolio or function and may dissolve Parliament.[19]

By vesting so much power in a single individual, the 1978 Constitution set the stage for what was to come. From 1978 to 2015, Sri Lanka experienced a centralization of authority in the executive, accompanied by a gradual erosion in the rule of law. Judicial appointments were politicized in this era, which led to a breakdown in the structural independence of the judiciary. Under President J.R. Jayewardene's tenure (1978–89), for instance, Supreme Court judges' homes were attacked, while other judges were locked out of their chambers when they ruled against the government.[20]

Sri Lanka's republican Constitutions also emasculated the judiciary in other ways. While both the 1972 and 1978 Constitutions included a comprehensive set of fundamental rights, they denied the courts any meaningful judicial review authority. For instance, Article 80 of the 1978 Constitution prevents judicial review of enacted laws. It merely permits courts to review proposed legislation in the abstract within a week of being placed on Parliament's official agenda. These Constitutions also did nothing to invalidate or limit long-standing emergency regulations. Sri Lanka was in an almost permanent state of emergency from 1971 to 2010, with the longest period of emergency rule occurring from 1983 (when hostilities began between the Sri Lankan government and the Liberation Tigers of Tamil Eelam (LTTE)) until 2001.[21] Article 15 of the 1978 Constitution permits fundamental rights

---

[17] Rohan Edrisinha, 'Sri Lanka: Constitutions Without Constitutionalism: A Tale of Three and a Half Constitutions' in Rohan Edrisinha and Asanga Welikala (eds), *Essays on Federalism in Sri Lanka* (Centre for Policy Alternatives 2008) 31.

[18] 1978 Constitution (n. 14) arts 42–4.

[19] 1978 Constitution (n. 14) arts 44, 70.

[20] Udagama (n. 6) 235; International Crisis Group, *Sri Lanka's Judiciary: Politicised Courts, Compromised Rights* (ICG 2009) 4 (International Crisis Group).

[21] Radhika Coomaraswamy and Charmaine de los Reyes, 'Rule by Emergency: Sri Lanka's Postcolonial Constitutional Experience', [2004] 2 *International Journal of Constitutional Law* 272, 273 (Coomaraswamy and Reyes).

to be restricted in the interest of national security, while Article 155 affirms the constitutionality of the Public Security Ordinance (PSO). The PSO was first instituted by the British in 1947 and, after subsequent amendments, permitted limits on parliamentary review of executive acts, prohibited judicial review, and suspended fundamental rights.[22] In 1979, President Jayewardene's government passed the Prevention of Terrorism Act (PTA). While initially intended as a temporary measure, it was made permanent in 1982. It permits preventative detention of suspects without judicial review for three-month intervals, for up to eighteen months. The PTA remains in force today despite strong domestic and international pressure to repeal it.[23]

In 2001, the Seventeenth Amendment to the Constitution of the Democratic Socialist Republic of Sri Lanka (17th Amendment) was passed with support across the political spectrum to depoliticize key areas of government. It created an independent Police Commission, Human Rights Commission, and Election Commission, among others. While the President would appoint members of these commissions, she could only do so with the consent of a newly established Constitutional Council. This Council comprised ten members, including the Speaker of Parliament, the Prime Minister, the Leader of the Opposition, one presidential appointee, five individuals nominated jointly by the Prime Minister and the Opposition Leader, and one person agreed upon by members of those parties other than those to which the Prime Minister or the Opposition Leader belonged.[24]

The 17th Amendment conferred authority to appoint judges of the Court of Appeal and Supreme Court on the Constitutional Council. This was seen as a positive development, seeking to protect the judiciary from undue executive interference and, more broadly, to move

[22] Coomaraswamy and Reyes (n. 21) 274–7.

[23] T. Ramakrishnan, 'Consensus on PTA's Repeal', The Hindu (Colombo, 4 January 2016) <http://www.thehindu.com/todays-paper/tp-international/consensus-on-ptas-repeal/article8062524.ece> accessed 12 April 2016; 'Letter to President Sirisena Re. Human Rights Situation in Sri Lanka', Human Rights Watch (New York, 26 February 2015) <https://www.hrw.org/news/2015/02/26/letter-president-sirisena-re-human-rights-situation-sri-lanka> accessed 12 April 2016.

[24] 1978 Constitution (n. 14) art 41A.

towards merit-based judicial appointments. Yet, for three main reasons, the Council was not particularly effective. First, the composition of the Council was problematic. It failed to include members of the judiciary or civil society and therefore relied on members of Parliament to exert a check on executive authority. As discussed, however, the 1978 Constitution makes the cabinet—and Parliament generally—subservient to the President, meaning that the Council did not actually assert independent appointment authority.[25] Second, the appointment of Chief Justice Sarath Silva in 1999 politicized the internal dynamics of the Sri Lankan judiciary. Silva broke with tradition to assign his allies to benches to decide particular cases and tightly controlled the appointment of judges to the JSC, which continued to appoint judges to the lower judiciary. He also controlled the budget for judicial training and reform, which he developed into a 'patronage system' to 'extract personal favors'.[26] Third, President Rajapaksa (2005–15) refused to convene the Council from 2005 onwards, retaining for himself the authority to appoint judges to the higher judiciary and members of the independent commissions.[27] This abdication of constitutional duty fundamentally undermined the Seventeenth Amendment and led to its supersession in 2010.

Extreme Politicization of Appointments (2010–15)

In 2010, the Eighteenth Amendment to the Constitution of the Democratic Socialist Republic of Sri Lanka (18th Amendment) came into force, displacing much of the 17th Amendment.[28] Under the 18th Amendment, the President regained sole authority to make appointments to the higher judiciary. The Amendment also abolished presidential term limits, allowing President Rajapaksa to campaign for a third term in 2015. While Rajapaksa was defeated in the 2015 presidential election, one could easily envision a President being elected to three or

---

[25] International Crisis Group (n. 20) 9.

[26] International Crisis Group (n. 20) 11.

[27] International Crisis Group (n. 20)10.

[28] For a detailed account of the 18th Amendment, *see* Rohan Edrisinha and Aruni Jayakody (eds), *The Eighteenth Amendment to the Constitution: Substance and Process* (Centre for Policy Alternatives 2011).

more terms. Under this scenario, a single individual could completely transform the judiciary in his image.

The 18th Amendment also abolished the Constitutional Council and replaced it with a Parliamentary Council consisting of the Prime Minister, the Speaker, the Leader of the Opposition, and two Members of Parliament nominated by the Prime Minister and Leader of the Opposition. This Council assumed responsibility for nominating members of independent commissions. As a result, such bodies—including the Human Rights Commission and the Permanent Commission to Investigate Allegations of Bribery and Corruption—would be 'independent' in name only. This is because at least three out of five members of the Council would be politically aligned with the President and, more fundamentally, because the President was no longer bound to follow the Council's advice. The 18th Amendment required only that the President 'seek the observations' of the Parliamentary Council.

This period also witnessed politicization in the judicial removal process. Chief Justice Shirani Bandaranayake's impeachment, and the controversy surrounding it, is a good illustration. In a 2012 Supreme Court judgment, Chief Justice Bandaranayake held President Rajapaksa's Divi Neguma ('uplifting lives') Bill unconstitutional. The Bill sought to establish a Department of Divi Neguma within the Ministry of Economic Development. This would have centralized all development-related activities under Basil Rajapaksa, the President's brother and Minister for Economic Development. The Chief Justice's opinion held that such delegation of authority violated the 13th Amendment to the 1978 Constitution, which had delegated these powers to the provinces and could not be altered without the consent of all provincial councils.[29]

On 8 December 2012, one day after the judgment was issued, Members of Parliament representing President Rajapaksa's United People's Freedom Alliance (UPFA) presented a motion before the Speaker of the Parliament to impeach the Chief Justice. The Speaker was Chamal Rajapaksa, another one of the President's brothers. The Speaker proceeded to appoint a Parliamentary Standing Committee (PSC) to conduct an inquiry in this matter. The PSC was widely criticized for first, consisting mostly of representatives from the ruling UPFA

---

[29] *In re a Bill Titled Divineguma*, SC Special Determination 1–3/2012.

coalition (seven out of eleven members); second, triggering several procedural issues that cast doubts on the fairness of the inquiry.[30]

Less than a day after the inquiry ended, the PSC found the Chief Justice guilty of several charges in the impeachment motion. She appealed this ruling to the Supreme Court, which held that the PSC inquiry was unconstitutional. Nonetheless, Parliament debated the impeachment motion and passed it along party lines with 155 MPs voting in favour, 49 against, and 11 abstaining. President Rajapaksa formalized the impeachment on 13 January 2013 and appointed his close associate and former Attorney General Mohan Peiris as the new Chief Justice. In a cruel irony, a few days before Chief Justice Bandaranayake was formally impeached, Parliament enacted into law the Divi Neguma Bill that she had ruled unconstitutional.[31]

These events brought into sharp relief the threat that an extremely politicized appointment and removal process posed to the judiciary. The powerful executive presidency instituted by the 1978 Constitution, combined with the 18th Amendment's removal of independent checks, eliminated any semblance of structural judicial independence in Sri Lanka.

Conclusion: Optimistic Signs Ahead

As it turned out, the impeachment of Chief Justice Bandaranayake was the nadir of executive interference in judicial affairs. In January 2015, Maithripala Sirisena defeated President Rajapaksa in the presidential election. Running as the opposition coalition's 'common candidate', Sirisena pledged to reverse many of the worst excesses of the Rajapaksa era, including the 18th Amendment.

Once elected, President Sirisena embarked on an ambitious 100-day reform programme that culminated with the passage of the 19th

---

[30] The main concerns were: (1) the PSC procedures and standard of proof were not clearly defined; (2) that all documents were not made available to the Chief Justice; and (3) that her lawyers did not have adequate time to review the evidence against her or to fully cross-examine witnesses.

[31] See Niran Anketell and Asanga Welikala, *A Systematic Crisis in Context: The Impeachment of the Chief Justice, the Independence of the Judiciary and the Rule of Law in Sri Lanka* (Centre for Policy Alternatives 2013).

Amendment in April 2015. This was perhaps the most significant constitutional amendment since President Jayewardene instituted the amendments to the 1972 Constitution that established the powerful executive presidency in 1978. The 19th Amendment, *inter alia*, reintroduced a two-term limit on presidential terms and reinstated the Constitutional Council and independent commissions.[32]

President Sirisena also called for parliamentary elections two years ahead of schedule, hoping that his coalition could gain a majority in Parliament. Elections were held in August 2015. Sirisena and Prime Minister Ranil Wickremesinghe united their coalitions to narrowly defeat former President Rajapaksa and his allies. They formed a national government, which pledged to enact a new constitution. On 5 April 2016, the Sri Lankan Parliament was converted into a Constitutional Assembly. A 21-member steering committee, led by Prime Minister Wickremesinghe, has been charged with soliciting public views on the new constitution and reporting back to the Assembly. The new constitution is expected to restore the parliamentary system of government in Sri Lanka.[33] It is hoped that the Constituent Assembly will also enact judicial reforms, particularly merit-based judicial appointments.

All told, Sri Lanka appears to be moving towards greater transparency and impartiality in its judicial appointments process. President Sirisena's government has enacted important reforms already, including the 19th Amendment, and the Constituent Assembly appears set to limit executive power substantially by abolishing the executive presidency.

I conclude with an important symbolic gesture, which suggests that the judiciary's structural independence can be restored. On 28 January 2015, less than a month after he assumed office, President Sirisena reinstated Chief Justice Bandaranayake on the grounds that she had

---

[32] T. Ramakrishnan, 'Sri Lanka Adopts 19th Amendment', *The Hindu* (Colombo, 29 April 2015) <http://www.thehindu.com/news/international/south-asia/sri-lanka-adopts-19th-amendment/article7151450.ece> accessed 12 April 2016.

[33] 'Lanka Sets up Formal Mechanism to Formulate New Constitution', *New Indian Express* (Chennai, 5 April 2016) <http://www.newindianexpress.com/world/Lanka-Sets-up-Formal-Mechanism-to-Formulate-New-Constitution/2016/04/05/article3364815.ece> accessed 12 April 2016.

been unlawfully impeached and the appointment of her successor Mohan Peiris was therefore void *ab initio*. She retired one day later, declaring in her farewell speech that 'an independent judiciary…would lead to a truly democratic country'.[34]

---

[34] 'Sri Lanka: Farewell Speech by Dr Shirani A. Bandaranayake, 43 CJ', *Sri Lanka Guardian* (Colombo, 10 April 2016) <http://www.slguardian.org/2015/01/sri-lanka-farewell-speech-by-dr-shirani-a-bandaranayake/> accessed 12 April 2016.

Appointments to the Supreme Court of Nepal

A New Beginning

21

SEMANTA DAHAL

In September 2015, the Constituent Assembly of Nepal passed the much anticipated and contested Constitution by an overwhelming majority. The Constitution was promulgated following eight years of intense and seemingly unending negotiations. However, the provinces carved to federalize Nepal have irked the elected political parties from Nepal's southern lowlands. The annoyance of these parties, which are politically active in Nepal's Terai region, has translated into continued protests which have often taken violent overtures and also resulted in Nepal's international borders with India being blockaded, with what is believed to be tacit Indian support.[1] The transition to the new Constitution also saw an experimental exercise of installing the Chief Justice of the Supreme Court to Chairman of the Council of Ministers, a position which is equivalent to that of the Prime Minister.

The full realization of the provisions of the new Constitution will take time, the length of which cannot be predicted since political parties are open to the demand of redrawing Nepal's federal map. In due course, the government may also have to consider some of the legitimate amendment proposals put forth by protesting parties. Within

---

[1] Puja Sen, 'Why Nepal's Ethnic Minorities Have Restarted Their Protest against the Constitution' (*Scroll.in*, 18 May 2016) <http://scroll.in/article/808280/why-nepals-ethnic-minorities-have-restarted-their-protest-against-the-constitution> accessed 20 May 2016.

four months of its promulgation, the first amendment to Nepal's Constitution has been made, with a view to ensure population-based proportional representation to state organs and electoral constituencies. Elections to the House of Representatives slated for 21 January 2018[2] will also be critical for full enforcement of the provisions of the new Constitution. Further implementation of this Constitution is not possible without the passing of several other legislative enactments.

The 2015 Constitution is Nepal's seventh and is unique in many respects, when compared with its predecessors.[3] Although, differences over the Constitution were settled in closed-room negotiations between top leaders of political parties, it is for the first time that a democratically elected body with strong gender and ethnic group representation voted on the motion whether or not to adopt the Constitution. This Constitution also transforms Nepal from unitary to a federal nation. Most crucially, the Constitution has the potential to make Nepal an inclusive state provided the proportional representation of disadvantaged people in state institutions is honestly implemented in practice.

Organization of the Judiciary

At the time when India awaited the outcome of the litigation in the *NJAC Case* on the process for appointing judges to its higher judiciary, Nepal was in the process of devising a constitution for herself. In a way, both neighbours were dealing with key questions relating to the balance of power between the different organs of the government. In India, the Supreme Court through its judgment in the *NJAC Case* preserved the power of appointments with the judicial collegium, while frowning upon the presence of the Law Minister (a member of the executive) and members of the public on the proposed NJAC.

Even though the Constitution federalizes Nepal into seven provinces, the unitary structure of the judiciary remains unchanged. The Supreme Court which exists at the highest level continues to remain the final arbiter of disputes and can pass rulings if the executive and the legislature act against the Constitution. The sanctioned strength of the

---

[2] Constitution of Nepal (Constitution) art. 296(1).

[3] Nepal previously has passed constitutions in 1948, 1951, 1959, 1962, 1990, and 2006.

Supreme Court in the new Constitution is twenty-one, inclusive of the Chief Justice.

The new Constitution establishes, for the first time, a permanent Constitutional Bench within the Supreme Court. Matters relating to (a) laws inconsistent with the Constitution, (b) inter-provincial and federal-provincial disputes, and (c) electoral disputes, fall under the exclusive jurisdiction of the Constitutional Bench of the Supreme Court. This Bench has been established to appease political parties who were demanding an independent Constitutional Court. The Constitutional Bench consists of the Chief Justice and four other Supreme Court judges appointed by the Chief Justice upon the recommendation of the Judicial Council.

The new Constitution introduces High Courts for each province. The extant sixteen Appellate Courts will be dissolved and the High Court for each of the seven provinces will replace them.[4] These High Courts will have to be established within a year from the date of the promulgation of the Constitution. Finally, at the lowest level the judicial powers are vested in the District Courts. Each district will have a District Court with original jurisdiction to try and settle all cases within its territory.

Supreme Court Appointments under Previous Constitutions

Nepal has learnt a lesson or two about judicial appointments from its experience of replacing and re-promulgating the Constitution at frequent intervals. The first four constitutions of Nepal and the legislations complementing them granted wide and discretionary authority to the executive for appointment of judges to the Supreme Court. The executive branch with the monarch at the helm was allowed to exercise his wisdom in the matter of appointments. The justices of the Supreme Court could be removed by the monarch if the commission appointed by him was of the opinion that judges misbehaved, were incompetent, or acted in bad faith.[5] Consequently, not just the appointment process

---

[4] Constitution (n. 2) art. 300.

[5] *See* Constitution of the Kingdom of Nepal, 1959 art. 57(4)(b). Such a commission with members appointed by the Monarch could be formed anytime for submitting a report to the Monarch about performance of judge's duty, misbehaviour, and incapacity.

but also the grounds for removal of judges were seemingly violative of the independence of the judiciary.

Genesis of the Judicial Council

It was only in 1990, after the promulgation of Nepal's fifth constitution, that the powers to select the judges of the Supreme Court, and to remove them (through an impeachment motion) were transferred from the executive to the Judicial Council and the Parliament, respectively. This was made possible because the Constitution of the Kingdom of Nepal, 1990 (1990 Constitution) was adopted following a popular people's movement which called for curtailment of the monarch's power and establishment of multi-party democracy in Nepal. The preamble recognized an independent judicial system as one of the fundamental features of the Constitution. Accordingly, an institution called the Judicial Council was introduced in the 1990 Constitution. Its constitutionally defined role was to make recommendations and provide advice with respect to appointment, transfer, and dismissal of judges. The Judicial Council also had the power to recommend disciplinary action against the judges. Under the 1990 Constitution, the Chief Justice was chairperson of the Judicial Council, and the other four members were the Minister of Law, two senior-most judges of the Supreme Court, and a distinguished jurist nominated by the monarch.

The Judicial Council was conceptualized by Bishwanath Upadhyaya, the chair of the 1990 Constitution Recommendation Commission. He later became the Chief Justice of the Supreme Court. With a majority of members from the judicial branch forming part of the Judicial Council, the appointment process was steered by the judges of the Supreme Court. Although the appointments made during the term of the 1990 Constitution were questioned for not bringing sufficiently competent judges to the Supreme Court, charges of appointments being politically motivated were only sporadic.

Confirmation by Parliamentary Hearing Committee

The introduction of the Judicial Council was considered an important step to ensure judicial independence. Hence, the Interim Constitution of Nepal[6] adopted in 2006 to end Nepal's Maoist conflict, abolish monarchy, and enable state restructuring by federalizing Nepal gave continuity to this institution with few modifications in its composition. The Chief Justice still headed the Judicial Council but the number of Supreme Court judges was decreased to one. Instead, the Interim Constitution provided for representation of Nepal Bar Association's nominated lawyer on the Judicial Council.[7] The monarch's nominee was replaced by the Prime Minister's nominee. The change in this composition was largely because most of the drafters of the Interim Constitution were members of the bar and their ostensible aim was to ensure appointments from the bar in the judiciary. The political parties had always lauded the role of the Nepal Bar Association in leading the country's democratic movement and thus did not object to the inclusion of a lawyer nominated by the Nepal Bar Association in the Judicial Council.

This new composition of Judicial Council introduced by the Interim Constitution also tilted the balance in favour of the executive. The Minister of Law and the person nominated by the Prime Minister served in the Judicial Council on behalf of the executive. Further, the lawyer nominated by the Nepal Bar Association was not expected to remain fully detached from the executive. This is because, even though the Nepal Bar Association is a professional organization, it holds elections to its executive committee by forming panels in line with the ideologies of the major political parties of Nepal. After consolidating the enhanced role of the executive in the appointments process, the Interim Constitution moved towards creating a significant space for the legislature. The second amendment to the Interim Constitution made compulsory a parliamentary hearing of judges who were nominated to the Supreme Court.[8] The Conduct of Business of Legislature-Parliament Rules, 2014 framed pursuant to the Interim Constitution granted the Parliamentary Hearing Special Committee (PHSC) the power to reject the names of the nominees, by a two-third majority. Thus, under the

---

[6] Interim Constitution of Nepal, 2007 (Interim Constitution).

[7] Interim Constitution (n. 6) art. 113(1).

[8] Interim Constitution (n. 6) art. 155(1) which was amended on 13 June 2007 by the Interim Constitution of Nepal (Second Amendment) Act, 2007, to include reference to appointments of judges and ambassadors.

Interim Constitution, all three branches of the state could exercise power in the matter of appointment of judges to the Supreme Court. During the term of eight years when the Interim Constitution was in force, the Judicial Council came in direct confrontation with the PHSC only once. In 2014, the PHSC asked for the official representative of the Judicial Council to be sent to it to explain the reasons behind recommending names of eight 'controversial' Appellate Court justices[9] for permanent position to the Supreme Court.[10] The Judicial Council refused to entertain PHSC's request citing the absence of a provision in the Interim Constitution which enabled the PHSC to summon the members and officials of Judicial Council before it. Eventually names of two judges—Justices Baidya Nath Upadhyay and Om Prakash Mishra were endorsed unanimously by the PHSC, while the names of Justices Gopal Parajuli, Deepak Raj Joshi, Govinda Upadhyay, Devendra Gopal Shrestha, Cholendra Shumsher Rana, and Jagdish Sharma Poudel were approved by voting.

Supreme Court Appointment Provisions in the New Constitution

The first Constituent Assembly elected in 2008 ventured into intense debate and explored judicial appointments in depth. The Committee on Judicial System of the first Constituent Assembly (CA I) tasked with the role of preparing a concept paper for the preliminary draft of the Constitution was divided, with the largest party in CA I, the Communist Party of Nepal (Maoist) (CPN-Maoist) standing firmly opposed to continuing with the Judicial Council. CPN-Maoist favoured creation of Special Judicial Committee within the Federal Parliament to make recommendation for the appointments of justices to the

---

[9] These eight judges were Justices Baidya Nath Upadhyay, Gopal Parajuli, Deepak Raj Joshi, Govinda Upadhyay, Om Prakash Mishra, Devendra Gopal Shrestha, Cholendra Shumsher Rana, and Jagdish Sharma Poudel.

[10] Pranab Kharel, 'House Panel Seeks Clarification: Tension Flares with JC Set to Snub PHSC Call', *The Kathmandu Post* (Kathmandu, 16 May 2014) <http://kathmandupost.ekantipur.com/news/2014-05-16/house-panel-seeks-clarificationtension-flares-with-jc-set-to-snub-phsc-call.html> accessed 16 May 2016.

Supreme Court.[11] The Special Judicial Committee it proposed consisted of the vice-chair of the Federal Parliament, Federal Law Minister and nine members elected from the Federal Parliament. Nepali Congress (NC), the second party in CA I stood against CPN-Maoist's proposal and reasoned that legislative recommendations to the posts of Supreme Court would centralize state powers in the Legislature and compromise judicial independence.[12] Unfortunately, CA I could not complete its task of constitution-making and was finally dissolved after the Supreme Court refused to extend its tenure beyond four years.[13]

In an unprecedented turn of events, a second round of elections to the Constituent Assembly (CA II) of Nepal was held in November 2013 under the leadership of Chief Justice of the Supreme Court, Khil Raj Regmi, who was made the Chairman of the Council of Ministers of the temporary election government to carry out the elections. The largest party in CA I, the CPN-Maoist was reduced to third position and NC and Communist Party of Nepal-United Marxist and Leninist (CPN-UML) secured first and second position respectively. With NC garnering a dominant position in CA II, its previous stance of appointing the judges to the Supreme Court upon the recommendation of the Judicial Council and following the completion of a parliamentary hearing process was incorporated in the 2015 Constitution.

Hence, the new Constitution retains the model of power-sharing between the executive, judiciary, and the legislature, which was first introduced in the Interim Constitution for the appointment of judges to the Supreme Court. As per Article 129(2) of the 2015 Constitution, the President appoints the Chief Justice upon the recommendation of the 'Constitutional Council', and other justices of the Supreme Court upon the recommendation of the Judicial Council. Prior to making these appointments, Article 292 makes it mandatory to conduct the

---

[11] Committee on Judicial System of the Constituent Assembly, *A Report Preliminary Draft with Concept Paper* (Constituent Assembly 2009) <http://www.ncf.org.np/upload/CA/concept_paper_Judiciary_System_ENG.pdf> accessed 16 May 2016 (CA Judicial System Committee Concept Paper).

[12] CA Judicial System Committee Concept Paper (n. 11) 77.

[13] Semanta Dahal, 'The Last Dance', *The Kathmandu Post* (Kathmandu, 29 November 2011) <http://kathmandupost.ekantipur.com/printedition/news/2011-11-28/the-last-dance.html> accessed on 16 May 2016.

parliamentary hearing of the nominees. Under this constitutional arrangement, the Constitutional Council for the Chief Justice, and the Judicial Council for other judges of the Supreme Court are the recommending bodies responsible to select and propose the names of potential appointees. The PHSC, one of the special committees of Parliament, is the confirming authority and the President is the appointing authority.

What Is the Constitutional Council?

The Constitutional Council was first founded by the 1990 Constitution, to make recommendations for appointment of officials to constitutional bodies including the Chief Justice of the Supreme Court. Such a body appeared in the Interim Constitution also and is now included in the 2015 Constitution. Under the 2015 Constitution, the Constitutional Council comprises the Prime Minister, the Chief Justice (or the Federal Minister of Law if the office of the Chief Justice is vacant and a recommendation has to be made for the same), the Speaker of the House of Representatives, Chairperson of the National Assembly, Leader of the opposition party in the House of Representatives, and Deputy Speaker of the House of Representatives.[14] Since the promulgation of the 1990 Constitution, the recommendations of the Constitutional Council for Chief Justice have not run into controversy because as a matter of convention it has followed seniority in proposing the names.

Structure of Judicial Council

The composition of the Judicial Council in the 2015 Constitution is similar to what existed in the Interim Constitution. In this five-member body,[15] the Chief Justice of the Supreme Court is the Chairperson and the Federal Minister of Law and the senior-most judge of the Supreme Court are *ex officio* members. The other two members to be appointed by the President are nominees of the Prime Minister and the Nepal Bar Association. The Prime Minister can recommend one jurist and the Nepal Bar Association can recommend either a senior advocate or an

[14] Constitution (n. 2) art. 284.
[15] Constitution (n. 2) art. 153.

advocate with at least twenty years of experience at the bar. The Prime Minister's appointee and the Nepal Bar Association's representative have tenures of four years. The only major variance from the Interim Constitution is that Article 285 of the 2015 Constitution makes parliamentary hearing of the nominees of the Prime Minister and the Nepal Bar Association compulsory.

Parliamentary Hearing Committee

The parliamentary hearing for appointment of judges to the Supreme Court, first introduced by the second amendment to the Interim Constitution, was an atypical endeavour for a country like Nepal where the Constitution had adopted parliamentary system as a form of government. This requirement of parliamentary hearing for appointments to the Supreme Court finds place in the 2015 Constitution as well.[16]

A significant role of the Parliament in confirming appointments to the Supreme Court is more common to presidential systems, like that of the United States of America (US), where the Senate can approve or reject presidential nominations. But unlike the clearly defined role of 'advice and consent' of the Senate articulated in the US Constitution,[17] neither the Interim Constitution nor the 2015 Constitution elaborate on the role of the hearing committee of the Parliament. Article 292(1) of the 2015 Constitution (comparable to Article 155(1) of the Interim Constitution) provides for a parliamentary hearing to be conducted 'in accordance with the provisions of the Federal law'. Only this constitutional provision does not equip the parliamentary hearing committee with sufficient powers to reject the names recommended by the Judicial Council. During the term of the Interim Constitution, such parliamentary hearing was conducted by the PHSC in accordance with the Conduct of Business of Legislature-Parliament Rules passed by the Legislature-Parliament in 2008. These rules framed under the Interim Constitution limited the size of the PHSC to seventy-five members of

---

[16] Constitution (n. 2) art. 292. As per Article 292, the parliamentary hearing is not only mandatory for the justices of the Supreme Court, but it also extends to members of the Judicial Council, chief and members of constitutional bodies, and ambassadors.

[17] Constitution of the United States 1787, s. 2.

Parliament and further empowered it to endorse or reject the names proposed for appointment to the Supreme Court. The Conduct of Business of Legislature-Parliament Rules, 2008 passed by CA I provided for unanimity for endorsement of proposed names, whereas the Conduct of Business of Legislature-Parliament Rules, 2014 passed after the formation of CA II allowed the PHSC to disapprove any name by two-thirds majority. Similar rules have not been adopted even after more than eight months having elapsed from the day of the promulgation of the 2015 Constitution and, as a consequence, a PHSC is yet to be formed by the current Parliament.

Unlike the Interim Constitution, the 2015 Constitution, however, specifies in its text itself the strength of the parliamentary hearing committee. The parliamentary hearing committee will consist of fifteen members with representation from both the Houses of the Federal Parliament.[18] According to Article 83 of the 2015 Constitution, the House of Representatives and the National Assembly are the two Houses of the Federal Parliament. The two Houses in accordance with Article 83 of the 2015 Constitution are yet to be formed, however for enabling the transition, Article 83(3) clarifies that all the business to be transacted by the Federal Parliament will be carried out by the existing Legislature-Parliament. It is worthwhile to note that the current legislature of Nepal is termed the Legislature-Parliament, which essentially exists as a transformed incarnation of CA II.[19]

Supreme Court Appointments Post-2015 Constitution

The transitional provisions contained in Part-33 of the 2015 Constitution gave continuity to the existing Supreme Court because of which justices serving in the Court were allowed to remain in service.[20] Thus, when the new Constitution came into force on 20 September 2015, there were ten vacant positions in the Supreme Court. One more position fell vacant after the retirement of Justice Girish Chandra Lal in January 2016.

---

[18] Constitution (n. 2) art. 292(2).
[19] Constitution (n. 2) art. 296.
[20] Constitution (n. 2) art. 300.

The transitional provisions of the 2015 Constitution, however, did not give continuity to the appointments made under the Interim Constitution of non-*ex officio* members of the Judicial Council.[21] As a result, fresh appointment of nominees of the Prime Minister and the Nepal Bar Association had to be made in accordance with the provisions of the new Constitution. Soon after the promulgation of the 2015 Constitution, Prime Minister Sushil Koirala of the NC hurriedly nominated Ram Prasad Sitaula to the Judicial Council.[22] But the parliamentary hearing for Ram Prasad Sitaula could not take place in the absence of the PHSC. Prime Minister Khadga Prasad Oli of CPN-UML, who assumed office on 12 October 2015, took advantage of the moment and withdrew Ram Prasad Sitaula's nomination.[23] The Nepal Bar Association also did not recommend its nominee for the Judicial Council citing the absence of the PHSC. As a consequence, Chief Justice Kalyan Shrestha had to head an incomplete Judicial Council, ambivalent of whether to make recommendations or not.

However because of the mounting pressure of backlog of cases pending disposal at the Supreme Court, the Judicial Council recommended eleven justices to the Supreme Court on 2 March 2016, six months after the promulgation of the 2015 Constitution. Of the eleven justices recommended, seven were elevated from the Appellate Courts, while the four remaining were from among senior advocates.[24] These nominations drew serious objection from the Speaker of the

[21] Constitution (n. 2) art. 301(2). Article 301(2) of the Constitution of Nepal continued the appointments of chief and other officials of the Constitutional Bodies only. Constitutional Bodies defined in Article 306(1) of the 2015 Constitution does not include the Judicial Council.

[22] Ram Sitaula was previously serving in the Judicial Council as nominee of Nepal Bar Association.

[23] 'Govt Cancels Sitaula's Hearing', *The Himalayan Times* (Kathmandu, 5 November 2015) <http://thehimalayantimes.com/nepal/govt-cancels-sitaulas-hearing/> accessed 16 May 2016.

[24] The seven Appellate Justices who were recommended were Justices Dipak Kumar Karki, Kedar Chalise, Meera Khadka, Sharada Prasad Ghimire, Biswombar Prasad Shrestha, Ishwor Khatiwada, and Ananda Mohan Bhattarai. The following senior advocates were recommended for Supreme Court judgeship: Hari Krishna Karki, Anil Kumar Sinha, Prakash Raut, and Sapana Pradhan Malla.

Legislature-Parliament. Besides, the Judicial Council was also questioned for picking names of senior advocates who were extremely active in political life.[25] The nomination of senior advocate Sapana Pradhan Malla, a former parliamentarian, who was elected to CA I under the proportional representation seats for CPN-UML, was particularly criticized because of her putative association with a political party. The 2015 Constitution, however, does not bar a former parliamentarian from being appointed as Supreme Court justice.

The Speaker of the Legislature-Parliament, Onsari Gharti Magar, immediately wrote back to the Judicial Council arguing that nominations were made by the Judicial Council without completing its full shape and that the parliamentary hearing of eleven nominees cannot be conducted owing to the absence of parliamentary rules for conducting the hearing. A turf war ensued between the Supreme Court and Judicial Council on the one hand and the Parliament on the other. The Judicial Council replied to the Speaker's letter and not only did it re-send the names of the eleven nominees but also reminded her of the constitutional provision that requires the parliament to conduct hearing. In addition, the Supreme Court in the writ filed before it declared the Speaker's letter *prima facie* invalid and issued an interim order against the Speaker and the Parliament Secretariat to conduct parliamentary hearing on the recommendations.[26] But political parties in the Legislature-Parliament were not able to agree even eight months after passing of the 2015 Constitution on the Conduct of Business of Legislature-Parliament Rules required to constitute the PHSC and conduct the hearings.

The disagreement between the coalition government led by CPN-UML and the main opposition party NC lay on the composition of the PHSC. The coalition government wanted to limit the size of the PHSC to fifteen in accordance with the requirement of Article 292(2) of the 2015 Constitution which states that the joint committee consisting of fifteen members of both Houses of the Federal Parliament

---

[25] Binita Dahal, 'Judicial Match-Fixing', *Nepali Times* (Kathmandu, 10 March 2016) <http://nepalitimes.com/regular-columns/Legalese/judicial-match-fixing-Nepal,674> accessed 16 May 2016.

[26] *Advocate Jyoti Baniya v. Speaker Onsari Gharti Magar*, 072-WO-0646 (Supreme Court of Nepal).

shall be formed for parliamentary hearing. But NC, which is the largest party and the main opposition, argued that pursuant to the 2015 Constitution, both Houses of Federal Parliament cannot be constituted until the next general elections, and hence, put forth a case for continuation of seventy-five member PHSC as it existed under the Interim Constitution. The larger the PHSC, the higher the probability of having lawmakers from various political parties in the PHSC. The PHSC can reject the names of judges recommended by the Judicial Council by a two-thirds majority. Hence the number and representation of each of the political parties on the committee could vitally block a politically motivated recommendation to the Supreme Court.

After a series of negotiations, the new Conduct of Business of Legislature-Parliament Rules was passed on 19 June 2016 under the 2015 Constitution, limiting the size of the PHSC to fifteen. The new PHSC has six members from NC, four from CPN-UML, two from CPN-Maoist, and one each from the Rastriya Prajatantra Party-Nepal and the Madhesi Janadhikar Forum-Loktantrik. One member from the Terai-based parties is yet to be appointed. PHSC has also decided to conduct hearings and has invited complaints against the proposed Chief Justice Sushila Karki and eleven Supreme Court justice nominees. It will be interesting to see if the PHSC will endorse names of all eleven Supreme Court justice nominees or question some of the recommendations of the Judicial Council for being politically tainted.

Meanwhile, Nepal has taken a significant step towards appointing Justice Karki as its first female Chief Justice. The Constitutional Council has already recommended her name for the top judicial job to replace the outgoing Chief Justice Kalyan Shrestha. She currently serves the Supreme Court as acting Chief Justice. Nepal had elected her first woman President, Bidhya Devi Bhandari, and first woman Speaker, Onsari Gharti Magar in 2015 after promulgation of the new Constitution, and if the name of Justice Karki is confirmed, Nepal will have a female trinity in the top-most positions in the state.

Conclusion

The spat that followed the promulgation of the new Constitution between the Judicial Council and the Parliament in the course of making the first appointments to the Supreme Court shows us the microcosm of what will ensue in future appointments. This is the consequence of overlap of powers between the three wings of the state. The appointment process to the Supreme Court cannot begin without the Chief Justice convening the meeting of the Judicial Council. In the Judicial Council's meeting, at the decision-making level, the Minister of Law, the appointee of the Prime Minister and the Nepal Bar Association's representative will be able to exert a significant influence in passing the recommendations. These three non-judicial members are representatives of political institutions and more often than not may come from different political affiliations or ideologies. In the end, the names recommended by the Judicial Council for appointment to the Supreme Court will have to go through screening of the Parliament with the risk of disapproval as well.

It is obvious why political parties wanted to exercise influence during the making of the Constitution. It will be wrong to assume that the Supreme Court works as a conservative legal institution. Most constitutional issues brought before the Supreme Court will have political overtones and the predisposition of the judges to political ideologies will have a bearing on their decisions. Further, political parties would want to ensure that their clientele and associates are favoured by the Supreme Court judges. Of course, political parties did not want to completely undermine judicial independence. This resulted in compromise and power sharing between the judiciary and political institutions in the process for appointments to the Supreme Court. However, this constitutional design has the potential to be a recipe for struggle between the executive, legislature, and judiciary. We have witnessed political manoeuvering in the first set of Supreme Court appointments itself after the new Constitution and such orchestration is only a sign of things to come.

Index

About the Editors and Contributors

Editors

Arghya Sengupta is the founder and research director at the Vidhi Centre for Legal Policy, New Delhi, India. He assisted the Union of India in preparing its written submissions in the *National Judicial Appointments Commission (NJAC) Case*. He graduated in law from the National Law School of India University (NLSIU), Bangalore, India in 2008, and obtained his B.C.L. from the University of Oxford, UK in 2009, where he was a Rhodes Scholar. While at Oxford, he completed his DPhil. on Independence and Accountability of the Indian Higher Judiciary and was a lecturer in Administrative Law at Pembroke College. At Vidhi, his areas of specialization are constitutional and administrative law. Sengupta writes regularly for national dailies such as *The Hindu* and *The Times of India*. He has also written for *Public Law* and *Law Quarterly Review* besides several other leading academic journals. He regularly advises the Union of India, state governments, and regulatory authorities on a range of legislation and regulation. He serves several law reform committees in India looking into data protection, institutional arbitration, immigration, and media reporting for court proceedings.

Ritwika Sharma is a candidate for the LLM (2017–18) at the Faculty of Law, University of Cambridge, UK. She assisted the Union of India in preparing its written submissions in the *National Judicial Appointments Commission (NJAC) Case*. She graduated in law from the Amity Law School (Guru Gobind Singh Indraprastha University), Delhi, India in 2013, and obtained an LLM from the National Academy of Legal Studies and Research (NALSAR) University of Law, Hyderabad, India in 2014. Subsequently, she was a research fellow at the Vidhi Centre for Legal Policy, New Delhi, India. At Vidhi, she worked with government departments and regulatory authorities on several projects, including the drafting of the Aadhaar (Targeted Delivery of Financial and Other Subsidies, Benefits and Services) Act, 2016, and exploring the possible contours of a conclusive land titling legislation for India.

Contributors

Rehan Abeyratne teaches law at the Chinese University of Hong Kong. He has a BA in political science from Brown University, USA and a J.D. from the Harvard Law School, USA. He taught law at Jindal Global Law School, Haryana, India from 2011 to 2016. At Jindal, he also served as assistant dean (Research) and as executive director of the Centre for Public Interest Law. His research interests include comparative constitutional law, human rights law, and public international law. His published works have appeared in the *International Journal of Constitutional Law*, *Asian Journal of Comparative Law*, *Nebraska Law Review*, *Yale Journal of International Law*, *Brooklyn Journal of International Law* and *George Washington International Law Review*, as well as in edited volumes published by Oxford University Press, and others.

Late **T.R. Andhyarujina** was a senior advocate in the Supreme Court of India, and an eminent jurist. Andhyarujina graduated in law from the Government Law College, Mumbai, India in 1957, and subsequently entered the bar as a counsel in the chambers of H.M. Seervai. He served as the Advocate-General of Maharashtra from 1993–5, and as Solicitor-General of India from 1996–8. In an illustrious career spanning almost six decades, he appeared as a counsel in several landmark cases, such as *Kesavananda Bharati v. State of Kerala* (1973), the *Parliamentary Privileges Case* (1965), *Vishaka v. State of Rajasthan* (1997), and *S.R. Bommai v. Union of India* (1993), among others. Andhyarujina appeared for the State of Maharashtra in the *National Judicial Appointments Commission (NJAC) Case*. In 2012, he authored *The Kesavananda Bharati Case: The Untold Story of Struggle for Supremacy by Supreme Court and Parliament*, his personal recollections of the proceedings in the *Kesavananda Bharati Case*.

T.R. Andhyarujina passed away on 28 March 2017 in Mumbai, at the age of 83. He is remembered as a stalwart of the Indian bar, and a scholar of constitutional law.

Gautam Bhatia is a practicing lawyer based in New Delhi, India. He graduated from the National Law School of India University (NLSIU), Bangalore, India in 2011, and read for the B.C.L. and MPhil at the University of Oxford, UK (2011–13), and for the LLM at Yale Law School, USA (2014). He has taught at NLSIU and the West Bengal National University of Juridical Sciences, Kolkata, India. His writings have appeared in *The Oxford Handbook for the Indian Constitution, The Max Planck Encyclopedia of Comparative Constitutional Law, The Australian Journal of Legal Philosophy,* and *Global Constitutionalism,* among others. Gautam's first book, *Offend, Shock, or Disturb: Free Speech under the Indian Constitution,* was published by Oxford University Press in 2015. He is presently at work on his second book, which is tentatively titled 'The Transformative Constitution'.

Chintan Chandrachud is an associate at Quinn Emanuel Urquhart & Sullivan, a leading law firm in London. He holds a PhD in law from the University of Cambridge, UK; master's degrees from the University of Oxford, UK and Yale University, USA; and a degree in law from the Government Law College, Mumbai, India. He is the author of *Balanced Constitutionalism: Courts and Legislatures in India and the United Kingdom,* which was published by Oxford University Press in 2017. His articles have been published in prominent journals and books, including *Public Law,* the *American Journal of Comparative Law,* and the *Oxford Handbook of the Indian Constitution.* He also writes frequently for Indian newspapers, including *The Hindu* and *The Indian Express.*

Semanta Dahal is an advocate practising in the Supreme Court of Nepal and a partner at Abhinawa Law Chambers, Kathmandu, Nepal. He graduated from the National Law School of India University (NLSIU), Bangalore, India in 2008, and obtained an LLM from the University of Nottingham, UK in 2010. Dahal has worked as a judicial clerk in the Supreme Court of India with Justice R.V. Raveendran. At present, Semanta advises the Government of Nepal on foreign investment and privately financed infrastructure projects including hydro concession, power purchase, highway PPPs, and municipal solid waste management, among others. He has published extensively on constitutional formation in Nepal and writes a regular column on judicial developments in Nepal for the *Kathmandu Post*.

Arvind Datar is a senior advocate in the Madras High Court. He completed his BSc (Hons) from the University of Bombay, India and graduated in law from the University of Madras, India. He joined the bar in 1980, and set up his independent practice in 1984. He has practiced before the Supreme Court of India, several High Courts, the Company Law Board, and various tax tribunals. In the *National Judicial Appointments Commission Case*, he appeared for the Service Bar Association of the Madras High Court, one of the petitioners. Datar has authored *Datar's Commentary on the Constitution of India*, and the *Guide to Central Excise–Law and Practice*. He is also the general editor of *A. Ramaiya's Guide to the Companies Act, 1956* and the chief editor of the 10th edition of *Kanga and Palkhivala's Law and Practice of Income Tax*. Along with Senior Advocate Soli Sorabjee, he has authored *Nani Palkhivala: The Courtroom Genius*, which was published in 2012.

Madhavi Divan is an advocate practicing in the Supreme Court of India. She completed a first-class honours degree in English from St. Stephen's College, University of Delhi, India and subsequently graduated in law from Pembroke College, University of Cambridge, UK. She began her independent practice as a counsel in the High Court of Bombay. Her areas of practice include constitutional law, media law, commercial law and environmental law. Divan has also appeared as a counsel for the Government of India in landmark cases such as the *National Judicial Appointments Commission Case*, the *Entry Tax Case*, and the *Triple Talaq Case*. In 2006, Madhavi authored *Facets of Media Law*, which is now in its second edition. She is on the Academic Council of the Maharashtra National Law School, Mumbai, and the editor of the *Indian Advocate*, the quarterly journal of the Bar Association of India.

A.K. Ganguli is a senior advocate in the Supreme Court of India. Ganguli was appointed amicus curiae by the Supreme Court in the case of *Suraz India Trust v. Union of India* (2011), where a petition was filed seeking reconsideration by the Supreme Court of its own judgments regarding the manner of appointment and transfer of judges. Ganguli is a renowned expert on arbitration in India. He is a member of several international institutions, such as the London Court of International Arbitration, Singapore International Arbitration Centre, and Asian Society of International Law. He also possesses extensive experience in matters on constitutional law, corporate laws, and interstate river water disputes. He is a recipient of the Justice V.R. Krishna Iyer Award sponsored by the Capital Foundation Society, New Delhi, India.

Arun Jaitley is the Minister of Finance and Minister of Corporate Affairs in the Government of India. He graduated with an honours degree in commerce from the Shri Ram College of Commerce, Delhi, India in 1973, and subsequently graduated in law from the Faculty of Law, University of Delhi in 1977. Subsequently, he practiced in the Supreme Court of India, and several High Courts. He was designated as senior advocate by the Delhi High Court in 1990. Jaitley was appointed Additional Solicitor General of India from 1989 to 1990. He has been part of the national executive of the Bharatiya Janata Party (BJP) since 1991, and has served as the Minister of Defence in the current, and as Minister of State for Information and Broadcasting, Minister of State for Divestment, and Minister of Law, Justice and Company Affairs in the previous governments formed by the BJP. He is currently a member of the Rajya Sabha from the state of Gujarat.

Sameer Khosa is an advocate practising in the High Courts of Pakistan, and a partner at Axis Law Chambers, Lahore, Pakistan. He read law at the University College London, UK and was called to the bar at the Honourable Society of Lincoln's Inn. Sameer obtained his LLM from the Columbia Law School, Columbia University, USA which he attended on a Fulbright Scholarship, and where he was named a Harlan Fiske Stone Scholar. He is also an attorney in the State of New York in USA. He is now based in Pakistan and handles commercial, constitutional, and administrative law disputes. He also frequently writes for various national newspapers on issues involving legal and current affairs.

Alok Prasanna Kumar heads the Bengaluru office of the Vidhi Centre for Legal Policy, where he is a senior resident fellow. He graduated from the National Academy of Legal Studies and Research (NALSAR)

University of Law, Hyderabad, India in 2008, and obtained his B.C.L. from the University of Oxford, UK in 2009. Between 2009 and 2013, he practised at the Supreme Court of India and Delhi High Court from the chambers of Mohan Pararasaran, the then Solicitor-General of India. He was also a senior resident fellow at the Vidhi Centre for Legal Policy, New Delhi, where he headed the Judicial Reforms Initiative from 2013 to 2016. Prasanna is the author of a monthly column in the *Economic and Political Weekly*, titled 'Law and Society'. His areas of academic interest are legal philosophy, constitutional theory, and taxation.

Chris McConnachie is an advocate practising in South Africa at the Johannesburg Bar. His areas of practice are constitutional law and human rights law. He obtained the BA and LLB degrees from the Rhodes University, Grahamstown, South Africa. He completed the B.C.L., MPhil, and DPhil at the University of Oxford, UK as a Rhodes Scholar. Chris is also an honorary research associate at the Rhodes University. He has clerked at the Constitutional Court of South Africa, appointed by former Chief Justice Pius Nkonzo Langa, and serving under Justice Chris Jafta.

Peter McCormick is a professor emeritus in the Department of Political Science at the University of Lethbridge, Canada. He graduated from the University of Alberta with a BA in 1968, the University of Toronto with an MA in 1969, and obtained a PhD from the London School of Economics in 1974. He taught at the Lakehead University and the University of British Columbia before joining Lethbridge in 1975. McCormick has authored *The End of the Charter Revolution*, which was published in 2015. He has also written commissioned reports on judicial appointment procedures in Canada for the Bastarache Commission of Enquiry (2010), and on judicial independence and judicial governance for the Canadian Association of Provincial Court Judges (2003). He is currently working on a biography of Canadian Supreme Court Chief Justice Beverley McLachlin, who will retire in fall 2018.

Pratap Bhanu Mehta is vice-chancellor, Ashoka University, Sonepat, India. He holds a BA (first class) in Philosophy, Politics, and Economics from St. John's College, University of Oxford, UK and a PhD in politics from Princeton University, USA. Mehta was previously president and chief executive of the Center for Policy Research, New Delhi, India. He has been a professor at Harvard University, USA and the Jawaharlal Nehru University, New Delhi, India and a participant in the Global Faculty Program at the New York University School of Law, USA. He has co-edited *Rethinking India's Public Institutions* (2017), *The Oxford Handbook to the Indian Constitution* (2016), and *The Oxford Companion to Politics in India* (2010), among other edited volumes. Mehta is editorial consultant to *The Indian Express*, where he writes a regular column. He also writes for *The Financial Times*, and is on the editorial board of *American Political Science Review* and the *Journal of Democracy*.

Suchindran B.N. is an advocate practicing in the Madras High Court and the Supreme Court of India. He graduated in law from the Indian Law Society's Law College, Pune, India in 2007, after which he joined the chambers of Arvind Datar. He began his independent practice in 2011, primarily on the original and appellate sides of the Madras High Court. He has appeared in a wide range of matters, including the constitutional challenge to the National Company Law Tribunal, and matters involving the interpretation of the statutory powers of the Petroleum and Natural Gas Regulatory Board, and the issue of entry of foreign law firms in India. Apart from commenting and writing on contemporary legal issues, Suchindran has a keen interest in the legal and political history of the Constitution of India.

Suhrith Parthasarathy is a practising lawyer based in Chennai, India. He graduated in law from the West Bengal National University of Juridical Sciences, Kolkata, India in 2008 and obtained an M.S. in Journalism from Columbia University, New York, USA in 2012. Parthasarathy focuses primarily on litigation work and appears regularly before the Madras High Court, as well as the National Company Law Tribunal, the National Green Tribunal, and the Income Tax Appellate Tribunal. In 2013, he established Focus Law, an independent boutique law firm in Chennai, which specializes in public law, and commercial and income tax litigation. Parthasarathy is a regular contributor to the op-ed pages of *The Hindu*. He has also published articles in a number of other dailies and magazines, including *The Indian Express*, the website of *The New*

Yorker, The Caravan Magazine, Open Magazine, The New York Times, and the *Economic and Political Weekly,* among others.

Raju Ramachandran is a senior advocate practising in the Supreme Court of India. He graduated with a degree in economics from St. Stephen's College, Delhi, India and subsequently graduated in law from the Faculty of Law, University of Delhi, India. He served as Additional Solicitor General of India from 2002 to 2004. He was appointed amicus curiae by the Supreme Court in the *Gulberg Society Massacre Case,* to defend Mohammed Ajmal Kasab in the *Mumbai Terrorist Attacks Case,* and the *Nirbhaya Case.* He is currently assisting the Supreme Court as amicus curiae in the *Sabarimala Temple Entry Case.* Ramachandran has authored *Professional Ethics for Lawyers: Changing Profession, Changing Ethics,* which was published in 2003. He also published *I've Been around for Some Time (Analyses, Reflections, and Reminiscences)* in 2016, which is a compilation of his select articles and interviews. He is the revising author of B.R. Agarwala's *Supreme Court Practice and Procedure* (2002), and co-editor of *Supreme but Not Infallible: Essays in Honour of the Supreme Court of India* (2000).

Mukul Rohatgi is a senior advocate practicing in the Supreme Court of India. He graduated in law from the Government Law College, Mumbai, India and subsequently trained as a junior counsel in the Chambers of Justice Y.K. Sabharwal, who later became the Chief Justice of India. Rohatgi has had a long-standing practice in the Delhi High Court. He served as the Additional Solicitor General of India from 1999 to 2004. In June 2014, he was appointed the 14th Attorney-General for India, a position he held till June 2017. During his tenure as the Attorney-General, he argued several significant cases for the Government of India, including the *National Judicial Appointments Commission Case,* the *Entry Tax Case,* the *Aadhaar-PAN Card Linkage Case,* and the *Triple Talaq Case.*

Gopal Subramanium is a senior advocate practising in the Supreme Court of India. He graduated in law from the Faculty of Law, University of Delhi, India. In 1993, he was designated senior advocate *suo moto* by the Supreme Court, one of the youngest in India's history to receive the designation. Subramanium served as Solicitor-General of India from 2009 to 2011, during which period he was also chairman of the Bar

Council of India. From 2005 to 2009, he served as Additional Solicitor General of India. He is also an Associate Member and Arbitrator with 3 Verulam Buildings Chambers, London, and a Judge at the Qatar International Court. Subramanium has contributed a chapter titled 'Writs and Remedies' in *The Oxford Handbook of the Indian Constitution* (2016), and co-edited the book *Supreme but Not Infallible: Essays in Honour of the Supreme Court of India* (2000). In 2009, Subramanium received the National Law Day Award for Outstanding Jurist from the President of India.

Mythili Vijay Kumar Thallam graduated in law from the National Academy of Legal Studies and Research (NALSAR) University of Law, Hyderabad, India in 2011. She was a judicial clerk in the Supreme Court of India from 2011 to 2012. Subsequently, she worked in the chambers of Raju Ramachandran from 2014 to 2017. She has assisted Ramachandran in various cases, including the *Nirbhaya Case*, the *Sabarimala Temple Entry Case*, and the appeal against Yakub Memon's death sentence. She is currently pursuing her LLM from the University of Michigan, where she is focusing on courses in constitutional law and criminal law.

K.T. Thomas is a retired judge of the Supreme Court of India. He obtained his BA from St. Albert's College, Ernakulam, India and subsequently graduated in law from the Madras Law College, India. Justice Thomas practised at the District Court, Kottayam and later, the Kerala High Court. In 1977, he was directly selected as District and Sessions Judge, securing first rank in the selection examination. He was elevated as a judge of the High Court of Kerala in 1985, and was appointed as Acting Chief Justice in 1995. In March 1996, he was appointed as a judge of the Supreme Court of India. Justice Thomas presided over the Supreme Court bench that confirmed the death sentence in the *Rajiv Gandhi Assassination Case* (1999). Justice Thomas retired from service in January 2002. In 2008, he chaired the Police Reforms Monitoring Committee, and the School Review Commission to Review the Functioning of the National Law School of India University, Bangalore. Justice Thomas wrote his autobiography, *Honeybees of Solomon— Memoirs of a Jurist*, in 2008, which is an account of his 25 years of judicial service.